LOS ANGELES IN FICTION

LOS ANGELES IN FICTION

A Collection of Original Essays
Edited by David Fine

University of New Mexico Press ● Albuquerque

Library of Congress Cataloging in Publication Data
Main entry under title:

Los Angeles in Fiction.

Includes index.
1. Los Angeles (Calif.) in literature—Addresses,
essays, lectures. 2. American fiction—20th century—
History and criticism—Addresses, essays, lectures.
3. English fiction—20th century—History and criticism—
Addresses, essays, lectures. I. Fine, David M., 1934–
PS374.L57L6   1984   813'.5'093279494   84-10430
ISBN 0-8263-0759-0
ISBN 0-8263-0760-4 (pbk.)

Design: B. Jellow

Contents

Acknowledgments

I am grateful to all the contributors, who took time from busy teaching and writing schedules to write these essays and make the various editorial changes I requested. I am indebted to Paul Skenazy and Liahna Babener, both of whom took on double assignments. I am particularly grateful to Professor Babener for assisting me as well in the editing of the manuscripts. She reviewed each essay thoroughly and professionally and made innumerable suggestions which have been incorporated into the text. Finally, I want to acknowledge my gratitude to Elizabeth C. Hadas, my editor at the University of New Mexico Press, for her expert advice, constant support, and help in guiding the manuscript through all the stages of preparation and production.

David Fine

Long Beach, California

Introduction

I

It is axiomatic that literary regionalism is the product of writers deeply rooted in, and committed to, the places about which they write. Mark Twain wrote that an author becomes little more than a superficial outsider "when he steps from the state whose life is familiar to him." Hamlin Garland, his contemporary, remarked that "the tourist cannot write the local novel." More recently, Lawrence Clark Powell, former UCLA librarian and a man who has written authoritatively on California and Southwestern literature, observed that to realize a true sense of place a writer needs regional roots, "the deep unconscious sources on which literature feeds."

However applicable such remarks may be to Northern and Central California writers like Frank Norris, Jack London, Robinson Jeffers, John Steinbeck, and William Saroyan, they do not account for the body of modern fiction that has given Southern California—Los Angeles and its surroundings—its literary identity. In fact, any discussion of the Los Angeles novel must begin with the observation that it is chiefly the work of the outsider—if not the tourist, then the newcomer. With a few exceptions, largely contemporary ones, its shapers have been men and women born elsewhere who for a time lived and worked in Southern California, frequently as script writers.

Southern California fiction dates back a full century or more, at least as far back as Helen Hunt Jackson's popular and still-in-print romance of mission life, *Ramona* (1884). But what can be called the first significant generation of Los Angeles writers—the generation that was to confer upon the city a modern fictional definition—did not appear until the 1930s. Sound came to the movies at the end of the twenties, and with it a demand for scripts. Throughout the thirties writers from all over the country—and from England—arrived in the film capital in response to the demand. James M. Cain, who was to write the first significant Los Angeles novel of the decade, came in 1931. John O'Hara followed in 1934, Nathanael West in 1935, Aldous Huxley and F. Scott Fitzgerald in 1937, Theodore Dreiser and Christopher Isherwood in 1939, and William Faulkner in 1940.

What drew the writers was the promise of high salaries and steady work. Some of them, though, disillusioned by the factory conditions at the studios and unhappy in the region, left after a short stay; others—Cain, McCoy, Huxley, and Isherwood among them—remained, joining earlier settlers like Raymond Chandler (since 1912) and Budd Schulberg (reared in Hollywood) to constitute an impressive local colony of writers.

Collectively, their screen achievements were modest, but within a few years after arriving on the West Coast, most of them wrote novels that gave the city its metaphoric shape, established a way of reading the Southern California landscape that would persist through successive decades into the sixties and seventies.[1] To a large extent it was their position as outsiders, their estrangement and sense of dislocation—expressed in moods ranging from fascination to revulsion and often a combination of the two—that gave the Los Angeles novel its peculiar ambience, that distinguishes it to the present day from the literature of other places, and makes it as a body of fiction so interesting.

The displacement experienced by the writers fostered a way of writing about the region that differed qualitatively from the way other regions have been written about. Places in fiction often have temporal as well as spatial dimension. Not uncommonly, a region's present is played against its past. Faulkner's South and Sherwood Anderson's Midwest come most easily to mind, places that reflect in microcosm larger national changes. By contrast, in Los Angeles fiction the West Coast present is set, explicitly or implicitly, against a past brought from another place—the Midwest, South, East Coast, or England. The contrast between the place left behind and the place discovered plays a strong role in the fiction, a point that is made in a number of the essays in this collection. Paul Skenazy, for instance, writing on the detective novel, says that "the story of the West inevitably becomes a story of the East, and of the complex interaction of the world left behind and the new life begun."

Nathanael West's *The Day of the Locust* (1939) makes the interaction quite explicit. Tod Hackett, fresh from the East Coast and Yale's School of Art, is painfully aware of the distance he has come and what it will mean for his art. Walking the streets of Hollywood, gazing at a human and architectural environment that violates his sense of propriety, he knows that he would "never again do a fat red barn, old stone wall or sturdy Nantucket fisherman." His derision, both amused and cynical, of the architectural facades he finds in the canyons above Hollywood Boulevard stems from the orthodoxies he has brought to the West. Only dynamite, he thinks, would be of any use against the line-up of "Mexican ranch houses, Samoan huts, Mediterranean villas, Egyptian and Japanese temples, Swiss chalets [and] Tudor cottages."[2] But his attitude becomes "charitable" when he remembers that such fantasies result from complete freedom in the use of building materials, impossible in the colder climate of the East Coast.

The anarchy of West's Los Angeles, its disregard for traditional, that is, eastern limits both on human behavior and the built landscape, is reflected in a persistent pattern of imagery linking bizarre and inappropriate human costuming, absurd role playing, and eclectic, counterfeit architectural design. The symbolic center of the pervasive masquerading in West's novel is the movie studio; his Los Angeles landscape appears as a vast annex to the back lot, a spillover onto the city's streets of what he calls "the dream dump,"

> a Sargasso of the imagination! And the dump grew continually, for there wasn't a dream afloat somewhere which wouldn't sooner or later turn up on it, having first been made photographic by plaster, canvas, lath, and paint. (p. 132)

Faddish costuming, like exotic architecture, reflects the compulsive role playing of the characters. Their masquerades grow out of the desperate need of a migrant population to cope with a landscape in which no traditional standards or authority governs. West's people, as Gerald Locklin notes below (Chapter 3), "have neither individual nor collective identity"; they attempt to find a place for themselves by aping a variety of movie-inspired styles. Hackett is amused by the people along Hollywood Boulevard who wear "sports clothes" that are not really sports clothes, but "fancy dress" or the clothes they wear to work—yachting caps, Norfolk jackets, Tyrolean hats, sneakers.

Aldous Huxley's *After Many a Summer Dies the Swan*, published in 1939, the same year as West's novel, also draws on bizarre costuming and fraudulent architecture to point to the collapse of traditional cultural standards. Jeremy Pordage, the narrator, just arrived from England, sees a woman shopping in a "hydrangea-blue strapless bathing suit, platinum curls, and a black fur jacket." Huxley's novel, like West's, is loaded with exotic architectural facades. Among them is the cemetery Beverly Pantheon, which contains, among other ersatz structures, "the Tomb of Shakespeare," the "Church of the Bard," and nude Greek statues that celebrate not the victory of spirit over matter, but exactly the opposite: the promise they offer, Pordage reflects, is one of everlasting tennis, swimming, and golf. Dominating Huxley's landscape is an enormous castle perched atop the Hollywood Hills. Gothic with a vengeance, the castle is "more medieval than any building of the thirteenth century." Like the Hearst Castle in San Simeon from which it derives its inspiration (just as the exotic cemetery parodies Forest Lawn), it is crammed with an eclectic assortment of pillaged Old World treasures.

Virtually all the writers were struck by the region's sham architecture, which they appropriated as metaphor for the absence of aesthetic control. In 1933 James M. Cain, two years in Los Angeles, described to eastern readers of *American Mercury* in an article he titled "Paradise," a bizarre landscape in which gas stations were built to look like the Taj Mahal and structures resembling giant oranges, windmills, mosques, and tea kettles were everywhere to be found. "There is no reward for aesthetic virtue here," he wrote, "no punishment for aesthetic crime."

Even before the thirties, however, this playing of East against West appears in the fiction. Mark Lee Luther's 1923 novel *The Boosters*, one of the more interesting of the prethirties novels,[3] anticipates the preoccupation of the next decade's fiction with the appropriation of the region's counterfeit architecture. George Hammond, a Boston architect down on his luck, is persuaded to seek a fresh start in Los Angeles where his wife's brother has already made a small fortune. Mrs. Hammond, the daughter of a "Forty Niner," sees the migration as a nostalgic retracing of her father's path across the Santa Fe Trail—albeit this time by pullman. As the train crosses the Colorado River and enters the Promised Land, the Hammonds are assailed by a fellow passenger, a genuine booster:

> It's the garden spot of the globe, and Los Angeles is the pick of the garden. . . . There she sits on her rolling hills—Our Lady, Queen of the Angels—the Sierra Madre at her back, the blue Pacific at her feet, the wonder city of the world.[4]

But the arrival in the city prefigures Hammond's disastrous encounter with Los Angeles. It is indeed a wonder city. The sky is overcast (though it is August), and the urban landscape is dominated by junkyards, orange juice stands, cheap souvenir shops, and parking lots. The house of Mrs. Hammond's brother is described as looking like a battleship—a mammoth, graceless rectangle. "The faults of structure," Hammond concludes, "were surpassed only by the sins of decoration. . . . The prevailing taste was one of costly and ugly gloom" (p. 21). Hammond has brought his New England with him, and nothing in the city pleases him.

He loathes the ubiquitous oil wells, palm trees, and tasteless architecture.

In the course of the novel Hammond's eastern crankiness subsides, largely through the influence of his brother-in-law's ex-wife, Anita, a descendant of the old mixed Anglo-Spanish settlers. She and her estranged husband are posed in the novel as opposite types. Spencer Ward represents the Yankee building spirit, hell-bent on exploiting the land for all it will bear materially, staking his claim on it as his father had done on the Mother Lode. Anita, the idealized issue of the California past, represents the alternative of living in harmony with the land, of preserving and conserving its natural beauty.

Both characters, of course, are stereotypes, stock figures in western—and California—literature, but functionally, they serve to allow Hammond, the displaced easterner, to define his own relationship to California. He throws his energies into the path Anita has shown him, devoting his architectural talents to the planning of buildings that combine his eastern legacy with a distinctively California design, much in the manner of the architect Irving Gill. At the novel's end Hammond is comfortably ensconced in a house in the Hollywood Hills, has shipped his library west, and is at work on the design for a model town in which every house is to be "the best of its type."

Luther's Los Angeles is both the best and worst of places. It is the land of the fast buck promoter and the simple-minded and race-conscious civic booster (anti-Japanese sentiment runs high among his boosters), but it is also the place that holds out the redemptive possibility of a new American landscape and identity forged by the impact of East and West. In a scene near the end of the novel, the Hammonds stumble on a New York State picnic in a park and notice sheets of paper hung on trees bearing the names of people hoping to locate East Coast neighbors. The names reflect the diversity of the California population and suggest to Hammond the metaphor of a new melting pot on the West Coast, a region that "by some chemistry of her own was . . . triumphantly blending the races into a single type."

The Boosters is no booster novel, nor is it simply a satire on the boosting spirit in the manner of Sinclair Lewis's Babbitt, published just a year before. It is, rather, an optimistic though cautious affirmation of Southern California possibilities. Set against the Los Angeles fiction of the thirties, however, it is an elegy to a dying vision, one that could be sustained through the growth years of the twenties but could not survive far into the depression decade.

The melting pot metaphor on which the novel ends suggests a parallel with, or throwback to, the immigrant fiction that in the unsettling years before and after the turn of the century formed a significant part of American urban literature.[5] Such novels play on the contrasts between Old World past and New World present and between expectation and actuality. The collision of the American promise and its betrayal is a recurring theme in this fiction, but the novels end, typically, with some kind of accommodation to the New World, expressed as a process of Americanization, a melting-pot fusion of cultures, or a commitment to a collective struggle for a new America.

For West, Cain, Fitzgerald, McCoy, and others, Los Angeles could not serve as setting for the regenerative possibilities of America. The dream, if it had once had potency, was behind them. Writing against the myth of El Dorado, they transformed it into its antithesis: that of the dream running out along the California shore. Collectively, the thirties writers superimposed upon the original myth what has been called the Los Angeles Anti-Myth.[6] The tension between myth and antimyth, between Southern California as the place of the fresh start and as the scene of the disastrous finish, recurs in almost all the fiction.

The characters in the Los Angeles novel have been for the most part seekers, men and women drawn hopefully or desperately to Southern California as the place of the new beginning or of the last chance. Among them have been opportunists like Sammy Glick and Frank Chambers; star-struck then disillusioned women like Gloria Beatty and Cora Smith; bewildered Englishmen like Jeremy Pordage and Dennis Barlow; tired, sick, and lonely Midwesterners like Homer Simpson and the "starers" who populate West's Hollywood; and those clients of Raymond Chandler's and Ross Macdonald's private eyes who have come to Southern California in an attempt to start over with a new name and new identity after a crime committed elsewhere.

Whatever the seekers were after, they were obeying the same westward impulse that drew hundreds of thousands to Southern California in the half century between the 1880s and the 1930s. From its Spanish founding in 1781 through the middle decades of the nineteenth century, Los Angeles remained sparsely populated, eclipsed by its cosmopolitan gold-rich northern neighbor San Francisco. With the collapse of the gold rush, the striking of a rail line into Southern California, and the carving up of old Mexican ranchos into hundreds of instant townsites, the city experienced the first of several successive booms. By 1920 the population surpassed for the first time, and for all time, that of San Francisco. By then oil had been discovered on the city streets, the movies had come, a 240-mile aqueduct had been engineered to bring water to a semi-arid land, and the world's largest man-made harbor had been dug. The California Dream, which had centered on San Francisco and the Mother Lode in the mid-nineteenth century, had been transformed into the Los Angeles dream.

That dream, both in its earlier Northern and later Southern California versions, died hard. It was founded on hope, and that hope had endurance. Kevin Starr, in *Americans and the California Dream, 1850–1915*, wrote:

> Whatever else California was, good or bad, it was charged
> with human hope. It was linked imaginatively with the
> most compelling of American myths, the pursuit of
> happiness. When that intensity of expectation was
> thwarted or only partially fulfilled . . . it could backfire
> into restlessness and bitterness. . . . As a hope in defiance
> of facts, as a longing which could ennoble and encourage
> but which could turn and devour itself, the symbolic
> value of California endured—a legacy of the Gold Rush.[7]

What sustained the dream in Southern California more than anything else was the climate. Miraculous curative powers were attributed to the weather. One result, a phenomenon which proved irresistibly seductive to the novelists, was that the city filled with invalids and health seekers—and in their wake a bizarre assortment of healers, spiritualists, psychics, and utopian reformers. Movements bearing such names as The Mighty I Am, Krotona, Mankind United, and Ham and Eggs flourished, and charismatic leaders like Katherine Tingley (the "Purple Mother" of Point Loma's Theosophy movement) and Aimee Semple McPherson (of the Four Square Gospel) electrified the faithful.

It is, of course, tempting to exaggerate the influence of cults and utopian schemes in the city's development, but what cannot be denied is their centrality in the city's fiction and folklore, their significance as metaphor. Spiritualists, medical quacks, and exotic imposters run rampant in the fiction of Nathanael West, Aldous Huxley, Evelyn Waugh, Raymond Chandler, Ross Macdonald, Thomas Sanchez, and Thomas Pynchon, reflecting the collapse of the boundary between reality and illusion.

Foi the British exiles Huxley and Waugh, the exotic cemetery provided a principal metaphor for that collapse. Huxley's use of architectural masquerades and classical statues more sensual, erotic, and athletic than spiritual, makes a mockery of the rituals of death and grieving. Waugh, as Walter Wells points out in his essay, drew his inspiration for Whispering Glades in *The Loved One* (1948) from the Glendale cemetery Forest Lawn, going one step beyond even that fantasy park in transforming it grotesquely into a movie set. But it is a movie set with a difference; the structures are not one-dimensional:

> When as a newcomer to Megalopitan studios he [Dennis Barlow] first toured the lots, it had taxed his imagination to realize that those solid-seeming streets and squares of every period and climate were in fact plaster facades whose backs revealed the structures of bill-boarding. Here the illusion was quite otherwise. Only with an effort could Dennis believe that the building before him was three-dimensional and permanent.[8]

The exotic cults and cemeteries, travesties of religious faith and significant ritual, and the exotic buildings, travesties of the world's architectural heritage, were appropriated by the writers as images of the failure in the West to distinguish the genuine from the fraudulent, art from artfulness.

As with the cults and the cemeteries, however, the case against regional architecture was one of exaggeration. Alongside the architectural gaucheries, the built Los Angeles environment has, since the turn of the century, contained a number of striking and innovative structures—the Pasadena bungalows of the Greene Brothers, the Art Deco department stores along Wilshire Boulevard, the "Streamline Moderne" commercial buildings of Stiles

Clements, Kem Weber, and others, and the modern "International," Bauhaus-inspired styles of Richard Neutra and Rudolph Schindler. But the fictional image of the city has been less one of architectural diversity than of confusion.

II

Landscape in the Los Angeles novel is always weighted with symbolic meaning. The fact that the writers, as outsiders, were playing the region contrapuntally against a home territory accounts to a large extent for the symbolic quality it acquired in fiction. The landscape offered itself readily to a vision of being cut off from a familiar sense of space.

To the writers who came in the thirties and in the following decades the symbolic possibilities of the landscape were obvious enough. The place embodied the contradiction of being a metropolitan center without itself having a geographically distinguishable center. Los Angeles took its shape in an uncharacteristic way for American cities: it grew not by pushing out centrifugally from a dense core, but by the separate development of towns often at considerable distance from one another, a process that had been going on since the 1880s. The old plaza, birthplace of the city, had become by the twenties simply one of a number of centers.

A place that has no clearly distinguishable center has no distinguishable periphery. Its low density and sprawling, horizontal appearance led historian Carey McWilliams to call the built environment "rurban," a middle landscape neither wholly rural nor urban. It became a city whose scope could be encompassed only by the automobile. The British architectural critic Reyner Banham noted that he had to learn how to drive to "read" the city "in the original." Municipal boundaries have never really defined Los Angeles. Its sprawl has lent an amorphous and ambiguous quality to the land that recurs in the fiction. The novelist's Los Angeles stretches up the coast to Malibu, down the coast to Long Beach, east to the desert resorts, and northeast to the San Bernardino Mountains. The city Raymond Chandler charted in his seven novels encompasses dozens of suburbs and several distinct ecologies. The detective novels of Chandler, Macdonald, and their followers have always given the feel of a city without either center or bounds. Robert Parker captures some sense of this chaotic spread in his recent detective novel *A Savage Place*. His Boston-based private eye, Spencer, is in Los Angeles on a case:

> I didn't know any place like it for sprawl, for the apparently idiosyncratic mix of homes and businesses and shopping malls. There was no center, no fixed point for taking bearings. It ambled and sprawled and disarrayed all over the peculiar landscape—garish and fascinating and imprecise and silly, smelling richly of bougainvillea and engine emissions, full of trees and grass and flowers and neon and pretense. And off to the northeast, beyond the Hollywood Hills, above the smog, and far from Disneyland were the mountains with snow on their peaks. I wondered if there was a leopard frozen up there anywhere.[9]

In addition to conveying a sense of limitless sprawl, the passage evokes some of the startling contrasts and discontinuities that mark the fictional Los Angeles. Such contrasts recur as metaphors for spatial incongruity: seacoast against desert; flat plain against rugged mountain; Mediterranean climate against smog-fouled air; palm trees against oil wells; flowers aginst neons. There is also the spatial contradiction posed by the appearance of luxury houses perched on (or over) the edge of sheer cliffs. Chandler writes of Pacific Palisades houses "hanging by their teeth and eyebrows to a spur of mountain and looking as if a good sneeze would drop them down among the lunch boxes on the beach." Lindsay Marriott, who lives precariously on the edge of a cliff above the beach in one of the houses referred to in the quotation, is the "fall guy," the patsy of Chandler's novel, set up to take the dive.

Houses in Los Angeles fiction are repeatedly used as indexes to character. Typically, they mirror the illusions and destructive fantasies of those who dwell in them. Jo Stoyte's "medieval" castle in *After Many a Summer Dies the Swan* reflects his maniacal obsession with immortality. The pretentious mansions of the rich and powerful in Chandler's novels offer illusions of their invulnerability. Their fortresses against the hills are elaborate masks of respectability which Marlowe, as detective, must penetrate. The deceptive facades behind which virtually all of West's characters live (Claude Estee's Mississippi plantation house, Homer Simpson's Irish/Spanish/Early American medley, the Greeners' turnip-domed apartment house) point to their hopeless confusion of reality and illusion. And James Cain's ordinary Spanish-styled middle-class houses are set contrapuntally, as I attempt to show in my discussion of Cain, against the extraordinary events that go on in them.

The spatial disarray of the built landscape has its counterpart in the temporal confusion presented by the absence of clearly delineated seasons. In two novels by easterners, Norman Mailer's *The Deer Park* (1955) and Alison Lurie's *The Nowhere City* (1965) the absence of seasons that conform to those of the East or Midwest signals the disappearance of time itself. In Lurie's novel Paul Cattleman, a New England–trained historian, sums up to East Coast friends what he has learned from a year in Los Angeles:

> The basic thing about L.A. . . . was that it lacked the
> dimension of time. . . . there were no seasons there, no
> days of the week, no night and day; beyond that there
> was (or was supposed to be) no youth and age. But worst,
> and most frightening, there was no past or future—only
> an eternal dizzying present. In effect the city had
> banished historians as Plato had poets from this
> Republic.[10]

Cattleman, in Lurie's bitter satire on Los Angeles, has been lured west by a research institute to write its history. What he learns, though, is that the institute has no interest whatever in history; history has no meaning in Los Angeles. He has been hired because the firm likes the idea of having a historian on its staff. And so after a year he returns to Massachusetts to teach. Meanwhile his wife, Katherine, whose early days in the city were marked by continuous headache and misery, has been discovering in the absence of history the freedom to remake herself. Nothing really counts in Los Angeles, she realizes, so one can do anything. "If there's no schedule," she is told by the hip Beverly Hills psychiatrist who serves as her guide, "then you are free to work out your own schedule. A place like this, Los Angeles, actually it's a great opportunity" (p. 173).

In the manner of West and Huxley, Lurie draws on the region's fantasy architecture as metaphor both for the confusion of reality and illusion and the collapse of the past into "the eternal dizzying present." Fresh from New England, Katherine and Paul rent a bungalow in a neighborhood called Vista Garden with no vista and no garden. The houses, all stucco, come in ice-cream colors, and their neighborhood looks like a stage set. Katherine, with her New England values, is appalled, but Paul is intrigued by houses in the shape of pagodas, grocery stores looking like Turkish baths, and drive-in milk bars topped by fifteen-foot plaster cows. Katherine tells a friend that coming in from the airport she passed a giant revolving cement donut. Like the enormous hole in the spinning donut, Los Angeles is to her a huge advertisement for nothing.

Images of disparity, both temporal and spatial, pervade the novel: smog against palm trees, flowers so huge as to appear artificial, a French Chateau crawling along the street on the back of a truck, crowds at the beach nearly naked against Merry Christmas signs, sun-lit store windows decorated with painted snow and ice, and sunbathers lounging beside an empty pool.

Some of this same sense of removal or liberation from an ordered sense of space and time is found in Norman Mailer's *The Deer Park*. The setting is not Los Angeles, but a desert resort called Desert D'Or, a few hours from Los Angeles. Modeled on Palm Springs, it is a watering hole for the movie colony. The town has no main street, and stores don't look like stores but living rooms where salespeople remove articles of clothing from hidden panels. One store is shaped like a cabin cruiser; through a porthole one can see a $30,000 necklace hung on a piece of driftwood. Everything in Desert D'Or is disguised to look like something else. Bars, where most of the activities of the movie people take place, are disguised as jungles, grottoes, or theater lobbies. With their false ceilings, irregular shapes, and garish colors, the bars distort the sense of time and space. Sergius O'Shaugnessy, the narrator, says of one bar, "Drinking in that atmosphere I never knew whether it was night or day, and I think that kind of uncertainty got into everybody's conversation."[11]

Mailer's novel is heavily indebted to *The Day of the Locust*, written sixteen years earlier. The characters in both works are compulsive role-players. Lulu Myers, the queen of Supreme Pictures is, like West's Faye Greener, constantly performing. Life is a series of roles, and she fails, like Faye, to distinguish living and acting. Neither character simply attempts to shape life to fit script; both suffer a pathological failure to distinguish the two. In both books architectural fantasies play a major symbolic role, and in both the landscape is seen through, or disguised by, the distorting lens of the artificial. West, to return briefly to his novel, consistently presents images of the natural world in terms of the unnatural. The edges of trees in the hills "burned with a pale violet light . . . like a neon tube," and the sky becomes a "blue serge sky" in which the moon makes an appearance "like an enormous bone button." What such images suggest is a sense of an organic landscape that has been corrupted and preempted by the materialistic and inorganic, a landscape from which we stand twice removed. It is the landscape of the cinema, the movie set, one produced by technical skill, by effective lighting and the use of props. And as such it symbolically defines the point where living and performing are indistinguishable.

Coupled with the cultural and architectural instability of the novelist's Los Angeles is the instability of the land itself. Natural as well as man-made disasters have furnished the plot line for much of the city's history and its fiction. The sun-drenched land which drew hundreds of thousands of seekers is also the land of destructive brush fires, droughts, floods, mudslides, and earthquakes. In two of the works discussed in this book, Fitzgerald's *The Last Tycoon* and Hisaye Yamamoto's short story "Yoneko's Earthquake," the 1933 Long Beach earthquake serves as a symbol of radical disjunction. It signals the end of one life for the major character and the beginning of another. In Fitzgerald's novel a flood on the studio back lot following the earthquake produces for Monroe Stahr the illusion of the resurrection of his dead wife. Kathleen, the look-alike, floats toward Stahr on a studio prop, the severed head of the Hindu god of destruction and dissolution, Siva. She is both the exhausted producer's restoration and his destruction. For Yamamoto's young heroine the quake similarly brings on the end of one stage of life and the beginning of another—in this instance, as Charles Crow points out in his essay, the end of childhood and the birth of the artist.

Other signs of instability on the landscape provide metaphors for the fiction. Periodically, the hot, dry Santa Ana winds—the kind Chandler and Joan Didion appropriate as the backdrop to violence—race through the canyons on their way to the sea, not only firing the tempers of Angelenos but causing the dry chaparral to explode in flames. The hills, no longer covered by protective brush, erode and become rivers of mud when the heavy winter rains come. Cliffs give way, dumping tons of mud onto houses and coastal highway below. The title story in Gavin Lambert's collection, *The Slide Area* (1951) offers an image of the encounter between cliff and ocean:

> High lurching cliffs confront the ocean, and are just beginning to fall apart. Signs have been posted along the highway, DRIVE CAREFULLY and SLIDE AREA. Lumps of earth and stone fall down. The land is restless here, restless and sliding. . . . The land is falling. Rocks fall down all over and the cliffs called Pacific Palisades are crumbling slowly down to the ocean.[12]

The menace of the ocean recurs as a motif in the fiction, signaling the fragility of life at its edge. The last act for many a Los Angeles character is played against the ocean: on a rickety pier over the Pacific in Horace McCoy's *They Shoot Horses, Don't They?*; in a car crash on the Coast Highway in James Cain's *The Postman Always Rings Twice*; and repeatedly in the detective fiction of Raymond Chandler and Ross Macdonald, whose hero Lew Archer hears, in *The Chill*, "the surf roaring up under the cottages and sucking at their pilings." For Macdonald there is still another ocean menace, as Jerry Speir's essay reminds us, a more contemporary one—the oil spill, bred by the mating of corporate greed and ecological fragility.

But it is fire which has always been the most frightening image. "The city burning," Joan Didion wrote in *Slouching Toward Bethlehem*, "is Los Angeles' deepest image of itself." A forest fire rages uncontrollably in Macdonald's *The Underground Man* "like flashes of heavy guns too far away to be heard," and the centerpiece of *The Day of the Locust* is Tod Hackett's apocalyptic painting of Los Angeles in flames.

Tod's painting, though, is just that—a painting, a metaphor within the larger metaphor for dream's end that is the novel itself. The betrayer of the dream—and the real subject of Tod's painting—is not nature's burning, but man's. The collapse of the high hopes projected onto the California landscape is depicted less often in images of natural destruction than in episodes of manmade violence.

Violence comes by the gun and, most appropriately for the locale, by the automobile. As Los Angeles emerged, in the 1930s, as the city on wheels, the car in fiction became the symbolic death instrument. The fast car on the Coast Highway came to represent the betrayed promise of freedom and high-speed mobility: the end of the road marks the end of the dream. As Paul Skenazy in his introductory piece on detective fiction notes, "the meeting place of ocean and road confirms that there is no turning back. Maybe this is part of the lesson of cars in the California story: the faster one travels the more one realizes that there is nowhere to go."

Still, the illusion of freedom, of mobility, of control over one's destiny has always been attached to the highway. Throughout American literature, the open road has been a principal metaphor for freedom and autonomy. The metaphor has been given special intensity in California fiction. Joan Didion, in *The White Album*, speaks of contemporary California freeway driving as "the only secular communion we have." Driving on the freeways is not the same as participating in them: participants think neither of where they came from nor where they are going, but "only about where they are." The experience requires "total surrender" to what she calls the "rapture of the freeway." Maria Wyeth, the beleaguered heroine of her 1970 novel *Play It as It Lays*, attempts desperately to give some order to her existence by speeding, without destination, along the freeways. She gets on the freeway at ten in the morning, packs her lunch so she won't have to stop, and travels all day:

> Again and again she returned to an intricate stretch south
> of the interchange where successful passage from the
> Hollywood onto the Harbor required a diagonal move
> across four lanes of traffic. On the afternoon she finally
> did it without once braking or losing the beat on the
> radio she was exhilarated, and that night slept
> dreamlessly.[13]

For Maria maneuvering on the freeway may be a way of playing it as it lays, of "creating order through the exercise of skills," as Charles Crow says of this passage. For Reyner Banham (who called the freeway one of the four distinct ecologies of Los Angeles) it may have offered the only way to read the city. but for most of the novelists, the California highway is a cul-de-sac. Like the highways traveled by Faulkner's Joe Christmas and by Fitzgerald's Jay Gatsby and Monroe Stahr, it marks the closing off of possibilities, not the opening to new experience. In James Cain's *The Postman Always Rings Twice* and *Double Indemnity*, in Fitzgerald's *The Last Tycoon*, in the detective novels of Chandler and Macdonald, and in Thomas Pynchon's *The Crying of Lot 49*, the car along the coast highway has reached the end of the line. Late in Pynchon's novel Oedipa Maas, her bearings lost, her purpose obscured, stands beside a dead telephone and a rented car facing the ocean. The scene sums up not only Oedipa Maas's enigma, but the plight of a good many other California seekers. Los Angeles, as metaphoric city, lies at the end of westward migration and aspiration.

III

Of the dozen essays that make up this collection Richard Lehan's opening essay, "The Los Angeles Novel and the Idea of the West," places the region's fiction in its broadest context. Drawing his illustrations from five novels—Fitzgerald's *The Last Tycoon*, West's *The Day of The Locust*, McCoy's *They Shoot Horses, Don't They?*, John Gregory Dunne's *True Confessions*, and Pynchon's *The Crying of Lot 49*—Lehan argues that Los Angeles represents as metaphor the culmination of the "Idea of the West," which had its origin in late seventeenth- and early eighteenth-century Europe. That idea rests on two principal articles of faith: first, that natural rights have priority over birth rights, and second, that as a consequence man's role is to control and dominate his environment, to impose his will upon the land for power and profit. The process of control through acquisition and technology that finds its early literary expression in Defoe's London was carried west across the Atlantic and then west again across the continent, going under such names as the Frontier Movement, Manifest Destiny, and the California Dream. In Los Angeles, a city almost literally carved out of a desert and dominated by technology—first the railroad, then the automobile—the process has reached its disastrous finale. Los Angeles, he holds, is the end product of a fraudulent dream, the place where the westward push culminates after two centuries in violence, exhaustion, and death.

The two essays that follow in the opening section of the

book, mine on James M. Cain and Horace McCoy and Gerald Locklin's on Nathanael West, suggest the ways three writers of the thirties have appropriated the human and architectural environment
of Los Angeles to reveal a pattern of hope giving way to frustration and violence. My essay tries to demonstrate that Cain and
McCoy, particularly in their first novels, *The Postman Always
Rings Twice* (1934) and *They Shoot Horses, Don't They?* (1935),
establish in tone, tempo, incident, and imagery the direction taken
by a number of subsequent Los Angeles novelists. Most specifically, I focus on the writers' use of the man-made landscape—the
roadside motor court, the dance hall at the edge of the ocean, the
car on the Coast Highway—as images of deception, metaphors for
betrayed hope. Locklin's essay discusses *The Day of the Locust* in
terms different both from Lehan's and from my own earlier remarks on West's novel. In contrast to Lehan's Hollywood-as-apoca-
lypse treatment of the work and my comments on West's handling
of the architecture of illusion, Locklin is interested first in the
structure of the novel, which he sees suggestively as "asymmetrical and horizontal" in keeping with the form of the city itself, and
second in the human landscape of West's "half world." The major
part of his eassay turns on what he sees as a pervasive pattern of
sexual neurosis infecting virtually all the characters, a pattern he
finds generally in West's fiction and in novels about Hollywood.

In the year in which *The Day of the Locust* appeared Raymond Chandler published *The Big Sleep*, the first of his seven
Philip Marlowe novels. Detective fiction, particularly in its tough-
guy, hard-boiled version, has since the thirties found a congenial
home in California's cities. Both San Francisco and Los Angeles
have long histories of corruption and violence linked inextricably
with the exploitation of gold, land, oil, and water. The brand of
detective fiction that took hold in Southern California first with
Chandler, then with Macdonald, was an exploration of the dark side
of the dream, the side that encouraged the rape of the landscape
and then allowed the plunderers to retreat into palatial homes,
their crimes buried in the past. Los Angeles, Chandler wrote in
his introduction to the collection *Trouble Is My Business*, is the
symbolic center of a "world gone wrong," a place in which the
streets "were dark with more than night." The tough private eye,

moving along those dark streets, became the vehicle for digging into the past, exposing the sources of corruption.

Paul Skenazy, in the first of three essays devoted to Southern California detective fiction (and the first of two pieces he has contributed to this volume), looks broadly at the genesis of the tradition and analytically isolates its components. His essay itself is a first-rate piece of detective work. He finds the tradition's sources in a number of places: in the archetypal western story with its self-reliant, resourceful hero, in British detective fiction, and, more directly, in the tough-guy stories appearing in the pulp magazine *Black Mask* and in the novels of Dashiell Hammett. Paul Cain's *Fast One* (1932), set in Los Angeles, Skenazy sees as the direct prototype of the novels of Chandler and Macdonald. Along with Hammett's Continental Op and the *Black Mask* detectives, Cain's private eye, Kells, asserts the antiestablishment ethic of the new detective. He affirms his independence of all systems, refuses to be bought, and remains loyal only to the obligations of his work. His power, his validation, Skenazy holds, comes solely through his ability to solve puzzles, to penetrate masks.

With Chandler, and then Macdonald, there is a shift away from Cain's and *Black Mask*'s world of speakeasies, saloons, and gangland crime and toward the new suburban world of Southern California, one in which the criminal rich live in elaborate fortresses up and down the coast. Unlike the traditional western story, which asserts that ideals from the past can be restorative, the Los Angeles detective story maintains that the past is the source of crime. It is the undisclosed event that occurred before the plot begins, the skeleton in the closet, that the detective must discover.

The dream of success is shown to be rooted in corruption and violence. Here Skenazy is echoing what Lehan has said more generally about the Los Angeles novel; their treatments of *The Big Sleep* bear this out. Skenazy, like Lehan, focuses on the Sternwood oil fields as the symbol and source of past defilement and the immediate link to blackmail and murder. Hidden in what is called a park below the family mansion, the wells are a potent symbol of the denial of accountability by the rich.

The attempt to hide the past, to build a new identity, is signaled in both Chandler's and Macdonald's fiction by the move from one neighborhood to another. "The California myth grants magical, transformative power to the alteration of place," Skenazy says. Encouraged by the mobility of the population and the open class structure, people create new identities. They change names and neighborhoods to wipe out traces of past crimes; they become what they appear to be. This is a point made both by Liahna Babener in her essay on Chandler and Jerry Speir in his essay on Macdonald.

Blackmail functions in detective fiction to pull characters back into the past. Skenazy, applying psychoanalytic terminology, likens the blackmailer to the superego, the punishing parent who must be eliminated if the secret, the unconscious, is to remain hidden from the world.

Liahna Babener's essay, "Raymond Chandler's City of Lies," the first of a pair of essays she has contributed, deals with many of these same ideas. Chandler's city, she holds, symbolizes the lie "that prosperity brings personal contentment and deliverance from the past." Wealth and the trappings of success cannot buy immunity from history. But in contrast to Lehan's cultural historical approach to *The Big Sleep* and Skenazy's psychoanalytic treatment of Chandler's work, she undertakes a detailed image study of the seven novels, isolating the dominant patterns that function to reveal the layers of deception.

Jerry Speir's study of Ross Macdonald's fiction provides an interesting contrast to Babener's essay, focusing as it does on his subject's characteristic use of the natural landscape of Southern California as the chief source of symbols. Babener's concern is with the manmade landscape; Speir's is with man's tenuous and invasive relationship to the organic world. In Macdonald's Southern California, the coastal region from Santa Barbara to Los Angeles, the rich live characteristically above the ocean in elaborate houses. But the rugged mountains and the endless ocean are there to remind them of their insignificance and the folly of past crimes. The menace of the ocean is always present, as are the enshrouding fogs, the sun blazing with a fury, and the hot winds that stir the dry brush to fire. In *The Underground Man* (1971) nature explodes in a devastating forest fire "in response to the moral outrage fostered by man." The outrage is man's egoism, his attempt to treat nature, Speir says, "as raw material for human exploitation."

Yet Speir reminds us that Macdonald is also a novelist of hope, and nature can be redemptive as well as destructive. The restoration of families at the end of *The Underground Man*, for instance, is accompanied by a rainfall that quenches the destructive fire. The tension in Macdonald's novels, ultimately, is not only between man and nature, but between dissolution and redemption.

A third section of the book, one that I have called "Perspectives," brings together three essays that approach the region's fiction from distinct vantage points. The first of these, Mark Royden Winchell's, examines the Hollywood novel since Nathanael West, differentiating between novels that purvey the Hollywood myth and those that show the antimyth. The former is represented in the essay by Fitzgerald's *The Last Tycoon* and the latter by Budd Schulberg's *What Makes Sammy Run?*. Fitzgerald, Winchell contends, accepted much of the original myth but had the misfortune of arriving and working in Hollywood at the end of its golden years, a fact that accounts for the elegiac tone of his novel. Focusing on the careers of the lead characters, Winchell sets Fitzgerald's and Schulberg's works against each other: both Monroe Stahr and Sammy Glick have risen from the Jewish Lower East Side of New York to Hollywood prominence, but while Stahr is an embittered and exhausted producer of some genius, Glick is an opportunist who symbolizes the corrupt and corrupting qualities of the film capital. (It was Schulberg, Winchell reminds us, who propagated the distorting image of Fitzgerald as victim of Hollywood in his novel *The Disenchanted*.)

Winchell sees Mailer as something of an inheritor of the Fitzgerald version. While he acknowledges that *The Deer Park* draws on the antimyth in its mockery of the hypocrisy and cant of the movie colony, its portrait of Charlie Eitel achieves a note of heroism. Earlier I discussed Mailer's work as having derived from West's, and I think the connection is strong (at one point quite explicit: Eitel is attempting a comeback with a screenplay that bears a strong resemblance to *Miss Lonelyhearts*); however, by comparing Stahr and Eitel as tragic figures, Winchell makes a convincing case for a Fitzgerald-Mailer link. He argues that the real influence of West is to be found in Joan Didion's *Play It as It Lays*, where the myth/antimyth dialectic resolves itself into a third term—the ironic or parodic vision,[14] a kind of anti-antimyth bent on demythologizing Hollywood that he finds generally in Didion's and her husband John Gregory Dunne's writings about the region. Winchell's essay is followed by Walter Wells's study of the Hollywood perspectives of two British exiles—Aldous Huxley and Evelyn Waugh. Both biographical and critical in scope, Wells's essay examines Huxley's letters and Waugh's diary as well as their Hollywood fiction to draw a picture of their disquieting careers in the film capital. Wells's discussion of Waugh's *The Loved One* is especially interesting. He treats it both as a satire on the film capital and as the novel that "internationalized the Hollywood novel." The setting is not the film studio but the Forest Lawn–inspired Whispering Glades cemetery. The connections between Hollywood and graveyard are abundant: architectural facades dominate the grounds; sound effects imitate the chirping of birds and buzzing of bees; the costuming and makeup of the "loved ones" rival MGM's best efforts; and Mr. Joyboy, the chief mortician who masterminds the whole enterprise, is the epitome of the Monroe Stahr–Sammy Glick figure creating roles for his inert actors. The graveyard, Wells asserts, is "the final resting place for a 2,500-year-old civilization." Written just after the war, it presents the symbolic landscape of European barbarism passed "from a defeated Germany to an ascendant America over the moribund body of English culture."

Kingsley Widmer has argued in an article, "The Hollywood Image" (*Coastlines* V, 1961), that there is a fundamental difference between the American and British novelists' vision of Hollywood. There is for Huxley and Waugh "a more general emotional and metaphysical contempt for the Hollywood Image." Whereas the native novelists—West, Schulberg, Mailer—satirize Hollywood as a national phenomenon, the British exiles measure it in broader, cross-cultural terms. Well's treatment of *The Loved One* as a work that internationalizes the Hollywood phenomenon would seem to support such a view.

Charles Crow's essay, "Home and Transcendence in Los Angeles Fiction" considers *The Loved One* along with three other works, Joan Didion's *Play It as It Lays* and two lesser-known pieces, Marc Norman's *Bicycle Riding in Los Angeles* and Hisaye Yamamoto's "Yoneko's Earthquake," which I alluded to earlier and which has been reprinted in James D. Houston's collection, *West Coast Fiction* (Bantam Books). Taking his cue from Whitman's "Facing West from California's Shores," Crow argues that an essential theme in Los Angeles fiction is the quest for home ("for the place of wholeness the wanderer has sought") and for transcendence ("which must follow when this resting place is found"). The quest, which gives life to all four works, may or may not be successful: Los Angeles holds out possibilities for personal and cultural renaissance as well as collapse. For Waugh's protagonist, there is, he holds, a kind of rebirth: Dennis Barlow undergoes the transformation to artist. Like Yamamoto's young heroine, he becomes an artist through "the savage destruction of innocence." Essentially, Crow is making the case against the case against Los Angeles. The city is more than the popular image would have it of fast driving, despair, drugs, and divorce. Even in Didion's work, the "most compellingly bleak of any writer," the true subject is not the sterility of Los Angeles but "the whole modern world, the way we live now."

The final section of the book, "Fiction as History," looks at four works written in the seventies that take their subjects from the historical record, works that transform public events into metaphor and symbol. Raymund Paredes focuses on the Mexican-American writer Oscar Zeta Acosta's *The Revolt of the Cockroach People* (1973), an autobiographical account of his involvement in the angry encounter of Chicanos and the white power structure in Los Angeles in the late sixties. Acosta, who is the model for the freaked-out Samoan lawyer in Hunter Thompson's *Fear and Loathing in Las Vegas*, is a man, Paredes writes, whose "excesses and paradoxes" match those of the city. "Los Angeles never drew the attention of a writer so much like itself." Acosta's Los Angeles, like Faulkner's South, is a place "cursed by its subjugation of a people and its willful destruction of a standing, vigorous culture." Los Angeles has rejected its very soul. The novel ends apocalyptically on the images of rioting in the barrios and the burning of the city's Hall of Records, after which Acosta leaves for San Francisco.

Paul Skenazy looks at two novels based on headlined events of the 1940s: John Gregory Dunne's *True Confessions* (1977), which takes its starting point from the unsolved "Black Dahlia" murder of Elizabeth Short in 1947, and Thomas Sanchez's *Zoot Suit Mur-*

ders, which centers on the wartime barrio riots of 1943. "Both novels," he writes, "serve as useful object lessons in the problems of writing about the Los Angeles past, the contradictions involved in historical revision, and the difficulties encountered in turning the melodrama of news headlines into the stuff of tragedy." Both employ the detective framework, and Skenazy focuses on how they depart from the tough-guy tradition of Chandler and Macdonald. Dunne's novel is the more successful of the two, a complex work that parodies the form as it plays against history as well. While he provides a killer for the Black Dahlia murder, the solution is accidental and only incidental. Nothing is really solved. Dunne's world is one of "absurd accidents and chance encounters." The ordered sequence of cause-effect central to detective fiction is undercut. Historical accuracy is subverted, too, "as if we are meant to see fiction as another, equally valid, plot structure, no more (if no less) significant or truthful than the historical record."

Sanchez's novel, by contrast, is a work of revisionist history, an attempt to affirm the Chicano rebellion either ignored or distorted by history texts. In this sense it is like Acosta's *The Revolt of The Cockroach People,* but Sanchez's novel, according to Skenazy, ends by oversimplifying social and political reality. The complex issues of racism and wartime paranoia are distorted and reduced to melodrama and to an Anglo love story.

Finally, in "Chinatown, City of Blight," Liahna Babener examines Robert Towne's screenplay based on the Owens River water scandal as an allegorical retelling of the Fall from Paradise. As she did in her essay on Chandler, Babener deals concretely and lucidly with the imagery and symbolism of the work, tracing the ways in which public and private morality, political and sexual taint, fuse in Towne's story.

Having said something about what is in the book, it remains for me to comment briefly on what is not in it. A collection of essays by different contributors will, by definition, be selective and cannot achieve the inclusiveness of a single-author book. A number of contemporary authors who have been writing about Los Angeles deserve mention, writers like Jill Robinson, Eve Babitz, Carolyn See, and Kate Braverman. Some would argue that John Fante deserves a place—as perhaps does his chief fan, the poet/novelist Charles Bukowski. Fante has written several Los Angeles novels,

the best known of which is *Ask the Dust* (1939). Christopher Isherwood's *A Single Man* (1951), a fine Los Angeles novel, is not discussed in the text. Only brief mention is given (in this introduction)
to John O'Hara's Los Angeles novel, *Hope of Heaven* (1938), and
Gavin Lambert's story collection, *The Slide Area* (1951). Recent
detective fiction is not discussed except in passing—the work of,
among others, Roger Simon, Andrew Bergman, and Stuart Kaminsky. And the police novels of the prolific ex-cop Joseph Wambaugh
have not been dealt with here—books like *The Black Marble, The
Glitter Dome, The New Centurions,* and his nonfiction novel, *The
Onion Field.*

In what it does cover the book attempts to be both representative and balanced. If it is a sampling, my hope is that it is a
fair one and that it provides both broad coverage of the major
themes and concerns of the regional Los Angeles novel and more
focused assessments of some of its principal practitioners—Cain,
West, Chandler, Macdonald, and others.

Notes

1. Of these writers, only Dreiser did not write fiction about Los
Angeles. O'Hara wrote a Los Angeles novel, *Hope of Heaven* (1938), not
by any standards one of his better works. Faulkner wrote only a short story
about the region, "Golden Land," a work which deserves more attention,
but in his brief time on the West Coast was the most successful of the lot
as a screenwriter, adapting for the screen Hemingway's *To Have and Have
Not* and Chandler's *The Big Sleep.*

2. Nathanael West, *Miss Lonelyhearts and The Day of the Locust*
(New York: New Directions, 1962), p. 61.

3. Among other pre-1930s Los Angeles/Hollywood novels deserv-
ing mention are Harry Leon Wilson's *Merton of the Movies* (1922), Upton
Sinclair's *Oil!* (1927), and the Graham Brothers' *Queer People* (1930), the
latter an immediate precursor of the Hollywood novels of the thirties.

4. Mark Lee Luther, *The Boosters* (Indianapolis: Bobbs-Merrill
Co., 1923) pp. 8–9.

5. Novels, for instance, by immigrants like Abraham Cahan,
Anzia Yezierska, and Elias Tobenkin and by nonimmigrants like Upton
Sinclair and Ernest Poole, who used immigrant material to focus atten-
tion on the exploitation of the working class.

6.   I am indebted here to the suggestions contained in J. U. Peters, "The Los Angeles Anti-Myth," *Itinerary Seven: Essays on California Writers,* ed. Charles L. Crow (Bowling Green, Ohio: Bowling Green State University Press, 1978), pp. 21–34.

7.   Kevin Starr, *Americans and the California Dream, 1850–1915* (1973; rpt. Santa Barbara and Salt Lake City: Peregrine Smith, 1981), p. 68.

8.   Evelyn Waugh, *The Loved One* (New York: Vintage Books 1948) p. 40.

9.   Robert Parker, *A Savage Place* (New York: Dell Publishing Co., 1981), p. 143.

10.   Alison Lurie, *The Nowhere City* (1965; rpt. Harmondsworth, England, and New York: Penguin Books, 1977), p. 309.

11.   Norman Mailer, *The Deer Park* (1955; New York: G. P. Putnam's Sons, Perigee Books, 1981), p. 3.

12.   Gavin Lambert, *The Slide Area* (1951; New York: Ballantine Books, 1972), p. 8.

13.   Joan Didion, *Play It as It Lays* (1970; New York: Bantam Books, 1971), p. 14.

14.   The triadic model he is using here is like that of R. W. B. Lewis, who in *The American Adam* discusses major American writers in terms of the parties of hope, the past and irony.

PART ONE

Starting Places

ONE

The Los Angeles Novel and the Idea of the West

Richard Lehan

F. Scott Fitzgerald's *The Last Tycoon* opens with Monroe Stahr moving east to west across the heavens. As the plane crosses the desert, Stahr looks down at the lights of Southern California in the far distance and thinks how far he has come from his youth in the slums of New York. He thinks also of America, a land whose westward movement has now been arrested by the sea.

Most of the action in Fitzgerald's as in so many other Los Angeles novels is engendered by these kinds of thoughts. The seed of these thoughts, the idea of the West, was carried from Europe across the Atlantic and then across a whole continent. The movement went by a number of names—Manifest Destiny, California Dreaming—but implicit in it were the assumption that natural rights took precedence over birth rights and the even more transforming belief that man must dominate his environment, impose his will upon nature and the land, and turn that control into wealth.

The idea goes back to the late seventeenth century and is depicted most clearly in Daniel Defoe's Robinson Crusoe.

A number of parallels exist between Crusoe's desire and that of the first Americans to survive in the wilderness. Both came from the Old World to the New, bringing with them an old set of myths and a new empirical/scientific state of mind. Both impose their will with the help of tools and rudimentary technology upon the land and bring it and the animals and the natives under their control. And before they are through, each has turned this control into wealth. In a premarket economy, money follows power, but in a market economy, power follows money, and in America that power led to control over the system, which encouraged nationalism and later imperialism, especially as the need for resources and a world market became greater.

Almost every city in the modern western world took its being from these imperatives, of course, but though Los Angeles is not unique, its image becomes different, perhaps because it is the last major city to grow out of the idea of the West. Further, Los Angeles was crafted out of the desert. Without the technology that would bring water, Los Angeles would never have become more than a village whose inhabitants struggled for life in an inhospitable environment. In the late nineteenth century, when two railroad lines met in Los Angeles, the city became a winter resort for wealthy Easterners. Later it became a mecca for more ordinary people who arrived from Indiana and Iowa in search of new life, and after that was inhabited by the technology that makes modern warfare and airfare possible, the Yoyodines of Thomas Pynchon's world. That Hollywood was among the first of the new industries to settle in Los Angeles only coupled the dreamer to the dream.

If the modern commercial city had its beginning in the eighteenth century, and if this city was transformed in the nineteenth century by the industrial revolution, such a city underwent a second transformation in twentieth-century Los Angeles, the first city in the western world to take its dimensions from the automobile—a fact that has determined its landscape and scale and overpowered a sense of human proportions. Probably no city in the western world has a more negative image than Los Angeles, depicted as it is on nightly TV as one vast freeway system, enshrouded in smog,

carrying thousands of dreamers to a kind of spiritual and physical dereliction. We often move in this world from a sense of promise to a sense of the grotesque, and hence to the violent and the apoc-
- alyptic. Los Angeles, the supreme embodiment of the secular city, is built on the same geographic parallel as Jerusalem, the embodiment of the holy city. The westward movement had its own way of playing jokes on us.

Whether Fitzgerald brought these ideas consciously to *The Last Tycoon*, I am not prepared to say, although I believe that he had a sense of most of them. Fitzgerald depicted Los Angeles as located at an end point in time and "filling up with weary desperadoes."[1] Somehow this image seems consistent with the image of the grunion who throw themselves on the beach in an act that would seem to promise something more than death: "They came in twos and threes and platoons and companies, relentless and exalted and scornful, around the great bare feet of the intruders, as they had come before Sir Francis Drake had nailed his plaque to the boulder on the shore" (p. 92). Something mysterious has been pushing man west (since Francis Drake and before), something seemingly inseparable from a kind of death (hence the reference to the grunion run). Thomas Pynchon will, we might say, bring these images to a conclusion in *The Crying of Lot 49*. In Fitzgerald's novel, Stahr himself seems to embody the process of westering; he is himself a weary desperado. A man who has dominated a new industry, has become a boy wonder and the very model of success, he now finds his energy depleted, the next struggle overwhelming, the next effort too much. The labor leader Brimmer, a Communist, cannot believe such a man holds up the system. But Brimmer only sees the shell of the man and fails to realize that Stahr is perhaps among the last (as suggested by the title) embodiments of Enlightenment individualism before it is replaced by the new corporatism and big unions:

> The split between the controllers of the movie industry, on the one hand, and the various groups of employees, on the other, is widening and leaving no place for real individualists of business like Stahr, whose successes are personal achievements and whose career has always been

invested with a certain personal glamor. He has held
himself directly responsible to everyone with whom he
worked; he has even wanted to beat up his enemies
himself. In Hollywood he is "the last tycoon." (p. 131)

What Stahr brought west was a dream spawned in feudal Europe,
transformed by the Reformation and the Enlightenment, and turned
into the frontier movement. This dream was codified around a personal sense of honor, a belief in the potential of self and technology,
and the desire to control others and to dominate what technology
had created. Fitzgerald came to believe that as the country moved
west, it lured the dreamer toward ideals that were in reality dead.
Such is the fate of Gatsby, and such also is the fate of Monroe Stahr,
whose story, Fitzgerald tells us, he set in "a lavish, romantic past
that perhaps will not come again into our time" (p. 141).

Fitzgerald could write with such conviction in *The Last
Tycoon* because he himself had experienced so many of the emotions that he gave to Monroe Stahr. After early success, he too had
come crashing down in the 1930s. He came to Los Angeles out of
need for money to sustain Zelda in an Asheville (life has its puns)
sanatorium and to pay off debts that stemmed from his own ill
health and despair. The novel brilliantly depicts the need of a sick,
tired man to start over again, his desire to sustain an earlier vitality that is gone forever. Fitzgerald could and did easily move from
himself to Monroe Stahr and from Stahr to a sense of destiny—that
is, a sense of cultural and historical process at work. Stahr's love
affair with Kathleen involves the need of the uprooted for roots
and a need to arrest time and reverse the process of which he
seems to be the end product. The mad drives through Los Angeles
at night that take them to the Pacific Coast Highway form an axis
between the home in Beverly Hills, in which he seldom lives since
he often sleeps at the studio, and the partly built home in Malibu,
which is as unfinished as his grand design. The rootlessness, the
misplaced desire, the horror of standing still, the need for fulfillment that seems inseparable from movement, the sense of being
incomplete in an unfinished home and in a city spawned by chance
between desert and sea—all of these feelings give an intensity to
the story of Monroe Stahr that cannot be separated from the world
in which it takes place.

Nathanael West's *The Day of the Locust* takes us several levels closer to Los Angeles as a kind of urban hell. West begins with many of the themes that would inform *The Last Tycoon;* he shows Hollywood as the end of a dream, to which one brings the unfulfilled self in the hope of success and material gain. But West does not concentrate on what is glamorous in this pursuit. Instead the focus is on shabby apartment houses, the loneliness of the displaced pilgrim, the burlesque that goes with grubbing a living as if the misery of survival is prelude to the dream.

Most different from Fitzgerald is West's belief that beneath the false glamor of Hollywood (both the place and the industry) is a brutal violence just waiting to erupt. West takes us to the edge of apocalypse, showing us in his satiric jeremiad a process playing itself out destructively. Nature itself seems to have given way to grotesqueries—to architecture that appears to result from an explosion in a time machine and houses that hang from hills like unnatural growths. It is a world where dwarfs unfold themselves out of rag piles in lonely corridors, where unwieldy hands jump about uncontrolled at the end of wrists, and where meat and fruit look unnatural in the neon-lighted bins of grocery stores.

In *The Day of the Locust,* people come to Los Angeles to realize their dream, or to retire, or to die. It is an end in itself, a world without a past where time can be renewed or terminated or where a person's fantasies can be warmed by the sun. West's novel reveals that part of what pushes people west is a sense of fantasy that often gives way to violence and death. No Los Angeles novel ends on a more violent note than *The Day of the Locust.* In West's world, youth and beauty have become commodities for sale in the market called Hollywood. Waiting to sell or buy leads to the terrible boredom that consumes so many lives in this novel and explains the need of so many to find some kind of excitement, whether it be the morbid interest of a funeral or the excitement of a movie premiere. Beneath the emptiness that neither ritual can relieve is a capacity for violence that seems atavistic, as if all restraint has finally given way on the edge of the Pacific.

Hollywood is one of the novel's sustaining metaphors. Not only is the place a dumping ground for dreams, but beneath the exterior of the film industry is something so thin that it collapses under the weight of life, transforming the heroic into the grotesque as when the Waterloo set collapses during the filming of the Napoleon movie, illusion giving way to reality, taking history with it. The Enlightenment era ended with Napoleon and Waterloo, now buried under Hollywood plywood and plaster. The violence of this scene is recapitulated three times in the novel—first in the scene in which Faye and Earle dance, then in the scene at the cock fight which gives way to the fight between Earle and Miguel, and finally in the scene at the movie premiere in which the characters in the novel seem to step into Tod's apocalyptic painting, "The Burning of Los Angeles," as if art has prophetically jumped ahead of history. The city's destiny, then, is to destruct, as if we have come to the end of a process, an end point in time.

Horace McCoy's *They Shoot Horses Don't They?* begins where *The Day of the Locust* ends—with the ending of a process, the judge reading the death sentence to Robert Syverten after he has already killed Gloria Beatty. The story of the killing makes up the novel, which is set at a marathon dance at the end of the Santa Monica pier. The dance itself, the commercial exploitation of the dancers who are pitted against one another until they literally drop, symbolizes the Hollywood experience. Both Robert and Gloria have come to Los Angeles seeking success. Like so many characters in Los Angeles novels, they meet by accident, two human beings randomly thrown together in the impersonal city. Robert misreads Gloria waving for a bus:

"I thought you were waving at me. . . ."
"What would I be waving at you for?" she asked.[2]

Out of such impersonality comes their mutual endurance of and finally Gloria's capitulation to the "merry-go-round" of life, ending with Robert shooting her at her request, while the tide of the Pacific beats on under them, nature itself capable of the greatest endurance, despite the shiny city as a monument to man's belief that he controls nature. Beneath the degrading process of the dance itself is, once again, a violence waiting to explode, as when Pedro tries to strangle his girlfriend and slashes Rocky's arm before he is blackjacked by Socks. No wonder Mrs. Higby and the Good Morals League try to stop the dance, but neither this dance nor the larger one it symbolizes can be stopped by good morals. The dance creates laws of its own, just as the city does. A kind of literary naturalism is at work, and what is left of civilization seems ready to give way to the atavistic. The shrewd control; the strong endure; and the battle becomes fiercer when the strong are the combatants: "I began to heel-and-toe faster than I ever had before," Robert tells us. "I knew I had to. All the weaklings had been eliminated. All these couples were fast" (p. 104).

When all but twenty couples have been eliminated, the dance ends with a brawl that leads to a shooting and two deaths. Only violence can break the rhythm. Robert and Gloria move out of the dance hall onto the pier and look up toward the lights of Malibu, "where all the movie stars live" and where Robert's dreams still take him. "Always tomorrow," Gloria tells him. "The big break is always coming tomorrow" (p. 124). As she says these words, a man "dragging a four-foot hammerhead shark" passes to make McCoy's point even more explicit. Gloria has had enough; she wants to get off this "whole stinking . . . merry-go-round" (p. 125), and Robert merely assists her. The absurd violence that has dominated the novel suddenly seems to have a purpose and is transformed into friendship. When one has become totally controlled by the system, when lost endurance makes the race useless, when the self loses even the illusion of fulfillment, then death is a release, one that acquires even larger significance because it takes place "out there in that black night on the edge of the Pacific" (p. 11), where many of these novels leave us.

Raymond Chandler's *The Big Sleep* begins and ends in the oil fields owned by General Guy Sternwood. As Marlowe looks out from the Sternwood mansion, he can see the fields in the distance:

> On this lower level faint and far off I could just barely see some of the old wooden derricks of the oilfields from which the Sternwoods had made their money. Most of the field was public now, cleaned up and donated to the city by General Sternwood. But a little of it was still producing in groups of wells pumping five or six barrels a day. The Sternwoods, having moved up the hill, could no longer smell the stale sump water or the oil, but they could still look out of their front windows and see what had made them rich. I don't suppose they would want to.[3]

In this novel Chandler, who worked for oil companies, draws a clear connection between their exploitation of the land and a moral recklessness that results.

Into this despoiled world comes Philip Marlowe, a kind of urban knight who desires to be honorable in a corrupt world, a kind of frontiersman transformed by the city. He follows a code that involves honor, courage, and pride in a job well done. In the tradition of the nineteenth-century detective (Dickens's Bucket and Conrad's Heat come to mind), he reduces the anonymity of city life, connects several sets of characters with one another, and helps put together the pieces of the narrative mystery. He is the human conduit through which necessary information must flow in order to solve that mystery.

Appropriately, the initial mystery involves the blackmailing of Carmen, General Sternwood's daughter, whose moral reckless-ness embodies her father's ruthless capitalism. I say "appropriately" because blackmail involves the use of information for purposes of extortion. General Sternwood's money, which has come from exploiting others, leads in this way to his own exploitation, and Marlowe must intercede between legal and illegal worlds, which turn out to be two sides of the same coin. Just a few miles from the Sternwood mansion, we enter the world of pornographic book shops and illegal gambling—the world of the mob whose motives, if not its methods, are substantially the same as those of Sternwood and his corporation.

In *The Big Sleep*, Carmen has murdered a man in the oil fields that made the family rich and is in turn about to be black-mailed. Carmen killed Rusty Regan when he would not return her love and tries to kill Marlowe for the same reason and even in the same place—the oil fields that supply the money that allows Stern-wood to act with impunity. Marlowe, however, refuses the $15,000 that would buy him off and that would bring him into the center of the Sternwoods' capitalistic system. Marlowe prefers to remain on the edge of the system, prefers to "go on being a son of a bitch" (p. 214) even though he will never escape being "part of the nasti-ness" (p. 216).

In *The Big Sleep*, Chandler takes us deep into the meaning of the idea of the West: he shows the moral consequences of a state of mind founded on commercial exploitation, the movement from the desire to control the land to the desire to control other people. This process always produces victims, in this case Rusty Regan and almost Marlowe himself. The big sleep of the title is death, of course, the force by which nature exercises its final dominance over the proud man and his belief that he can control all that is outside him. The big sleep is the great equalizer in this novel, the moment when "oil and water" (the sources of wealth in the West) are not different from "wind and air" (p. 216)—and Rusty Regan no different from General Sternwood. So the big sleep restores a kind of balance for the dead, but not for the living.

The novels that I have been discussing were all written in the thirties and reflect a good deal of the disillusionment with the capitalistic system at the height of the depression. But the theme of the West as I have been using it in this essay is not limited to a particular time period. If we jump a generation ahead to certain novels of the sixties and seventies, we find the same concerns, even if the narrative context is understandably different.

John Gregory Dunne's *True Confessions* is a remarkable case in point. Dunne's novel is about two brothers: Tom and Desmond Spellacy, who grow up in the slums of Boyle Heights; one becomes a detective lieutenant in the Los Angeles police force, the other a monsignor and the cardinal's righthand man in the Los Angeles diocese: "Cops and priests, that's what the Heights was famous for."[4] Despite their very different vocations, their lives are connected by the city itself and unexpectedly by the murder of Lois Fazenda, a Los Angeles prostitute whose corpse has been found cut in two in a vacant lot. The link between the two brothers and Lois Fazenda is Jack Amsterdam, a Southern California contractor who embodies the desire to develop everything in sight, and who holds seventeen million dollars in building contracts from Desmond Spellacy and the diocese.

Amsterdam's influence is pervasive and pernicious. He not only dominates the building industry in Southern California (other contractors' rigs mysteriously blow over when they submit competing bids), but he seems omnipotent in the underworld as well, running a chain of whorehouses, rigging prize fights, and forging green cards for illegal immigrant Mexicans, among other enterprises. In *True Confessions*, as in other Los Angeles novels of the

1960s and 1970s, the worlds of General Sternwood and Eddie Mars have become one. The lives of both brothers intersect with Amsterdam's—Des's because of his position as business manager for the church, and Tommy's because he was once Amsterdam's "bagman" and is now the chief investigator in the Lois Fazenda case.

Lois was a part of Amsterdam's stable of girls. Even Desmond has chanced to meet her in a car in which he is being driven back from the racetrack. The evil that Amsterdam and his world exude thus touches everyone, and from Amsterdam's greed and desire to control comes all the action of this novel. At one point, Tommy Spellacy reflects, "Jack Amsterdam. Every time I turn around, there's Jack. Lois Fazenda does a good deed and it's one of Jack's rackets. That goddamn maze" (p. 213). Maze indeed. But like the good detective he is, Tom Spellacy can find his way through the maze—through the maze of the city and then the maze of facts— until he makes the lines connect: "connect the consecutive numbers with lines and a picture begins to emerge" (p. 261).

Marlowe, of course, has to make similar connections in *The Big Sleep*, and like Philip Marlowe, Tom Spellacy comes to realize that he is part of the emerging picture, and so is his brother, the priest. No one escapes from the system and its effects—a system that had its origins in both religious and economic beliefs on a different continent three centuries or more before the novel takes place. In *True Confessions*, Dunne rewrites the myth of original sin. Tom Spellacy reflects that both cops and priests share a belief in original sin, but original sin in this novel comes not from taking the apple from the tree but from cutting down the tree itself and developing the site.

The murderer of Lois Fazenda, an Encino barber by the name of Harold Pugh, has nothing to do with the principals of the novel. His brutal act serves ony as agency, to call attention to the system itself and the mentality that generates and keeps it going. *True Confessions* ends on the desert where Desmond Spellacy, now old and on the verge of death, was long ago exiled after his connection with Lois Fazenda has led to his disgrace. This exile is, he tells us, his salvation, his absolution, because it has freed him from the system. Los Angeles as a city took its being by overpowering the desert. But the closing of *True Confessions* calls our attention to the tenuousness of this victory over nature. At the end, Tom looks into the far distance and sees "a sandstorm beginning to build up" (p. 340). Anyone who has lived in Southern California knows how fire, flood, and sand challenge the very occupancy of place, and challenge as well man's Enlightenment pride in his mastery of what he creates. Dunne has convincingly shown how such pride is misplaced and how we are all victims of our master designs.

The novel of the sixties that most directly treats the idea of the West is Thomas Pynchon's *The Crying of Lot 49.* The central character in Pynchon's work is Oedipa Maas, who discovers that she has just been made the executrix of Pierce Inverarity's estate. Pierce is the ultimate descendant of Robinson Crusoe, a kind of Howard Hughes industrialist/ developer. Through his understanding of the commercial system and his use of technology, he has controlled the land and turned his complex holdings into a massive fortune. Oedipa (as her name suggests) is the modern woman who must come to terms with the legacy of the father (in her case a kind of father/ lover). What she discovers is that this legacy is America itself:

> She had dedicated herself weeks ago, to making sense of what Inverarity had left behind, never suspecting that the legacy was America. . . . her love [for him remained] incommensurate with his need to possess, to alter the land, to bring new skylines, personal antagonisms, growth rates into being. "Keep it bouncing," he told her once,"that's all the secret, keep it bouncing."[5]

In this novel Pynchon seems clearly to have been playing with the ideas of Henry Adams. Pierce Inverarity has created the world of the Dynamo, embodied in Yoyodine, the modern Southern California plant that has moved us beyond the industrial revolution into a new dimension of business and technology. Oedipa is the woman in this world (the metaphorical equivalent of the Virgin) who must pit her whole emotional and intelligent being against what Pierce has created: she may never come to understand what his state of mind has spawned.

It is also clear that Pynchon is working with many of the major ideas of Max Weber and R. W. Tawney, especially their belief that capitalism had its origins in Puritan thought and belief. Pynchon adds this dimension to the novel with a discussion of a Puritan sect, the Scurvhamites,and by the use of a Jacobean play, *The Courier's Tragedy,* a version of which may have been an attack on Puritanism. The play introduces us to a secret organization, Trystero, that may have had its origins in the late Renaissance as a counterforce to the Thurn and Taxis monopoly in the Low Countries, controlled by the Baron of Taxis. As Enlightenment capitalism spread West, the Trystero counterforce spread with it; disguised as black-faced Indians when it hit the frontier, its soldiers prey on the Pony Express and Wells Fargo until they hit the Pacific, where "their entire emphasis [was] now toward silence, impersonation, opposition masquerading as allegiance" (p. 130). Their acronym W.A.S.T.E. (We Await Silent Trystero's Empire) suggests that they take their being from the idea of entropy, the tendency of energy in a fixed system to run down. Indeed, their source of renewal seems to come from taking into themselves the human dereliction, the failures of one kind or another, the System uses up. They are intent in their belief that machines cannot go on forever, leaving waste by-products; they also seem to believe that the communication and information systems (including the mail) through which power is sustained, can be undermined, leaving silence. Out of this entropic waste and silence will come the death of the System, and once again we have the suggestion of an apocalypse.

The Crying of Lot 49 presupposes that the Puritan, middle-class, commercial, capitalistic, industrial, technological process is subject both to thermodynamic entropy, which creates waste, and communication entropy, which creates silence. The by-product of this process is a third kind of entropy, human, which leads to an army of outcasts, of derelicts and failures, who make up the core of Trystero. This army of men and women operates as a counterforce to the commercial processes that have ravaged the land as they have moved silently west through history.

An understanding of the commercial process seems to rest with Oedipa, or so she has come to believe. But since she is part of the process herself, it becomes impossible for her to verify her suspicions. All the signs become self-referential, suggesting paranoia, in this world where Los Angeles is named San Narciso and motor hotels are named Echo Court.

When capitalism took its being from Puritanism, the world had a reference point in God. In its three hundred years of development, capitalism substituted the Self for God, leaving Oedipa with signs that have no meaning outside the self-enclosed world that Pierce Inverarity has left her. At the very end of the novel, "She stood between the public phone booth and the rented car, in the night, her isolation complete, and tried to face toward the sea. But she had lost her bearings" (p. 133). Such is the fate of the new detective at what seems to be a juncture in history. Oedipa holds a dead phone, caught between the machine (the rented car) and the Pacific, lost in the isolation of the world Pierce Inverarity created. This enigmatic ending is a fitting conclusion to the novel that offers us the most complete and sustained handling of the idea of the West.

Notes

1. Scott Fitzgerald, *The Last Tycoon* (New York: Charles Scribner's Sons, 1941), p. 80. Further references are cited parenthetically in the text.

2. Horace McCoy, *They Shoot Horses, Don't They?* (1935; New York: Avon Books, 1969), p.19. Further references are cited parenthetically in the text.

3. Raymond Chandler, *The Big Sleep* (1939; New York: Random House, Vintage Books, 1976), p. 18. Further references are cited parenthetically in the text.

4. John Gregory Dunne, *True Confessions* (New York: E. P. Dutton & Co., 1977), p. 8. Further references are cited parenthetically in the text.

5. Thomas Pynchon, *The Crying of Lot 49* (1966; New York: Bantam Books, 1967), p. 134. Further references are cited parenthetically in the text.

TWO

Beginning in the Thirties: The Los Angeles Fiction of James M. Cain and Horace McCoy

David Fine

Writing on James M. Cain in *The New Republic* in 1975, Kevin Starr, author of *Americans and the California Dream*, observed: "Something happened in Southern California in the 1930s. Some new vision of evil rushed in upon the American consciousness." Starr's retrospective on Cain was occasioned by the appearance of *Chinatown*, a film that recovered for the seventies some part of that dark thirties–L.A. mood so closely identified with Cain:

> Roman Polanski has of late caught that '30s feeling of moral depravity and unending doom in the film *Chinatown:* a sense of brooding evil just beneath the movie-tone surface of Southern California life. . . . In Los Angeles during these years death seemed everywhere; and a mood of excess and disaster, strange and sinister, like flowers rotting from too much sunshine, pervaded the city.[1]

What Polanski (with a script by Robert Towne) caught in his celebrated film was a vision that emerged not only in Cain's Los Angeles novels but also in those of a number of other novelists who took up residence in the film capital in the thirties. Both Cain and Horace McCoy arrived in 1931. Both came from backgrounds in journalism—Cain in Baltimore and New York, where he wrote for such ranking journals as *The American Mercury*, the *Baltimore Sun*, and the *New York World;* and McCoy in Dallas, where in addition to his work as a reporter he acted with the Dallas Little Theatre (hoping, in coming to Hollywood, to break in as an actor as well as a screenwriter).

Neither had yet published a novel, but within a few years of their arrival on the coast each published a short novel that steered Los Angeles fiction onto the path it was to follow in the years ahead. Anticipating Nathanael West's *The Day of the Locust*, Raymond Chandler's *The Big Sleep*, and Aldous Huxley's *After Many a Summer Dies the Swan*—all published in 1939, a kind of *annus mirabilis* in Los Angeles literary production—Cain's *The Postman Always Rings Twice* (1934) and McCoy's *They Shoot Horses, Don't They?* (1935) mark the real starting place of the Los Angeles novel, a regional fiction obsessively concerned with puncturing the bloated image of Southern California as the golden land of opportunity and the fresh start. For Cain and McCoy, Southern California was not the place of new beginnings but of disastrous finishes. Dissolution and collapse have been the essential themes of the L.A. novel ever since.

As the last stop on the continent, Southern California was heir to the contradictory myths of the nineteenth-century frontier, the place both of the second chance and, for the novelists, of recurring violence and calamitous endings. Cain and McCoy offered no analysis of these themes; rather than probing into sociological causes for the collapse of the West Coast dream they show us, instead, concrete instances of it, metaphors for disaster and dissolution drawn from a manmade and natural landscape of flimsy makeshift architecture, highways that go nowhere, claustrophobic dance halls, glaring sunlight, destructive winds, and the ever-present ocean. Where the continent comes to an abrupt end against the cliffs bordering the Pacific, the road, and with it the dream, comes to an end as well.

For Cain the road, with its deceptive promise of mobility and freedom, provides the chief metaphor for the betrayed promise of the West. The high-speed adventure recounted in *Postman* begins and ends on the California highway, and the rapid-fire telling of the tale is consistent with its dominating image. "They threw me off the hay truck about noon," the narrative begins. The pace never slows. In the next paragraph, Frank Chambers, a tramp who has hitchhiked up the coast from the Mexican border town of Tijuana, stumbles on the Twin Oaks Tavern, "a roadside sandwich joint" with filling station and "a half dozen shacks that they called an auto court." A few short paragraphs later he discovers the proprietress, whose "lips stuck out in a way that made me want to mash them in for her." Before Chapter 1 ends, he has taken a job at the Twin Oaks, and when the second chapter closes a few pages later, he already has his wish:

> I took her in my arms and mashed my mouth up against hers . . . "Bite me! Bite me!"
> I bit her. I sunk my teeth into her lips so deep I could feel the blood spurt into my mouth. It was running down her neck when I carried her upstairs.[2]

By the end of Chapter 3 the pair have decided to kill Nick, Cora's husband.

The book moves so fast that its structure has always seemed to its critics more like a movie script than a novel. Albert Van Nostrand wrote that the novel was "like a movie 'continuity,' " and was "a scenario the moment it was published." Kevin Starr remarked that Cain's fiction "rushes forward with the headlong pace of a writer who has left everything save narrative on the cutting room floor." Commenting on the body of Cain's 1930s fiction, Edmund Wilson wrote that his novels are a kind of "Devil's parody of the movies."[3]

Inevitably, Cain's four L.A. novels, written between 1934 and 1941, just before the heyday of American *film noir* and European new realism, found their way quickly to the screen. Like McCoy, Cain found a more admiring audience in Europe, and the first screen adaptations, significantly, were continental. As early as 1939 *Postman* was the basis for a French film *Le Dernier Tournant* and three years later was the source for Luchino Visconti's first film, *Ossessione*, the progenitor of Italy's neorealist cinema. Hollywood followed the European lead, filming *Double Indemnity* in 1944, *Mildred Pierce* in 1945, and *Postman* in 1946. With the revival of interest in *film noir* in recent years the three have become regular offerings in campus and revival movie houses. Bob Rafelson's recent film remake of *Postman* and Lawrence Kasdan's *Body Heat*—an original screenplay set in Florida but almost a remake of *Double Indemnity*—attest to Cain's continuing presence in, and influence on, American film. Even *The Embezzler*, the least known of Cain's four L.A. novels—a novella that reverses the usual Cain formula with its happy ending and its focus on an attempt to *undo* a crime—reached the screen in a 1940 version called *Money and the Woman*. Cain's non-L.A. novels, too, have been the basis for a number of Hollywood films, including *Serenade*, filmed in 1956 and set partly in L.A., and, most recently, *The Butterfly*.[4]

So Cain, who came to Los Angeles from the East Coast to write for the movies and remained a studio hack, had the peculiar fate of becoming a writer whose works not written for the screen exist most memorably on the screen. Reading Cain, Kevin Starr wrote, is a "mixed media event," to which we bring the images derived from hours "spent wisely or not too wisely at matinees or before the leperous white light of the late show."[5]

Some of this same fate is shared by his contemporary Horace McCoy, whose 1935 novel *They Shoot Horses, Don't they!* is known today thanks largely to Sydney Pollack's 1969 screen version. While the popularity—and critical success—of the film may have contributed to some interest in McCoy's novel, it is likely that only a few of the people who saw the film had even heard of the author or the novel. McCoy, who remained in Hollywood for twenty years and contributed to about a hundred films, survives for his American audience chiefly through the movie rendition of his first novel, made fourteen years after his death and thirty-four after its initial publication.

With the almost back-to-back publication of the two novels, the two writers were quickly linked—both to each other and to the new hard-boiled school of fiction that was surfacing on the West Coast. Edmund Wilson included them among his "boys in the back room" in a 1940 group portrait of the West Coast tough-guy writers, wrongly naming Hemingway as their chief source and wrongly describing McCoy as a follower of Cain.[6] Although Wilson gave only a few lines to McCoy—an equivocal judgment buried in a paragraph on Cain—it was the Cain linkage, echoed by other critics, that rankled the author: "I do not care for Cain's work," McCoy wrote, "although there may be much he can teach me. I know this, though—his continued labeling of me as of 'the Cain school' (whatever the hell that is) and I shall slit either his throat or mine." McCoy, in fact, had written the unpublished story upon which his novel would be based as early as 1932 and completed a draft of the novel in 1933, before *Postman* appeared. McCoy's real kinship is with the group associated with *Black Mask*, a mystery tabloid whose contributors included Dashiell Hammett, Raymond Chandler, and Erle Stanley Gardner. Between 1927 and 1934 McCoy published sixteen stories in *Black Mask*, and Captain Joseph Shaw, the journal's editor, named McCoy as among "the older writers who helped establish the *Black Mask* standard."[7]

In fact one writer did not influence the other; rather both began their writing careers at a time when a tough, detached, cynical stance had taken strong hold in American writing. *Black Mask* fiction and the hard-boiled detective novels of Hammett, the proletarian fiction of Mike Gold and others, and Cain's and McCoy's own experience as journalists were certainly influential. So, too, was the new tough attitude emerging in drama and film—in plays like Eugene O'Neill's *The Hairy Ape*, Ben Hecht and Charles MacArthur's *The Front Page*, and Robert Sherwood's *The Petrified Forest*; and, even more significantly, in gangster films, like Mervyn LeRoy's *Little Caesar*, the first talking gangster movie (1930—based on W. R. Burnett's 1929 novel), William Wellman's *The Public Enemy* (1931), and Howard Hawks's *Scarface* (1932). When Cain and McCoy wrote their first novels they were joining what had become by the mid-1930s a clearly established tough-guy tradition in American narrative writing.

The similarities between the two first novels not only make comparison inevitable but throw the very substantial differences into relief. To begin with the similarities, both are stories of collapsed hope—a theme that would preoccupy more than one generation of L.A. novelists. Both focus on the violent shattering of the dreams of a pair of seekers who have come to the West Coast chasing its fabled promise. Like their authors—and about 70 percent of the Southern California population in the 1930s—the protagonists of both books are newcomers. Frank Chambers is a drifter and con man with a criminal trail stretching across the county. Cora Papadakis is an Iowa girl named Smith who came to Hollywood after winning a high school beauty contest and wound up working in a hash house before settling into a dull marriage. The principals in *They Shoot Horses*, Robert Syverten and Gloria Beatty, are migrants from small towns who hope to break into movies as extras. In both works the male has been condemned to execution for the violent death of the female, but the "murder" in each case is conceived ironically—a deed resulting from an act of intended kindness or compassion: Frank is rushing the pregnant Cora to a hospital after a threatened miscarraige when the car hits a culvert wall and she is killed instantly; Robert accedes to Gloria's wish to be dead, expressed again and again in the novel, and puts a bullet in her head, the only way, he realizes, she can be taken out of her unending misery. Both stories, moreover, are told in first-person flashbacks by the comdemned males, a confessional narrative stance that has the effect of implicating the reader as confidant and arousing some sympathy for the doomed men.

As narrators the two men are very different. Except for a few lapses into sentimentality which in context are almost comical and plain silly (e.g., "I kissed her. Her eyes were shining up at me like two blue stars. It was like being in church."—p. 24), Frank remains tough, detached, and dispassionate. Robert, by contrast, is romantic and naively optimistic. He daydreams about being discovered by a talent scout, becoming a famous director, and driving a fancy car. The tough quality of McCoy's novel derives not from the language and tone of its narrator, but from the unremitting hardness and cynicism of Gloria and the relentless brutality of its subject matter.

There is another significant difference in the way the tales are narrated. Cain's narrator tells his story in straight, unframed chronological flashback; it is only in the last chapter that the death-row perspective of the telling is revealed. McCoy's novel is framed from the beginning by the murder trial—the present tense of the novel. It opens on the judge's words, printed alone on the page in capitals: THE PRISONER WILL STAND. Each of the thirteen

chapters or episodes of the narrative is preceded by another frag-
ment of the judge's sentence in increasingly larger type face until
the final words of the book, MAY GOD HAVE MERCY ON YOUR
SOUL, are printed boldly across the whole page. The chapters
themselves, beginning with the third, are reflections, acts of memory by the condemned man as he stands before the judge. The
events of the thirty-seven days of the marathon leading up to the
killing and arrest are compressed into the moment of actual senten-
cing. There are also a number of italicized passages throughout
the text that signal Robert's present-time reflections interrupting
his replaying of the past. The effect is that of overhearing the
thoughts of a condemned man, not of being told a story. We read
Cain's novel as a series of events leading to a resolution held back
from the reader; we read McCoy's with the knowledge that everything has already happened. Sydney Pollack remarked that the
structure of *They Shoot Horses* is almost that of "flashforward,"
an effect he tried to achieve in the film by making the marathon
the present and using flashforwards to the trial.[8]

Whatever the narrative differences, however, the novels are
structurally alike in their persistent circularity. In McCoy's the
circularity is achieved by the back and forth shifts in time and by
the endless back and forth movement of the marathon dancers,
accompanied by the relentless ebb and flow of the ocean beneath
their feet. "The whole business is a merry-go-round," Gloria says
at one point. "When we get out of here we're right back where we
started" (p. 76). As the lame horse on that merry-go-round, however, Gloria will end not where she started but in her sought-after
death. In *Postman* the circular path is the highway, doubling back
on itself, betraying its promise of mobility, and leading not to
freedom, but to Frank's and Cora's deaths. Every action in *Postman*—to intensify its circularity—elicits a counteraction, a bizarre
recapitulation. Events are rhymed or doubled. There are two murder attempts. At the second attempt, botched but successful,
Nick's final sounds bounce back on the lover-accomplices across
the desolate canyon as a horrible echo. Frank betrays Cora, whom
he calls both kitten and hellcat, by going off with a female lion
tamer. The cagey criminal lawyer who wins their acquittal is named
Katz. The cat that ruined the first murder attempt by climbing a
ladder (Cora's escape route), stepping on a fuse box, and short-

circuiting the lights returns in the form of a baby puma sent by Frank's lover, tipping off the betrayal to Cora.

Such images of circular motion, of movement and return, action and reaction, become for Cain metaphors for futility. In *Postman* the highway is the recurring setting for disaster. Frank and Cora bash in Nick's head on a road in the mountains above Malibu Beach, "the worst piece of road in L.A. County," and Cora in a grotesque rebound is killed in a bloody crash on the Pacific Coast Highway, not far from the murder site. It is an appropriate irony. Since the 1920s the automobile on the open highway has been a central component of the California—and American—Dream. Cain's characters behind the wheels of their cars experience a sense of liberation from both the constraints of the depression and the consequences of their acts. For his desperate heroes the fast-moving car fosters both a sense of power and control over one's destiny and, at the same time, a feeling of separation or insulation from the influence of others and a constraining social environment. Cars provide not only mobility, but that private space essential to the American Dream.[9] Caught up in the illusory promise of the highway, Frank announces to Cora, "I'm talking about the road. It's fun, Cora. . . . I know every twist and turn it's got. And I know how to work it, too. Isn't that what we want? Just to be a pair of tramps, like we really are?" (pp. 21–22).

But Cora knows the road too, and knows it leads nowhere: "You've been trying to make a bum out of me ever since you've known me but you're not going to do it. . . . I want to *be* something" (p. 145). What Cora wants to be is a commercial success. She wants to use the insurance money claimed from the murder of her husband to refurbish the Twin Oaks. She sets up a beer garden outside under the trees with striped awnings and bright lanterns to attract passing motorists. The perversity of Cora's dream of respectability and mothering domesticity, grounded in a brutal murder, is blatant. The Twin Oaks Tavern, where the pair make love, plot a murder, and then clash, is the perfectly realized backdrop for Cain's high-speed adventure. Sprawled alongside the California highway, the makeshift diner, filling station, and auto court is the place where the polar embodiments of the American Dream—highway and home, mobility and domesticity—collide.

In presenting his male protagonist as the unencumbered drifter with his dream of the open road, Cain not only provides a powerful Depression image, but joins his first novel to a long native literary tradition of the hero on the road stretching back to (and beyond) Whitman, Twain, and Cooper. Moreover, he introduces what is to become a dominant metaphor in L.A. fiction in the years ahead. The vast and varied terrain of Southern California—foothill, canyon, shoreline, desert—provided regional novelists with ready-made images for fluidity, mobility, and a deceptive sense of freedom. As L.A. became increasingly a city on wheels, the central figure in the L.A. novel became the man—or woman—in the driver's seat. Raymond Chandler's and Ross Macdonald's private-eye heroes roam the landscape by car, and recently in such novels as Joan Didion's *Play It as It Lays*, Roger Simon's *The Big Fix*, Thomas Pynchon's *The Crying of Lot 49*, and John Gregory Dunne's *True Confessions*, high-speed movement across an endless California landscape is a recurring theme.

In Cain's other L.A. novels as well, car and highway are the prevailing images. *Double Indemnity* begins with Walter Huff, an insurance salesman, driving from Glendale to Hollywood; almost immediately he is involved in a murder-for-love-and-insurance scheme like that in *Postman*, but executed with considerably more ingenuity. Nirdlinger, the husband, is killed in his own car and Huff is shot by his lover-accomplice Phyllis (murder always curdles love into hate in Cain's fiction) while sitting in a car in Griffith Park waiting for her in order to kill her. The novel is almost a gazetteer of L.A. street names, a grand auto tour of Southern California, a fact not lost on Billy Wilder, who did the superb 1944 film (with a Raymond Chandler assist on the script). Huff is almost constantly behind the wheel of his car. He drives from his house in the Los Feliz district to his office downtown, south to the oil fields of Long Beach, west to Santa Monica on the coast (to park with Phyllis's daughter Lola and watch the moon rise over the Pacific), to Glendale, Burbank, Hollywood, and Griffith Park.

For Mildred Pierce, the heroine of Cain's last L.A. novel, fast driving is a source of exhilaration, pleasure, and even sexual excitement. Like Frank Chambers, she craves highway speed, equating—and confusing—geographic mobility with liberation.

One of her first acts after her husband walks out on her is to claim the family car. Behind the wheel, she transcends her restrictive depression environment:

> She gave the car the gun, excitedly watching the needle swing past 30, 40, and 50. At 60 . . . she eased off a little on the gas, breathed a long, tremulous sigh. The car was pumping something into her veins, something of pride, of arrogance, of regained self-respect, that no talk, no liquor, no love, could possibly give.[10]

Through much of the novel Mildred speeds from one to another of the three suburban restaurants she commands in Glendale, Beverly Hills, and Laguna Beach. Her scramble for wealth and status takes the metaphoric shape of a journey from her tract home in Glendale to the mansions along Pasadena's exclusive Orange Grove Avenue, where her lover and future husband, Monty Beragon, lives. The social distance between her depression present and the future she covets is expressed spatially as the distance along Colorado Boulevard between the two suburban cities. The one represents the limitations of the age, the other the freedom of the dream. The wish seems within reach for a time, but, like Walter Huff, she is denied it because the love-object—here Mildred's daughter Veda—proves more ruthless and predatory than she. The dream always remains just beyond her grasp. In a key scene that compresses the futility of her quest into an image, Mildred is trapped in her car between Glendale and Pasadena in a flash flood and is forced to abandon it, climb a hill, and stagger home in the middle of the night "through the worst storm in the annals of the Los Angeles weather bureau." Reyner Banham's *Los Angeles: The Architecture of Four Ecologies* names the freeway as one of four clearly defined ecologies in the city. (The others are seashore, hills, and flat plains.)[11] Although Cain wrote his L.A. novels before the elaborate freeway system was constructed, the roads and highways connecting the suburban towns making up greater Los Angeles are the places where his people do much of their living. They are distinct habitats within the larger habitat. When Mildred needs to talk to her ex-husband, they characteristically take to the road. In the brief 1936 novel *The Embezzler*, which Cain included in his collection *Three of a Kind,* Dave Bennett, the narrator, does much of his thinking along the California highway, even measuring time in miles ("I thought about that for a few miles").

Architectural structures, often linked with the highway, are another major source of Cain's symbolism. The improvised highway stop, obsolete now in an age of Holiday Inns and Travelodges, was a conspicuous part of the 1930s landscape. That this meeting ground of high-speed mobility and domesticity becomes a battleground for Frank and Cora is thematically central to Cain's first novel. A significant part of the lure of Southern California in the boom of the twenties was the promise of the detached house. Houses in every conceivable historic design found a place in the instant townscape of the twenties and thirties. Novelists found an inexhaustible supply of images of disparity and dislocation in the eclectic building styles of Southern California. Chandler used the monumental, pretentious fortresses of the new rich again and again as metaphors for the deception and corruption of those who rose to power in the city. The exotic structures described by West and Huxley are almost spillovers from the studio back lots— "gothic" castles, fairy-tale cottages, Mississippi plantation houses, Egyptian sphinxes (actually real estate offices), and other such counterfeits.

Cain avoided this kind of exaggerated architectural imagery. Instead, he set his characters typically in the "Spanish" style houses of white stucco with red tile roofs favored by many of the subdividers as "authentic" evocations of the region's past. These ordinary houses served Cain both as ironic contrasts to the extraordinary actions and behavior of their inhabitants—commonplace domestic facades behind which adultery, murder, and extortion were played out—and, in their banality, expressions of the frustrations, failures, and betrayed dreams of his people. Houses externalized the mental states of their owners.

Consistently, he underscored the monotony of the architecture. The Twin Oaks Tavern is "like millions of others in California." The first description of the "House of Death" in *Double Indemnity*—located in Hollywoodland, a 1920s subdivision along Beechwood Avenue above Hollywood Boulevard and beneath the famous sign—combines a flat ordinariness with a sense of the grotesque in its incongruous details:

> It didn't look like a House of Death when I saw it. It was
> just a Spanish house, like all the rest of them in
> California, with white walls, red tile roof, and a patio out
> to one side. It was built cock-eyed. The garage was under
> the house, the first floor was over that, and the rest of it
> was spilled up the hill any way they could get it in.[12]

Inside, he piles on more symbolic details. Although the house has
a living room "like every other living room in California," the most
conspicuous features in it are "blood-red drapes" run on iron spears,
red velvet tapestries, and a "Mexican" rug made in Oakland, California. The insisted-on conventionality, set against its "cock-eyed"
floor plan, the blood-red domination of its interior, and the rug
carry elements of deception which run through the novel.

Mildred Pierce opens with a description of a house which
with a few changes could be *Double Indemnity's* "Death House."
Bert Pierce, a real estate developer who went broke in the crash
and is about to walk out on Mildred, mows the lawn of his Glendale house, "a lawn like thousands of others in southern California. . . . The house, too, was like others of its kind: a Spanish
bungalow, with white walls and red-tile roof" (p. 8). Inside is "the
standard living room sent out by department stores," including a
"crimson velvet coat of arms" and "crimson velvet drapes, hung
on iron spears." A withered attempt at suburban elegance, the
Pierce home, "mortgaged and remortgaged," reflects the twenties'
image of the good life shattered by the depression.

Bert Pierce is the prototypical California real estate developer. Having inherited 300 acres of land in Glendale which he
unsuccessfully tried to farm, he became a subdivider, "a community builder, a man of vision, a big shot." The houses he builds
reflect the Southern California promise, typically featuring three
bedrooms and a bath for each bedroom. His tract contains a sales
office "built like a home, to stimulate the imagination of customers." Significantly, ten years before the novel opens, Bert had
seduced Mildred, then eighteen, in the model home, and Mildred,
largely to win over Veda, the spoiled product of that seduction,
transforms it into the first of her three restaurants after Bert's
failure. To complete the cycle, Mildred's business failure, coming a
decade after her husband's, is in part the result of Veda's treachery.

Mildred Pierce's three restaurants, like the Twin Oaks

Tavern, bridge the opposing versions of the dream, fusing auto-mobility and domesticity. They are precursors of the drive-in res-taurant, which beginning in the thirties became major enterprises in Southern California's "linear cities." Along with the new stream-lined supermarkets (built behind parking spaces) and drive-in the-aters, they became the characteristic commercial structures in an age and place dedicated to the marriage of business and the auto-mobile. With their oversize parking lots and neon signs, Mildred Pierce's roadside restaurants acknowledge the automobile and anticipate the drive-in, but still retain the image of the traditional restaurant where patrons leave their cars and are served inside.

Mildred Pierce reflects a major shift in Cain's fiction away from the tough-guy, first-person stance of his earlier works to a more lyrical, and traditional, third-person narrative. In place of his earlier lean, spare prose and his rapid-fire action sequences pre-sented almost in outline, the novel is a detailed portrait of middle-class life and dreams spanning the decade of the thirties. Like Theodore Dreiser and Sinclair Lewis, Cain charts intimately the day-to-day existence of his leading character. The reader coming to the novel for the first time is dazzled by the massing of details and (seemingly) factual information Cain offers. Even *Double In-demnity*, with all its insider's talk about the insurance business, doesn't adequately prepare one for all the lore he doles out, partic-ularly about the restaurant business. The novel epitomizes what David Madden called Cain's "inside dopester strain." He gives us the countless details of running a restaurant—serving a table, bak-ing pies, cooking chicken croquettes, operating a cocktail bar. We learn, with Mildred, how to balance three plates on one arm and even how to deal with the sexual harassment of customers ("Even a leg feeler, if properly handled, could be nursed into a regular who left good tips").

Still, the novel obeys the formula Cain established at the beginning of his career. The ironic vision which informs all his L.A. novels is that of the dream-come-true turning into nightmare. Driven by sexual passion or a passion for wealth, or both, Cain's protagonists commit desperate acts, experience a taste of victory, and then lose everything. Of the Cain hero, Edmund Wilson wrote, "His fate is forecast from the beginning; but in the meantime he has fabulous adventures—samples, as it were, from a *Thousand*

and One Nights of the screwy California Coast."[13] Cain himself said of his fiction that "the reader is carried along as much by his own realization that the characters cannot have their particular wish and survive, and his curiosity to see what happens to them."[14] Elsewhere, he explained his formula in terms of the "love rack," an expression he claimed he got from his friend and mentor, the screenwriter Vincent Lawrence, to whom he dedicated *Postman*. Murder, Cain wrote, is always written from "the least interesting angle, which was whether the police would catch the murderer." He wanted instead to write from the angle of the effect the crime had on the perpetrators. "They would find. . . . that the earth is not big enough for two persons who share such a dreadful secret, and eventually turn on each other."[15]

Frank and Cora beat a murder rap and collect the insurance money but can't escape each other; the price they pay for their action is distrust and suspicion. They turn on each other at the trial and afterward live in fear that one will betray the other. "We're chained to each other, Cora," Frank says, and then shifts to a metaphor that recapitulates the grizzly murder scene: "We thought we were on top of a mountain. That wasn't it. It's on top of us, and that's where it's been ever since that night" (p. 175). Deception and double-dealing run through the novel. The trial itself is a travesty of justice, a duel fought for wholly personal ends by a shrewd district attorney and an even shrewder criminal lawyer. When Cain's characters feel most in control, they are least so. Early in the novel Nick Papadakis, overjoyed at hiring Frank to help out at the Twin Oaks, rushes off at Frank's urging to order a new neon sign to replace the old bulb sign blown down during a fierce Santa Ana wind. While he is in the city ordering the sign—which will carry the Greek and American flag, two hands shaking, and the legend, "Satisfaction guaranteed"—Frank is in bed with Cora. A little later Frank goes off to Glendale to pick up money playing billiards. He is good, but not good enough. He tries to con an opponent by letting him win when the stakes are low; when the stakes are raised, the opponent takes him for everything he has.

Each of Cain's protagonists gets taken when he or she feels most secure in the attainment of the forbidden wish. Walter Huff nearly gets away with the perfect crime, but his lover-accomplice turns out to be a psychopathic killer with no qualms about killing him. *Mildred Pierce* contains no murder—a shortcoming the movie version remedied in an attempt to translate it as *film noir*—but it follows a similar pattern: Mildred with three successful restaurants operating and a Pasadena home on the horizon is brought to her knees by a daughter capable of greater scheming than she.

While Veda Pierce in her unmitigated selfishness and cruel opportunism is by far the most distasteful of Cain's women, Cora Papadakis and Phyllis Nirdlinger are more elemental in their pursuit of money and status. Phyllis, in particular, is perhaps the most brutal and cold-blooded female in the period's fiction, a vampire who masquerades grotesquely in a red silk shroud, white makeup, and a dagger in her hand and who has murdered more than one victim before she meets Huff and entices him into murdering her husband. The woman who uses men for her own ends, whose ruthless ambitions and machinations equal or surpass those of the male, is a stock figure in the crime fiction of the period. But even Dashiell Hammett's Brigid O'Shaughnessy, whom Sam Spade unmasks in the famous ending to *The Maltese Falcon*, and Raymond Chandler's duplicitous females like Carmen Sternwood, Helen Grayle, and Eileen Wade are the weak sisters of Phyllis Nirdlinger.

In Horace McCoy's two L.A. novels the women are less destructive than self-destructive. More pessimistic, cynical, and consistently more aware than their male partners, they turn their aggressiveness inward, into suicidal impulses. If Phyllis Nirdlinger is the deadliest of the females in the period's fiction, Gloria Beatty in *They Shoot Horses, Don't They?* is the most nihilistic, the most death-obsessed. Her thoughts constantly turn on death. Just after meeting Robert Syverten, she says to him: "Why are all these high-powered scientists always screwing around trying to prolong life instead of finding pleasant ways to end it? There must be a hell of a lot of people in the world like me—who want to die but haven't the guts—" (p. 23).

Gloria is, like Cora, one of the Hollywood dream chasers, but her past has already molded her in a cynicism that Hollywood can only harden. In Texas she had been the victim of an uncle's sexual advances, lived miserably with a number of men, and attempted suicide. Recovering from the effects of poison in a hospital, she began reading movie magazines—another source of infection—and migrated to Hollywood in a desperate last gesture.

Although the narrative comes to us through the courtroom reflections of Robert, Gloria's vision dominates the novel and determines its outcome. It is a nihilistic vision; nothing matters, nothing is immoral, nothing meaningful. Lee Richmond, one of the novel's recent critics, remarked that with the exceptions of West's *Miss Lonelyhearts* and *The Day of the Locust* McCoy's novel is "indisputably the best example of absurdist existentialism in American fiction," anticipating Sartre's *La Nausée* (1938) and Camus' *L'Etranger* (1942) in France.[16] Indeed, as Richmond documents, the novel was widely discussed in France, and McCoy's name was linked with Hemingway's and Faulkner's on the continent in the late thirties and early forties.

The contrast between Robert and Gloria is that between traditional native optimism and absurd existential awareness. Robert brings to the West Coast an innocent hopefulness, a literal belief in the Gospel of Hollywood; and she the debilitating awareness that the world doesn't square with hopes, logic, or conventional morality. Like the other participants, they join the dance marathon for the meals and lodging, the possibility of prize money, and the hope (which Gloria sees as a ruse) of being discovered by a producer. The cumulative exhaustion has the effect, though, in Robert's case of subverting a too-easily-held optimism, and in Gloria's of corroborating and intensifying her death wish. When Robert, "out there on the black night on the edge of the Pacific," obliges Gloria by putting a bullet in her head, he is indicating that if he has not quite come around to her nihilistic vision, he has come a long way toward it.

The dance marathon serves McCoy as a symbol of deception, of the betrayed Southern California promise. On one level it is pure theater—an elaborate, staged spectacle cynically manipulated by its gangster-promoters to draw crowds of thrill seekers. It is almost a parody of the Hollywood dream factory. On another level it is a potent metaphor for the end of the road. Like the highway that circles back on itself for Frank Chambers, the dance floor represents movement without progress.

Dance, traditionally a celebration of life, becomes in the novel a rite of death. There are no celebrants and no winners, only an abrupt and crashing halt after thirty-seven days, 879 hours of futile movement. The futility is underscored by the insistent presence of the ocean "pounding, pounding against the pilings all the time." Robert feels it whether he is moving across the floor or resting on his cot during the ten-minute break the dancers have every two hours. "Through the legs of my cot I could feel the ocean quivering against the pilings below. It rose and fell, rose and fell, went out and came back, went out and came back" (p. 51).

The ocean is the perfect accompaniment to the *danse macabre*, its relentless ebbing and flowing the cosmic counterpart to the drugged movement of the dancers. The pier, "rising and falling and groaning and creaking with the movements of the water" is almost an extension of the bodies of the dancers. The once hopeful Robert recalls how previously he romanticized the ocean:

> I used to sit for hours looking at it, wondering about the
> ships that had sailed it and never returned, about China
> and the South Seas, wondering all sorts of things . . . But
> not any more. I've had enough of the Pacific. (p. 28)

As mental construct or physical presence the Pacific Ocean persists as an image in L.A. fiction, one which evokes a sense of arriving at the end of the line, the border of dreams, the place where the road and the hope run out. In the crime novels of Cain, Chandler, and Macdonald, and in Robert Towne's *Chinatown* script, the edge of the Pacific, the site of the elaborate homes of those who have made it, is the recurring scene of brutal murder. In *Postman* Nick is killed on a cliff above Malibu Beach, lured there by Cora's desire to see where the movie stars live. When Robert and Gloria emerge from the dance hall onto the pier after the marathon is shut down, Robert points to the lights of Malibu up the coast, "where all the movie stars live."

At this point in the narrative two fishermen pass, dragging a four-foot hammerhead shark. "This baby'll never do any more damage," one says to the other. The appearance of the dead predator comes almost as an echo of Robert's remark seconds earlier. He had been looking back at the dance hall where they had spent the last thirty-seven days. "So that's where we've been all the time. . . . Now I know how Jonah felt when he looked at the whale" (p. 123). The dance hall is the demon which has swallowed, then expelled them. The image is claustrophobic, reflecting Robert's constant feeling of entrapment. During the marathon, to open the door and face the sun was to risk disqualification. Every day he tried to steer Gloria into a triangle of sunlight that came through the double windows of the beer garden above the dance floor for ten minutes a day. The sun functions as a counterimage to the ocean, an evocation of life:

> I watched the triangle on the floor get smaller and
> smaller. Finally, it closed up altogether and started up
> my legs. . . . When it got to my chin I stood on my toes,
> to keep my head in as long as possible. . . . In a moment
> it was gone. (p. 48)

Robert has been trying desperately to keep his head above water. The cliché is intentional: the dance hall is not only the belly of the whale but also a sinking ship, the dancers a desperate crew seized increasingly by exhaustion and impotence. Whatever hope Robert has brought to the dance has been undercut by the endless round of meaningless movement, the brutalizing competition of the derbies, and the senseless and degrading extravaganzas engineered to titillate a thrill-seeking audience. When Gloria urges Robert to "pinch hit for God," he does so without reflection, recognizing at least some part of himself in her black despair. Early in the novel, before they enter the marathon, he had responded glibly to her expressed wish to be dead: "I know exactly what you mean." But he *doesn't* know until the night of the killing. One of the arresting policemen asks him why he did it, and he replies, "They shoot horses, don't they?" Gloria is the suffering horse of the title, but while Robert is her executioner, her mercy killer, his act also gives expression to his own growing estrangement from the world in which he had placed all his hope, a point underscored by his refusal to offer any legal defense at his trial or even to listen to the words of the judge.

McCoy's other L.A. novel, *I Should Have Stayed Home* (1938), is a blunter indictment of the meretriciousness of the dream, a weaker, more discursive, and more confused work, both a satire on the dream factory and a farce riddled with movie-colony stereotypes. The leads are again a young pair of seekers who begin with opposing expectations and attitudes. Ralph Carston is hopeful and romantic in temperament; Mona Matthews is tough and disillusioned. One difference, though, is that Ralph, unlike Robert Syverten, never loses his optimism, his expectation that he will be a star. Another is that Mona, while possessing some of Gloria Beatty's cynical and embittered vision, has none of her paralyzing hopelessness. She remains hard but opportunistic. A third character, Dorothy Trotter, takes on Gloria's consummate despair. Arrested for shoplifting, Dorothy escapes prison, steals a car, and is rearrested. Soon after, she hangs herself with a stocking in her cell. A reporter taking pictures at the morgue asks for the death instrument, and Mona places some fan magazines in the dead girl's hand: the Hollywood publicity network with its small-town-girl-makes-good message is the death instrument.

Ralph and Mona share (chastely) a bungalow on Vine Street. Nearby on Hollywood Boulevard a giant sign reads: "All Roads Lead to Hollywood—And the Pause that Refreshes!"[17] In a tiny nieghborhood park, Ralph sees a middle-aged woman dressed in black lay a wreath at a shrine to Valentino. Ralph, who has come west on the strength of a promised screen test and then never hears again from the producer, continues to dream of his big chance. The novel takes on some comic life when he is ensnared by the rich, nymphomaniacal widow Ethel Smithers, setting up McCoy's burlesque version of the film capital. Mrs. Smithers is Mrs. Layden, "the champion dance marathon fan" of *They Shoot Horses*, carried to an extreme of explicit lust. A collector of young men, she tries to seduce the simple-minded hero by showing him pornographic movies in her private screening room. The Hollywood denizens attached to Mrs. Smithers are the stock figures of movieland folklore—homosexual actors and lesbian screen goddesses, nymphomaniacs and their troup of gigolos, cynical, hard-drinking writers and tyrannical producers. They are the people West, Fitzgerald, Schulberg, and Mailer would later portray with considerably more subtlety.

Although very different in tone and ambience from *They Shoot Horses*, *I Should Have Stayed Home* has something in common with the earlier novel. There are, among other similarities, the constant display of theatrics and showmanship, the exploitative use of sex, and the failure of traditional sources of authority and morality in the competitive drive for status and fame. Most important, it shares with the earlier work the sense of the West Coast as the place not of new beginnings but of disastrous finishes. Dorothy is dead, and Mona, at the end, signals her surrender by accepting a magazine ad proposal and marrying a Central California farmer. Only Robert continues to dream of success in Hollywood. His persistent guilelessness mars the book's effectiveness as an indictment, frustrating our every effort to muster some identification with him as narrator.

There are, it should be added, two interesting characters in the novel—the writer Heinrich, who can't find work until he discovers he can attract attention by continually playing the clown, and the studio publicist Johnny Hill, a quasi-radical and disillusioned idealist who sells out at the end and becomes Ralph's successor as Mrs. Smithers's gigolo. In their political savvy, both are foils to the naive narrator. But they aren't enough to redeem the book.

I Should Have Stayed Home might have been saved by a controlling metaphor with the potency of the dance marathon; loose and sprawling, it lacks the tautness, the symbolic compression, of the earlier novel. Both Cain and McCoy in their tougher and leaner first novels were able to do what they could not do as successfully in their subsequent novels—concentrate their fables in powerful images drawn from the built environment, images which would help carry the weight of their themes. The haphazard Twin Oaks Tavern spread along the California highway and the old dance hall pitched over the edge of the Pacific provided them with symbolic landscapes they were not to find again.

In *Postman* and *They Shoot Horses* Cain and McCoy gave a literary identity to Los Angeles. They made available to their successors the principal metaphors for deception, illusion, and loss. For Nathanael West, Raymond Chandler, Ross Macdonald, Norman Mailer, Joan Didion, Alison Lurie, and John Gregory Dunne, among others, the betrayed promise of the West Coast would be expressed in images of deceptive, fraudulent architecture; highways that dead-end against the Pacific; rootless characters engaged in compulsive, aimless, and futile motion; and human relationships that dissolve in greed, lust, and violence.

Notes

1. Kevin Starr, "It's Chinatown," *The New Republic*, 26 July 1975, p. 31
2. James M. Cain, *The Postman Always Rings Twice* (New York: Alfred A. Knopf, 1934), p. 15. Subsequent references are cited parenthetically in the text.
3. Albert Van Nostrand, *The Denatured Novel* (Indianapolis: Bobbs-Merrill Co., 1960), pp. 126–127; Starr, p. 31; Edmund Wilson, "The Boys in the Back Room," in *Classics and Commercials: A Chronicle of the 1940s* (New York: Farrar, Straus & Giroux, 1950), p. 22.
4. A list of the adaptations of Cain's novels is contained in Stewart Weiner, "They're Raising Cain (James M., That Is)," *Los Angeles Magazine*, April 1980, pp. 240–47; Frank Krutnik in "Desire, Transgression, and James M. Cain," *Screen* 23, no. 1 (1982):31–44, discusses Cain and American *film noir*, focusing chiefly on *Double Indemnity* and *Mildred Pierce*.
5. Starr, p. 32.
6. Wilson, pp. 19–20.
7. Both quotes in this paragraph are in Thomas Sturak, "Horace McCoy's Objective Lyricism," in *Tough Guy Writers of the Thirties*, ed. David Madden (Carbondale: Southern Illinois University Press, 1968), p. 146.
8. Sydney Pollack, foreward to the screenplay, in *They Shoot Horses, Don't They?* (New York: Avon Books, 1966), p. 134. Further references to the novel are indicated parenthetically in the text. The flashforwards were generally attacked by the film's reviewers; see Paul Warshow's interesting discussion in "The Unreal McCoy," in *The Modern American Novel and the Movies*, ed. Gerald Peary and Roger Shatzkin (New York: Frederick Ungar Publishing Co., 1978), p. 35.
9. See David Laird, "Versions of Eden: The Automobile and the American Novel," *Michigan Quarterly Review* 29 (1980):639–51.
10. Cain, *Mildred Pierce* (1941; Cleveland: World Publishing Co., 1944), p 67. Subsequent references are cited parenthetically in the text.
11. Reyner Banham, *Los Angeles: The Architecture of Four Ecologies* (Harmondsworth, Middlesex, England: Penguin Books, 1971), pp. 213–21.
12. Cain, *Double Indemnity*, in *Three of a Kind* (New York: Alfred A. Knopf, 1944), p. 217. Subsequent references are cited parenthetically in the text.
13. Wilson, p. 21.
14. Cain, Preface to *The Butterfly* (1947 New York: Random House Vintage Books, 1979), p. x.

15. Cain, Preface to *Three of a Kind* (New York: Alfred A. Knopf, 1944), p. xii.
16. Lee Richmond, "A Time to Mourn and a Time to Dance: Horace McCoy's *They Shoot Horses, Don't They?*," *Twentieth Century Literature* 17 (1971):91.
17. McCoy, *I Should Have Stayed Home* (New York: Alfred A. Knopf, 1938), p. 8. Subsequent references are cited parenthetically in the text.

Bibliographic Note

The first full-length treatment of Cain's life, Ray Hoopes's *The Biography of James M. Cain* (Holt, Rinehart and Winston, 1982) has recently appeared. It's almost straight biography—543 pages of it, plus afterword, a chronology, notes, bibliography, filmography, and index—and for criticism of the novels we need to turn to other sources. David Madden's *James M. Cain* (Boston: Twayne, 1970) is a good starting place. The only pre-Hoopes book-length study of the author, it offers some biography but is chiefly concerned with the works. Madden has been, over the years, Cain's most prolific critic. Among his articles, which focus largely on Cain and the tough-guy tradition, are "James M. Cain and the Pure Novel," *The University Review* 30 (1963):143–48; "James M. Cain and the Twenty Minute Egg of the Hard Boiled School," *Journal of Popular Culture* 1 (1967):178-92; and "James M. Cain and the Tough Guy Novelists of the Thirties" in *The Thirties: Fiction, Poetry, Drama*, ed. Warren French (Deland, Fla,: Everett/Edwards, 1955, 1976), pp. 63–71. Joyce Carol Oates has written shrewdly of Cain and the tough guy in "Man Under the Sentence of Death: The Novels of James M. Cain" in *Tough Guy Writers of the Thirties*, ed. David Madden (Carbondale: Southern Illinois University Press, 1968), pp. 110–28.

Cain's Southern California novels are the subjects of articles by Thomas Reck, "James M. Cain's Los Angeles Novels," *Colorado Quarterly* 22 (1974):375–87; and David Fine, "James M. Cain and The Los Angeles Novel," *American Studies* 20 (1979):25–34. Among shorter pieces on Cain that deserve mention are Kevin Starr, "It's Chinatown," *New Republic*, 26 July 1975, pp. 31–32; John Leonard, "The Wish of James Cain," *New York Times Book Review*, 2 March 1969, pp. 2, 48; and Ray Hoopes, "An Appreciation of James M. Cain," *New Republic*, 22 July 1978, pp. 23–26. The last, written following Cain's death, is interesting largely for quoting a number of well-known writers on Cain.

Cain and McCoy were linked conspicuously, if briefly, in Edmund Wilson's 1940 piece, "The Boys in the Back Room," reprinted and enlarged in *Classics and Commercials: A Literary Chronicle of the 1940s* (New York: Farrar, Straus, 1950), pp. 19–56. Among recent critics there has been little effort to link the two. A notable exception is by Walter Wells, a contributor to this volume, a fine chapter, "The Postman and the Marathon," in his *Tycoons and Locusts: A Regional Look at Hollywood Fiction in the 1930s* (Carbondale: Southern Illinois University Press, 1973), pp. 14–35. Wells draws strong parallels between the two first novels of Cain and McCoy and relates them to his overall theme of dissolution in Southern California fiction.

The fullest treatment of McCoy is Thomas Sturak's unpublished dissertation (UCLA, 1967), *The Life and Writings of Horace McCoy, 1897–1955*. Sturak's article, "Horace McCoy's Objective Lyricism," in the Madden collection cited above, pp. 137–62, develops some of the material cited in the dissertation and remains the best single article on McCoy's fiction. Mark Royden Winchell, a contributor to this volume, has recently published a balanced assessment of McCoy's achievement for the Boise State Western Writers pamphlet series (1982). Lee Richmond's "A Time to Mourn and a Time to Dance: Horace McCoy's *They Shoot Horses, Don't They?*, *Twentieth Century Literature* 17 (1971):91–99, develops the novel's existential themes which Harry Levin addressed earlier, and only briefly, in "Some European Views of Contemporary American Literature," *American Quarterly* 1 (1949):264–79. *I Should Have Stayed Home*, not surprisingly, has received attention only in general studies of the writer's work and in reviews. The review in the *Saturday Review of Literature*, 19 February 1938, p.4, is worth citing for its reviewer's sarcastic comment that the novel allowed McCoy to "get all of his bile [about Hollywood] out of his system in a short, bitter, name-calling novel."

There are several useful studies of Cain and McCoy on film. Cain on screen is treated in Parker Tyler, *The Magic and Mystery of the Movies* (New York: Holt, 1947), pp. 175–89 (on *Double Indemnity*) and pp. 211–29 (on *Mildred Pierce*); and in Gabriel Miller, *Screening the Novel: Rediscovered American Fiction in Film* (New York: Frederick Ungar Publishing Co., 1980), pp. 46–63 (on *Postman*). The most astute study of Cain on film is Frank Krutnik, "Desire, Transgression, and James M. Cain" in the British film journal *Screen* 23, no. 1 (1982):31–34, which connects Cain's fiction to *film noir*, focusing on *Double Indemnity* and *Mildred Pierce*. June Sochen, "Mildred Pierce and Women in Film" *American Quarterly* 30 (1978):3–20, is suggestive and insightful.

The screen version of *They Shoot Horses, Don't They?* is treated perceptively in Paul Warshow, "The Unreal McCoy" in *The Modern American Novel and the Movies* (New York: Frederick Ungar Publishing Co., 1978) pp. 29–39. Warshow's essay is in part a response to director Sydney Pollack's foreword to the published script which appeared in the Avon paperback edition of the novel (1966), pp.133–36. The film is also discussed in Gabriel Miller, *Screening the Novel* (cited above), pp. 64–83.

THREE

The Day of the Painter;
the Death of the Cock:
Nathanael West's
Hollywood Novel

Gerald Locklin

It used to be a commonplace of essays such as this to decry the lack of critical and popular attention accorded the novels of Nathanael West. To continue that tradition, however, in the wake of book-length bibliographies and a seeming dissertation assembly line would be disingenuous indeed. *The Day of the Locust* is now considered by many the best novel ever written about Hollywood. Lillian Hellman has called it "the only good book about Hollywood ever written."[1] But to what extent is the novel truly *about* Hollywood? And why do even the book's admirers tend to find at least one major feature of it unsuccessful?

One of the first commentators to complain of the novel's alleged lack of focus was Stanley Edgar Hyman: "I think that *The Day of the Locust* ultimately fails as a novel. Shifting from Tod to Homer and back to Tod, it has no dramatic unity."[2] A. M. Tibbetts, one of West's severest critics, concurs in this indictment:

67

The shift in person is not very successful, and the point
of view moves without apparent reason from Tod
Hackett to Homer Simpson and back again. It is
interesting to notice, by the way, that neither of the two
main characters was the original narrator, which further
complicates the point of view. West was, I think, not
quite sure where to focus his material.[3]

But there is no real shift of person in the novel. The chapters
describing Homer alone are narrated in a manner perfectly consistent with the rest of the book. And, as shall be seen, Tod and
Homer (and West) have a good deal in common.

The major structural principle of the novel is the emana-
tion of a point of view from "the painter's eye," the eye of Tod
Hackett's imagination.[4] *The Day of the Locust* is the story of the
painting "The Burning of Los Angeles." Just as Tod Hackett does
preliminary sketches of landscapes, crowds, and individuals, so
West desultorily builds toward his final chapter. Because West was
employed as a screenwriter during the period in which the novel
was written, a good deal has been made of cinematic techniques.
West seems to me, however, to be working much more in the style
of his protagonist's art than following what he would probably have
characterized as his own subliterary method of earning a living.
For one thing, only the most experimental of movies would dare
to proceed at the leisurely and seemingly aimless pace of this novel.

Tod is in a situation similar to West's own. He has been
brought to the coast by a talent scout who was impressed by his
drawings for an exhibit at the Yale School of Fine Arts. Thus, like
West, he faces the dilemma of reconciling his creative work with
his commercial labors. He provides an apologia for himself, and
by implication, for West: he asserts that, despite his background
and training, his old masters, Winslow Homer and Thomas Ryder,
(He apparently means Albert Pynkham Ryder, perhaps confusing
him with Thomas Eakins) would have to give way to new ones—
Goya and Daumier.[5] At any rate, West's writing was never in the
American grain, as was already evident in the Dadism and European erudition of his first novel, *The Dream Life of Balso Snell*.[6]

The passage does throw light on West's real antecedents for
the purpose of this novel, painters schooled in distortion, carica-
ture, satire, and prophecy. This recognition helps to alleviate the

difficulty some critics have had with West's world. An early review complained that "it needs . . . most of all, perhaps, a few ordinary, everyday people (of whom there must be a few even in Hollywood), to lend perspective."[7] West anticipated this problem:

> If I put into *The Day of the Locust* any of the sincere, honest people who work here and are making such a great progressive fight, those chapters couldn't be written satirically and the whole fabric of the peculiar half-world which I attempted to create would be badly torn by them.[8]

A major task for Tod is the classification of the people who inhabit this peculiar metropolis. He isolates, on the bases of appearance and behavior, three major groups. The first of these, identified by its costuming, is the "masqueraders":

> The fat lady in the yachting cap was going shopping, not boating; the man in the Norfolk jacket and Tyrolean hat was returning, not from a mountain, but an insurance office; and the girl in slacks and sneaks with a bandanna round her head had just left a switchboard, not a tennis court. (p. 261)

The implication is that this celluloid-inspired culture is an aping of other times and places, a playing of roles by people who have neither individual nor collective identity. Hollywood provides a second group, the "starers," who serve as an audience for these masqueraders:

> . . . they loitered on the corners or stood with their backs to the shop windows and stared at everyone who passed. When their stare was returned their eyes filled with hatred. At this time Tod knew very little about them except that they had come to California to die. (p. 261)

This group is volatile because it is most sensitive to the disparity between the dreams churned out by Hollywood and reality. West called the first draft of the novel, considerably different, *The Cheated*, and the cheated have survived as "the starers."

The major characters in the novel belong to yet another group, the "dancers" or "performers":

> Abe was an important figure in a set of lithographs
> called "The Dancers" on which Tod was working. He
> was one of the dancers. Faye Greener was another and
> her father, Harry, still another. They changed with each
> plate, but the group of uneasy people who formed their
> audience remained the same. They stood staring at the
> performers in just the way that they stared at the
> masqueraders on Vine Street. It was their stare that drove
> Abe and the others to spin crazily and leap into the air
> with twisted backs like hooked trout. (p. 264)

An invidious comparison is often drawn between the unified structure of *Miss Lonelyhearts* and the seemingly looser construction of *The Day of the Locust*. But West's Hollywood novel is consistent in form with both the art of its painter-protagonist and the apparent shapelessness of the region. Both West and Tod are matching form to irregular material. The architecture of houses in Hollywood persistently reveals this irregularity:

> When he noticed that they were all of plaster, lath, and
> paper, he was charitable and blamed their shape on the
> materials used. Steel, stone and brick curb a builder's
> fancy a little, forcing him to distribute his stresses and
> weights and to keep the corners plumb, but plaster and
> paper know no law, not even that of gravity. (p. 262)

New York, a city of granite and steel skyscrapers and iron bridges, depends on mathematical symmetry for its very existence. But the Los Angeles observed by West (and by Tod) stretched, asymmetrically, into canyons, hills, and desert. *Miss Lonelyhearts* requires, structurally, a balance of forces: Lonelyhearts versus Shrike; the healthy love for Betty versus the unhealthy love for Doyle. West had to find a new form, asymmetrical and horizontal, for Los Angeles, a two-dimensional canvas producing the illusion of energy. He drew partial inspiration from the painters of apocalyptic panoramas, particularly Breughel and Hieronymus Bosch. They would almost certainly endorse West's meticulous reconstruction-of-the-reconstruction of Waterloo and the final blocking out of Tod's painting, "The Burning of Los Angeles." Both scenes involve the kinesthetics of crowd movement and collective emotions. In the novel as well as in the painting, individuals, as colorful as they may seem in close-up, are ultimately swallowed up by the masses or mobs.

West substitutes for conventional plot a technique of symbolic description and of isolated revelatory scenes. The novel does occupy a span of time, but the reader senses until near the end almost no forward motion, and West goes backward to sketch a character's history almost as often as he goes forward. West objected to Clifton Fadiman's naming him a Surrealist, and I would also consider the term an exaggeration, but there is a surreal tendency in painters such as Salvator Rosa, Franceso Guardi, and Monsu Desiderio, those "painters of mystery and decay" that Tod eventually settled upon as masters: "For Guardi and Desiderio there were bridges which bridged nothing, sculpture in trees, palaces that seemed of marble until a whole stone portico began to flap in the light breeze" (p. 353). And they are appropriate to Hollywood in scope. Desiderio's painting "The Tower of Babel" reminds one of a studio preparing for a Cecil B. DeMille epic, and Guardi's "Ascent of a Balloon over the Canale della Guidecca in Venice" is uncannily like the film images of *Around the World in Eighty Days.* Some critics, taking the term in a broader sense, have argued for a closer identification of West with Surrealism:

> The paintings and writing of their official school
> affected him profoundly when he came across them in
> Paris, and his feeling for their destructive derision, their
> preoccupation with decay and degeneracy and
> disintegration was indisputably empathetic. . . . Like the
> Surrealists, West often used enormous incongruities to
> make his points, but unlike them, he preferred to distill
> his perceptions into images and situations that were
> painfully barren of minutiae.[9]

Furthermore, cubistic description or characterization, which is a staple of the cartoonlike renderings in *Miss Lonelyhearts*, is not altogether abandoned in *The Day of the Locust*, where Tod Hackett's personality is "like a nest of chinese boxes" (p. 260), and where West continues his affinity with Picasso's stylistic flexibility and catholicity. The novel is "painted" in the manners of many masters, all of whom transformed surface realities in the service of personal vision. Painting inspired West to a new formal principle for fiction. He related all problems of technique and interpretation to painting, and the analogy served as a unifying principle and as a source of original effects. When one views the world of *The Day* through the painter's eye, important new insights emerge.

West painted Hollywood first as a historical microcosm, a closed system in which to observe the decline of the West. Richard Gehman notes how perfectly Hollywood served as a microcosm "because everything that is wrong with life in the United States is to be found there in rare purity, and because the unreality of the business of making pictures seemed a most proper setting for his 'half-world.' " The "half-world" can be extended to include all of Western civilization. Echoes of other times and places pervade the costuming and architecture of the studios, the residential streets, and the restaurant rows. The decay of Hollywood, as V. L. Lokke has demonstrated, is meant to prefigure the decay of civilization:

> What West discovered in Hollywood was only the
> advanced stage of a sickness which was spreading
> through the whole of contemporary society. And there
> was no cure in sight. It is impossible to extract hope from
> any of West's novels: . . . . all reflect a belief that history
> is discontinuous, that the present civilization can neither
> draw upon the past nor contribute to the future, and that
> with the impending collapse into a new barbarism, we
> are witnessing the end of the whole process. His plea for
> the Apocalypse includes no millennium; and there is
> ample reason for believing that West saw complete social
> collapse, not as a first act towards social reconstruction,
> but rather as a last act of mercy.[10]

West appropriated Hollywood not only as a microcosm of society but also as a metaphysical symbol, a house of mirrors illuminating the eternal disparity between appearance and reality. To this end, he carried the motif of the facade throughout the work, representing falsity in such images as the front of the "San Berdoo" apartments, the public relations of the movie industry, the dead horse in Claude Esteés pool, Harry's facial transformations, Mrs. Schwartzen's face and neck, and the social performances of Faye Greener. Hollywood emerges in the novel as a symbol of metaphysical deception, as objectification of West's pessimism: Life is, was, and ever shall be a lie.

Hollywood is also a real city, a city West knew intimately, and the novel's characters are not so nearly allegorical that they cease to remind us of human beings. They represent a great variety of human types, but they have in common a suffering that is largely the result of sexual frustration, a suffering that extends to Tod himself. This sexual alienation, central to West's vision and a recurring motif in novels about Hollywood, frames my discussion of *The Day of the Locust's* characters.

What Tod consistently refers to as the "boredom" of the "starers" may more accurately be termed their sexual unhappiness or sexual alienation, a condition that breeds sadomasochism. Similarly, it is sexual unfulfillment that makes the dancers dance and makes Tod paint, and paint what he paints, and paint it the way he paints it. A good deal of projection is involved in Tod's art and, I think, in West's as well. When Tod finds Abe in the corridor, he "couldn't help wondering what had happened in the woman's apartment." Abe grudgingly dubs the woman "a lollapalooza—all slut and a yard wide" (pp. 264–65).

Tod himself falls violently for Faye's sexuality, although "her invitation wasn't to pleasure but to struggle, hard and sharp, closer to murder than to love. If you threw yourself on her, it would be like throwing yourself from the parapet of a skyscraper. You would do it with a scream. You couldn't expect to rise again." As for Faye: "She wouldn't have him. She didn't love him and he couldn't further her career. She wasn't sentimental and she had no need for tenderness, even if he were capable of it" (p. 271).

At Claude Estee's party—in a house which is a replica, Hollywood-style, of a Mississippi plantation home—Mrs. Schwartzen embarasses the men by declaring she "adores smut." And is it overinterpreting to take the imitation dead horse in the pool as a phallic figure of death, especially when "its legs stuck up stiff and straight and from its mouth, which was set in an agonized grin, hung a heavy, black tongue" (p. 274)? Claude Estee's comic amplifications upon love as a vending machine, a valise, and so forth, are in the manner of the sadomasochistic Shrike (in *Miss Lonelyhearts*). And Tod predictably announces that prostitution and pornography "depress" him. What doesn't? Nevertheless Tod reluctantly proceeds with the others at the Estee party to Mrs. Jenning's brothel, a triumph of "skillful packaging," where they view a stag movie. But the film breaks at the climax of *La Predicament de Marie*, mimicking the novel's persistent titillation-frustration pattern.

Homer's sexuality is also suspect. Like Miss Lonelyhearts, Homer is afraid of his sexual urges: "He somehow felt that his only defense was chastity, that it served him, like the shell of a tortoise, as both spine and armor. He couldn't shed it even in thought. If he did, he would be destroyed" (p. 313). And like Miss Lonelyhearts, Homer indulges in masochism: "But he couldn't let well enough alone. He was impatient and began to prod at this sadness, hoping to make it acute and so still more pleasant" (p. 315).

Even Faye, who drives men wild with desire (and torments her father by singing "Jeepers, Creepers") and who, though calculatingly selective, is certainly not chaste, is herself onanistic. She has evolved an elaborate system of daydreaming, by which she mentally thumbs through a deck of favorite dreams until she finds the one to suit that day's romantic needs. Wilhelm Stekel's explanation of such daydreaming is apropos:

> The paraphiliac [onanistic daydreamer] identifies himself with his object; he feels himself into it so that he can experience both conditions: triumph and defeat, power and subjection, activity and passivity, male and female, resistance and the overcoming of it. The specific scene which he is always wanting to repeat is a drama, a fiction, in which he as the author feels with the actors, suffers, and enjoys. This fiction has as its purpose to withdraw him from the real world. All these paraphiliacs are dreamers and have to force themselves to the daily duties of life.[11]

Tod's onanism, which recalls Lonelyhearts and the men of Delehanty's, takes the form of dreams of rape: "He expressed some of his desire by a grunt. If he only had the courage to throw himself on her. Nothing less violent than rape would do" (p. 320). In this inversion of the eternal triangle, Homer, Faye, and Tod all exercise their sexuality in the imagination or in pantomime.

West perceives the relationship between these fantasies and fiction, and he hints that Faye's technique bears similarities to his own:

> Although the events she described were miraculous, her description of them was realistic. . . . She . . . seemed to think that fantasy could be made plausible by a humdrum technique. (p. 320).

When Faye does move from fantasy to reality, it is as a prostitute. To pay for her father's funeral, Faye turns tricks for Mrs. Jenning. Tod, jealous as a schoolboy, confronts her with the perils of venereal disease, the potential ruination of her youth and beauty. Ironically, this last-ditch threat does dissuade her.

An even more troubling victim of corrupted sexuality, however, is Homer's neighbor, the epicene child actor Adore Loomis, who has mastered a repertory of suggestive songs, complete with abdominal writhings:

> Mama doan wan' no glass of gin,
> because it boun' to make her sin,
> An' keep her hot and bothered all the day. (p. 364)

Squirming in discomfort at a movie with Homer and Faye, Tod, after listening to Adore's lyrics, has the first intimation that he may not be untainted by the weakness of those he satirizes. By now the reader should realize that Tod is bound to his models by sexual alienation and by a tropism toward death: "He began to wonder if he didn't suffer from the ingrained morbid apathy he liked to draw in others. Maybe he could only be galvanized into sensibility and that was why he was chasing Faye" (p. 365). He is sufficiently unsettled by the thought to avoid Faye for a number of months while he searches out the Hollywood faddists. In the Church of Christ, Physical; the Crusade Against Salt; and the Temple Moderne, he finds people who have repressed but have not succeeded in sublimating their sexuality; to the contrary, it threatens to implode. At the Temple of the Third Coming, Tod watches an angry Jeremiah railing against modern decadence. Tod does not despise the man or his listeners because he knows they are the potential destroyers of civilization. And even if they have not quite succeeded, the present-day reader is not apt to peruse this chapter with a purely antiquarian interest.

When Tod next sees Faye and Homer, their unsacramental honeymoon is over. Time breeds boredom, and boredom, for Faye, who is not used to it, is conducive to persecution of Homer. Throughout the novel, sex is virtually synonymous with sado-masochism. At a night club, Faye humiliates the teetotaling Homer. Tod feels for his rival, but he has problems of his own. Like Lonely-hearts in the cab with Mary Shrike, Tod asks Faye to sleep with him. He does not plead love or money; he simply begs for mercy. Faye insists that she can't do it—probably because sex is her only weapon and she knows she dare not devalue it by charity. It is also to be noted that Tod is grateful to Faye, after she turns him down, "for having behaved so well, for not having made him feel too ridiculous." She has often been described by critics as a bitch, and her sexuality is indeed the magnetic and motivating center for much of what action takes place in the book, but she cannot help her role as the pursued one any more than the men can help pursuing her.

At the nightclub, she taunts Homer (whose own name suggests "homo") for not knowing what a fairy is. When Tod tries to prompt him "by forming the word 'homo' with his lips" (p. 371), Homer says "momo," which may suggest that mother who is absent from all the major characters' lives except Adore Loomis's. The nightclub, shaped like an enormous slipper (another example of Hollywood fantasy architecture) provides still another facade in the form of a female impersonator.

To relieve her boredom, Faye has invited Earle and Mig to live at Homer's. Homer likes the young man, but is bothered by their gamecocks and especially by their one hen, a horrible symbol of misogyny: "You never saw such a disgusting thing, the way it squats and turns its head. The roosters have torn all the feathers off its neck and made its comb all bloody and it has scabby feet covered with warts and it cackles so nasty when they drop it into the pen" (p. 372). Although the hen and Faye are as unlike as possible in appearance, both are scavengers. Homer continues, "I wouldn't touch that thing for all the money in the world. She's all over scabs and almost naked. She looks like a buzzard. She eats meat" (p. 373).

The mangy sex object furnishes a thematic transition to the most famous of West's scenes, one of the most memorable in literature: the cockfight. It is one of the very few scenes in the book that approximates pure action. There seems no question that the death of their cock is a crippling blow to the sexuality of Abe, Tod, and Claude. Moreover, the dwarf's final, frantic efforts to revive his outmatched dying bird partake of a transparent and ambiguous sexuality:

> Abe, moaning softly, smoothed its feathers and licked its
> eyes clean, then took its whole head in his mouth. The
> red was finished, however. The dwarf blew away its
> feathers from under its tail and pressed the lips of its vent
> together hard. When that didn't seem to help, he inserted
> his little finger and scratched the bird's testicles. It
> fluttered and made a gallant effort to straighten its neck.
> (pp. 382–83)

Miguel laughs, but Earle, the white parody-cowboy, "handled the dead cock gently and with respect." Tod passes the whiskey as at a wake and, as Hopkins might phrase it, it is his own phallicism and that of his friends he grieves for.

Josephine Herbst called this cockfight the one heroic battle in West's novels.[12] This assessment is not quite accurate since Abe's subsequent attack on Earle inside the house has a heroic as well as comic quality (and is at least partially successful). One can imagine Hemingway admiring the courage of the cock and of Abe, but since physical courage appears rarely in West's fiction, it would seem that he found that virtue less common in his world and considered it less of a consolation. Physical courage, for West, seems not so much a moral victory as simply a better way of losing. All of West's characters lose. They have all been handed a "cold deck," to use Abe's phrase. Of course, we sometimes forget that Hemingway's protagonists lose also.

Instances of disordered sexuality (sometimes subtle, sometimes blatant) proliferate throughout the later chapters of the book. Faye sends Homer's hands into a masturbatory tic. Homer calls Tod "Toddie" and Tod spits back "Homie." In a frankly Oedipal scene, Abe tugs at Earle's pants and later dashes himself against the Goliath's groin. Similarly Oedipal, Tod hesitates to follow Faye into her bedroom, preferring to follow Claude's suggestion, "Let's blow." Other sexual overtones include Abe's calling Homer a "quiff" and then having his nose tweaked. Abe calls Tod a "punk" and says of Earle, "I fixed that buckeroo, " which, in a veterinary sense, he just about has. But, for all the "special extensions" necessary for him to drive his car, Abe is the only man still willing to "go see some girls."

Faye accuses Homer of a voyeuristic spying on her, and Earle leaves his boots as if to taunt, "Can anyone here fill us?" Homer, now over the edge, curls into a fetal position, the Original Coil or Uterine Flight of Tod's college abnormal psych text.

Tod displays his masochism at Hodge's saddlery store, offering "Mexicans are very good with women." He imagines Faye being hugged to the sagging belly of "a savage with pork-sausage fingers and a pimpled butt." He gives himself over to an elaborate fantasy reminiscent of the Fatty Arbuckle case in which he stars as the rapist of Faye in a parking lot, armed with a cold water bottle. Interrupted, he is not even able "to start the rape going again."

The novel's apocalyptic finale is a textbook example of repressed sex seeking its expression in violence. The riot is incited by a "pervert," Homer, who stomps to death the sadistic Adore Loomis. Tod becomes wedged in such a way that "his whole leg as high as the groin throbbed." Tod manages to free a battered young girl from an old man who "had one of his hands inside her dress and was biting her neck." The conversation turns to "one of them pervert fellows" who "ripped up a girl with a pair of scissors" in St. Louis. Double-entendres upon "the wong tool" abound.

Tod's own participation in the apocalyptic masterpiece upon which he meditates in the midst of this chaos is to pick up a small stone and throw it before continuing his flight. This is the gesture of the artist, and neither Tod nor West seems to put much stock in its effectiveness. Taken away in a police car, Tod laughs and "begins to imitate the siren as loud as he could" (p. 421). Faulkner ended *The Sound and the Fury* with a similarly mindless outcry against disorder. Here in Hollywood, both Tod and his society seem to have disintegrated, to have come apart.

But have they? Tod has "had the presence of mind" to decline a ride to the hospital and to give the police Claude's address. Ambulances and law enforcement seem to be functioning adequately. In other words, the riot has not turned into utter anarchy or revolution. The "Burning of Los Angeles," the subject matter of his painting, has taken place only in Tod's imagination.

Tod had earlier considered the possibility that his predictions might not come true:

> He told himself that it didn't make any difference
> because he was an artist, not a prophet. His work would
> not be judged by the accuracy with which it foretold a

future event but by its merit as painting. Nevertheless,
he refused to give up the role of Jeremiah. He changed
"pick of America's madmen" to "cream" and felt almost
certain that the milk from which it had been skimmed
was just as rich in violence. The Angelenos would be
first, but their comrades all over the country would
follow. There would be civil war. (pp. 334-35)

In more than forty years since the publication of *The Day
of the Locust,* Los Angeles has seen blacklists and demonstrations
and the Watts riots and radical demographic change and epidem-
ics of drugs and herpes, but neither the city nor the rest of the country has yet to host a second Civil War. Maybe one is just around
the corner, but if so it may still be asked whether the causes will
be those that West has indicated. This is not to disparage West's
many valid sociological observations, or the historical and aesthetic value of his meticulous preservation of the surfaces of Southern Californa.[13]

But I do mean to suggest that the vision and values of Tod
and West are highly personal ones and that Tod's (and probably
West's) is highly colored by psychosexual neurosis. This is not a
purely objective depiction of Los Angeles. It is the story of Tod's
life in Hollywood, and Tod's life is a very lonely one.

A good deal of projection is involved in Tod's art and, I think,
in West's as well. After his romantic marriage in the last year of
his life, "West noted that he was no longer interested in pessimistic writing; in the future—and not just because such art sold—he
planned to write simple, warm, and kindly books, one of which
he had already planned."[14]

It was Daniel Aaron's opinion that "West's image of a tortured demented world grew out of a deep personal anguish and that
in the dislocations of society he found the symbols of his private
state."[15] In spite of the tendency of Jay Martin's impressive biography to emphasize West's amiability and normality,[16] I find it
hard to wean myself from the evidence of James Light's early study,
which, along with friends' reminiscences, pointed to a man deeply
troubled by his rejection of his Jewishness, by an unsatisfactory
relationship with his parents, by his disappointment at the lack of
reception accorded his work, and, most important, by an alienation from satisfactory romantic involvements. But it does not

really matter what West the man was like. All that matters is that a major theme, perhaps *the* major theme, of all his fiction is blighted, blocked, or twisted sexuality. It would be a mistake to read *The Day of the Locust* as social history without taking into account the psychology of Tod Hackett and that of its author.

I would be reluctant to join others in calling *The Day of the Locust* the best novel ever written about Hollywood because I would not know how to compare it fairly with works by, say, Charles Bukowski, John Fante, or John Gregory Dunne. While Bukowski and Fante both knew the Hollywood of West's time period, and while both conveyed the roughness and perils of the place, they often celebrated those same features of diversity which are evidence to West of a dishonest and disjointed culture. It may be that West remained essentially a New Yorker to the end of his brief life.

Nonetheless, *The Day of the Locust* is one of the most original and painstakingly realized works of fiction in our literature, and it deserves its place, on aesthetic, sociological, and psychological grounds, in the first rank of American art.

Notes

1. Lillian Hellman, *An Unfinished Woman* (Boston: Little, Brown and Co., 1969), p. 63.

2. Stanley Edgar Hyman, *Nathanael West* (Minneapolis: University of Minnesota Press, 1962), p. 45.

3. A.M. Tibbetts, "The Strange Half-World of Nathanael West," *Prairie Schooner* 34 (1960):12.

4. Cf. Donald T. Torchiana, "The Painter's Eye," in *Nathanael West: The Cheaters and the Cheated*, ed. David Madden (Deland, Fla.: Everett/Edwards, 1973), pp. 249–82; and Joan Zlotnik, "Nathanael West and the Pictorial Imagination," *Western American Literature* 9 (1974):174–78. I was, however, employing the term, "the painter's eye," and developing ideas from it as early as my 1964 dissertation, "A Critical Study of the Novels of Nathanael West" (University of Arizona).

5. *The Complete Works of Nathanael West* (New York: Farrar, Straus, 1957), p. 261. All further references to the work are to this edition and indicated parenthetically in the text.

6. Gerald I. Locklin, "The Journey into the Microcosm," in *Madden*, pp. 23–56.

7. Louis B. Salomon,"California Grotesque," *The Nation*, 15 July 1939, p. 79.

8. Quoted in Richard B. Gehman, Introduction to *The Day of the Locust* (New York: New Directions, 1950), pp. ix–x.

9. Ibid., p. x.

10. V. L. Lokke, "A Side Glance at Medusa: Hollywood, the Literature Boys, and Nathanael West," *Southwest Review* 46 (1961):45.

11. Wilhelm Stekel, *Sadism and Masochism: The Psychology of Hatred and Cruelty*, trans. Louise Brink (New York: Liveright, 1939), 1:56.

12. Josephine Herbst, "Nathanael West, " *Kenyon Review* 33 (1961):611

13. Cf. David M. Fine, "Landscape of Fantasy: Nathanael West and the Los Angeles Architecture of the Thirties," in *Itinerary Seven: Essays on California Writers*, ed. Charles L. Crow, (Bowling Green, Ohio: Bowling Green University Press,1978). pp. 49–62.

14. Quoted in James F. Light, *Nathanael West: An Interpretive Study* (Evanston, Ill.: Northwestern University Press, 1961), p. 182.

15. Daniel Aaron, "Waiting for the Apocalypse," *Hudson Review* 3 (1951):636.

16. Jay Martin, *Nathanael West: The Art of His Life* (New York: Farrar, Straus & Giroux, 1970).

Bibliographic Note

West scholars are fortunate to have at their disposal *Nathanael West: A Comprehensive Bibliography*, by William White (Kent, Ohio: Kent State University Press, 1975) and *Nathanael West: An Annotated Bibliography of the Scholarship and Works*, by Dennis P. Vannatta, with a foreword by Jay Martin (New York: Garland Publishing, 1976).

The most thorough biography remains Jay Martin's *Nathanael West: The Art of His Life* (New York: Farrar, Straus & Giroux, 1970), but James F. Light's *Nathanael West: An Interpretive Study*, 2d ed. (Evanston, Ill.: Northwestern University Press, 1971) should not be ignored.

The biographical studies by Martin and Light contain extensive treatments of the works as well. Other book-length studies include *Nathanael West: The Ironic Prophet*, by Victor Comerchero (Syracuse, N.Y.: Syracuse University Press, 1964), *Nathanael West's Novels*, by Irving Malin (Carbondale: Southern Illinois University Press, 1972), and *The Fiction of Nathanael West: No Redeemer, No Promised Land* (Chicago: University of Chicago Press, 1967).

Pamphlets include Stanley Edgar Hyman's *Nathanael West* (Minneapolis: University of Minnesota Press, 1962) and Nathan A. Scott's *Nathanael West: A Critical Essay* (Grand Rapids, Mich.: William B. Eerdmans, 1971).

Two major critical collections are *Nathanael West: The Cheaters and the Cheated*, ed. David Madden (Deland, Fla.: Everett/Edwards, 1973) and *Nathanael West: A Collection of Critical Essays*, ed. Jay Martin (Englewood Cliffs, N.J.: Prentice-Hall, 1971).

Among the many noteworthy uncollected essays and reviews are Tom Burke's "The Day of the Locust," *Esquire*, September 1974, 120–26, 174–75; Clifton Fadiman's review in *The New Yorker*, 20 May 1939, pp. 78–80; Richard Gehman's introduction to the 1950 New Directions edition of *The Day*; V. L. Lokke's "A Side Glance at Medusa: Hollywood, the Literature Boys, and Nathanael West," *Southwest Review* 46 (1961):35–45; Louis B. Salomon's "California Grotesque," *The Nation*, 15 July 1931, pp. 78–79; John Sanford's "Nathanael West," *The Screen Writer* 2 (December 1946):10–13; Budd Schulberg's "Literature of the Film: The Hollywood Novel," *Films* I (1940):68–78; A. M. Tibbets's "The Strange Half-World of Nathanael West," *Prairie Schooner* 34 (1960):8–14; and Robert Van Gelder's "A Tragic Chorus," *The New York Times Book Review*, 21 May 1939, pp. 6–7.

Since the compilation of the White and Vannatta bibliographies, *The Day of the Locust*, partly but perhaps not entirely because of the movie, seems to be occupying an increasing proportion of the energies of West scholars. Recent publications include J. T. Ward's "The Hollwyood Metaphor: The Marx Brothers, S. J. Perlman, and Nathanael West," *Southern Review* 12 (1976):659–72; David M. Fine's "Landscape of Fantasy: Nathanael West and Los Angeles Architecture of the Thirties," in *Itinerary Seven: Essays on California Writers*, (Bowling Green, Ohio: Bowling Green University Press, 1978), pp. 49–62; and *The Modern American Novel and the Movies*, ed. Gerald Peary and Roger Schatzkin (New York: Frederick Ungar Publishing Co., 1978). Dissertations on West emerge annually.

PART TWO

Los Angeles and the Detective Novel

FOUR

Behind the
Territory Ahead

Paul Skenazy

I

> The panting pursuit of danger
> is the pursuit of life itself.
> Henry James
> Preface to *The American*

The hard-boiled narrative emerged as a peculiarly American form in a distinctly American voice in the early 1920s; in December 1922 to be exact, in two tentative, unpolished stories published in *Black Mask* magazine: "The False Burton Combs," by Carroll John Daly, and "The Road Home," by Peter Collinson (Dashiell Hammett). These crude beginnings gave little hint of the immense future popularity and cultural impact of such tales. But for sixty years, they have transcribed the shadow side of American life. The transcription has been reductive, exaggerated, and repetitive; still, it has mirrored this complex period with enough fidelity to have helped define our self-conceptions. Writers like James M. Cain, Raymond Chandler, and Ross Macdonald (Kenneth Millar), in particular, have so invaded our Los Angeles imaginings that their idiosyncratic hallucinations have become our regional assumptions. Their works create and dominate many of our insights into the spirit of this city and its citizens.

The power of the early hard-boiled stories came, as Raymond Chandler later noted, from their "smell of fear":

> Their characters lived in a world gone wrong, a world in which, long before the atom bomb, civilization had created the machinery for its own destruction, and was learning to use it with all the moronic delight of a gangster trying out his first machine gun. The law was something to be manipulated for profit and power. The streets were dark with something more than night.[1]

The precise nature of that "something" changed with each writer, and altered as history shifted from the 1920s' "carnival by the sea" to the 1930s' search for a buddy with a spare dime, to and through our several later wars, booms, busts, and fads. At once realistic and as formulaic as a fairy tale, the hard-boiled novel began as an outgrowth of the English detective story, borrowed some motifs from the Western genre, and even stole characteristic gothic trappings. And somehow the form that resulted has become a peculiarly appropriate translation of Los Angeles life.

II

> Thrillers are like life. . . .
> [They're] what we've all made
> of the world.
> Graham Greene,
> *The Ministry of Fear*

Stories of the manipulation of governments by gangsters dominated the tough-guy novels of the 1920s. Such tales exist independent of geography; rather, they inhabit the historical circumstances common to almost all American urban society in the decade. They take their cue from the legends and actions of bootleggers and racketeers, and echo the daily big-city headlines.

America's self-conception and social reality changed dramatically in this period. What Robert Wiebe in *The Search for Order* calls the United States' "island communities" of the late nineteenth and early twentieth century—isolated small-town worlds—lost much of their cultural influence, and their isolation.[2] The change began decades earlier with the massive European migrations and the industrialization of the turn of the century. The end of the war brought returning soldiers eager to work, already removed from families and childhood communities. Prohibition represented the power of the older, traditional, America and paradoxically revealed the seductive strength of the lawless.

A subsistence morality that had dominated America since the eighteenth century was giving way to a consumer economy. These conflicts of old and new were enacted primarily in the cities, which were the symbolic and real heartland of the decade. According to the national census of 1920, urban centers outpopulated rural areas for the first time. The urban world also increasingly invaded the rural through the expansion of cities beyond earlier boundaries, and through new forms of transportation and communication. Magazines, mail-order catalogues, and newspapers brought reports of the city to the small towns. Movies and radio linked the "islands" through common voices and experiences. Cars entered the daily life of the populace, redefining the nature of distance. Local autonomy, which Wiebe calls the "heart of American democracy" before 1920, gave way to "managerial government."

Among the most curious responses to these changes in the 1920s was the nation's fascination with murder.[3] Frequent, sensational trials like that of Mrs. Hall and Snyder, of Fatty Arbuckle, and of Leopold and Loeb, provided real-life melodrama with the morning coffee. As Charles Merz noted at the time, the trials presented a "single set of facts" on which the nation could "test its moral values."[4]

Several popular literary forms provided similar structured playgrounds of violence for their readers. The English detective novel, for example, offered life through a time and class warp. Writers like Agatha Christie and Dorothy Sayers retain a faith in the power of the intellect to clarify the muddled and to order the seemingly chaotic, and of the local social system to maintain itself despite such minor interruptions and inconveniences as dead bodies. These novels offer nostalgia for a traditional moment and place. They pay homage to manners, relationships, and behavior rendered archaic by modern forms of warfare and violence. The genre is dedicated to rule, and to a society that conforms to—and thereby confirms—expectations.

Those willing to allow more realistic unruliness into their entertainment turned to the native, hard-boiled tales published in the several pulp magazines of the time. There were, for example, pure gangster tales, like W. R. Burnett's *Little Caesar* (1929).[5] These were essentially class tragedies, describing the rise and fall of the poor, illiterate, neighborhood child who became a powerful gang leader. Such works were inverted mirrors of their times, describing the rapid fortunes available to the aggressive, skillful organization man of the 1920s in underworld terms—as well as the inevitable crash that followed success.

The detective version of the gangster myth added a wrinkle—the morally ambiguous but ultimately loyal and dependable detective. Although invariably delighting in the pleasures of power and manipulation, the detective is finally able to reject temptation. He declines the achievement-oriented, financially defined power structure of American society, opting instead for his own independent point of view.

In Dashiell Hammett's *Red Harvest* (1929) and *The Glass Key* (1931), for example, alliances between bootleggers and gamblers rule city politics. Both books are about power: how it works, who works it, what it does and can do to and for those who have it. Hammett and his detective are not shocked by crime, nor do they expect a different world to result from solutions to crimes. What Erle Stanley Gardner refers to as Hammett's "peculiar attitude of aloofness and detachment" comes from this nihilism. Revelation of the causality of murder accomplishes little or nothing. There is no one to reveal things to, because the world of these books is corrupt or corruptible. Everyone knows from the beginning how the political structure works and who runs it, and the murders and criminality are only a minor part of these political arrangements.

The problem for the Op in *Red Harvest* is to destroy the government/bootlegging structure; the way to do this is to tell tales behind people's backs, break down the commonality of purpose among the thieves and killers, and make them fight each other.

The Op therefore doesn't so much attempt to disclose the truth as to "stir things up" by planting believable, useful lies. *Harvest* ends with the Op giving Personville back to Willsson, the "Czar" of the city, "all nice and clean and ready to go to the dogs again."[6]

In *The Glass Key*, the issues are more complicated, involving questions of personal loyalty and friendship. But again the political problem is who will rule, not whether government might ever be free from corruption. The novel ends with the political boss ready to "dynamite" his own disloyal machine and spend "four years cleaning house and putting together an organization that will stay put. . . . I'll get the city back next time and by then I'll have done my housekeeping."[7]

Even when a writer set his gangster plot in Los Angeles, there was little to suggest that the change of venue affected the form. California did, however, emerge as a curious conditioning agent on occasion, as in Paul Cain's *Fast One* (1932). Most of the book retains the traditional formula of such tales. No single mystery focuses the action in the novel; each killing is solved in an episodic series of scenes connected only by the antiheroic figures of Kells and his enemy Rose. There is no altruism, no expectation of reform. Only when Kells is personally betrayed does he confront Rose and sacrifice himself to avenge a friend's death.

The atmosphere reminds one more of the enclosed space of Manhattan than of a sprawling Pacific landscape. As Carolyn See notes, "The characteristic Hollywood descriptions are missing: there are no flowers, fruits, clear skies, movie stars."[8] One gangster lives on an island off the coast; two others have gambling boats moored offshore. Otherwise, *Fast One* is a world of interiors in apartments and hotels. Kells often walks from place to place. Movement is noted only by lists of street names:

> He went out and walked up Ivar to Yucca, west on Yucca the short block to Cahuenga. . . . They went down Santa Monica Boulevard very fast, turned north on La Brea. . . . They went up La Brea to Franklin, over Franklin to Cahuenga, up Cahuenga and Iris to Cullen's house.[9]

Descriptions of environment imply that people live within and are affected by their habitat. In *Fast One*, the characters, tone, story, and themes have been imported. Los Angeles is a Manhattan suburb:

> Things are pretty hot back East. . . . Now, I'm going to
> move *all* my interests here, the whole layout. I'm going
> to take over the coast. . . . I've got the finest organization
> in the country. . . . Los Angeles county is big enough for
> everybody . . . but things have got to be under a single
> head. . . . Organization is the thing. We'll organize
> gambling, the bootleggers, the city and state and federal
> police—*everything*. (pp. 127, 130)

Crime in these early thirties' gangster tales is corporate, and the mentality monopolistic. Conglomerates fight for control of the market. Los Angeles is a business venture. The gangster is merely a modern version of the nineteenth-century investor or land speculator, traveling in the wake of the first settlers, and a step ahead of the civilizing standard bearers of law and order.

Kells refuses to join any of the rackets organizations. He too has come west to escape the "heat" of the East, but he has come to "play," as is no longer possible in New York. In this sense, he is reliving the Natty Bumppo story, removing himself from civilization when it encroaches on his personal freedom.

In saying no to offers of power and position, Kells articulates the antiestablishment ethic of the tough detective hero who has bought out of all institutional arrangements and values:

> I've never worked for anybody in my life and I'm too old
> to start. . . . I don't like the racket, anyway. . . . the whole
> god-damned business gives me a pain in the belly. . . .
> [When two men] tried to frame me . . . [they] made me
> mad and I fought back. I was lucky—I took advantage of a
> couple breaks and got myself into a spot where I could
> have some fun. . . . I guess I'm not commercially
> inclined. It's not my game. . . . (p. 131)

The detective figure like Kells rejects the promise of America; he refuses to court William James's "bitch goddess success." Kells, and Hammett's detectives—the Op, Beaumont, and Sam Spade—express their achievement most through what might be called their negating capability. In a world defined by and through ownership—of land, of money, of beauty, of other people—superior character is articulated by the refusal to be bought, or to possess (and hence be vulnerable to the loss of) any more than is essential. The detective's power lies in the act of rejection. He temporarily joins society during a case but remains estranged from its values. His denial confirms his capacity to distinguish impulse from necessity, passion from decision. He chooses confinement, control, and the obligations of his work over the satisfactions of a culture that caters to its animal, instinctual desires.

Which is not to say that there isn't an element of greed and the passion for achievement to the detective. But his power comes from knowledge; he wins by learning secrets and solving puzzles. Discovering the weaknesses of his clients, he confirms his own superiority by rejecting their style of life. This negating skill is ironically his "payoff," an ethical and moral one-upmanship. His ability to know and solve is his equalizer, his passion, and his vindication. It validates his isolation from a community that both repels and hires him.

In the nihilistic world of *Fast One*, however, there is no alternative satisfaction available to Kells. He denies himself a separate peace through his loyalty to a friend and need to revenge him. And Cain denies him even the redemption of that surrounding landscape worth notice which ministers to the wounded spirits of his jaded successors in Chandler and Macdonald. Instead of the region's untamed sense of possibility, Cain takes advantage of land's end to represent Los Angeles as an execution chamber, in which people destroy themselves in the effort to survive with dignity.

Throughout the novel, Kells prepares for an escape from the West back to New York City, but he keeps postponing the return to his earlier life. Instead, the story—and Kells's life—ends with a car chase along the California coast through rain and fog. The car, the cliffs, the fog, and their cumulative destructive force are images that will be repeated time and again in the Los Angeles mythology; exactly the same landscape of tragedy appears only two years later in James M. Cain's *The Postman Always Rings Twice* (1934), for example. For Kells, the meeting of ocean and road confirms that there is no turning back. Maybe this is part of the lesson of cars in a California story: the faster one travels, the more one realizes that there is nowhere to go. In the last scenes of the book, Kells is "alone in the darkness" at the edge of the continent as "life went away from him."

The extraordinary determinism and passivity of the novel's

last line disappears from tough-guy fiction by the late 1930s. One sees a similar tone in Horace McCoy's *They Shoot Horses, Don't They?* (1935) and at moments in James M. Cain's *The Postman Always Rings Twice* and *Double Indemnity* (1936). But there is far less of it in Raymond Chandler, where people have the privilege of making their own destinies, such as they are, through greed and idealism. Chandler and Cain also portray their characters within a physical landscape that is more than just a record of street names. And their protagonists are no longer financial manipulators but seekers and dreamers, cruelly fumbling their way through others' lives toward a vision of self-possession.

III

> The love story and the
> detective story cannot exist,
> not only in the same book—one
> might say in the same culture.
> Raymond Chandler, Diary

The tale of power politics never completely disappears from Los Angeles fiction. It even returns to center stage in the 1970s, in novels like Roger Simon's *The Big Fix* (1973), where the underworld becomes the military-industrial complex. But gangland and municipal crime assumes a secondary position for writers like Raymond Chandler and Ross Macdonald. Their serial accounts of land's end are more concerned with the lives of quiet desperation lived in suburbs and behind not-so-protective shrubbery borders and brick walls.

Chandler and Macdonald come to the detective story without Hammett's personal experience in detective work, or knowledge of street life. Their familiarity with police procedure comes primarily from books, and their street jargon represents a kind of linguistic slumming. Both men self-consciously choose the detective form for their work; both are critical social analysts taking advantage of and testing the limits of a popular form.

Furthermore, both view not only Los Angeles but America as outsiders. Chandler was born in Chicago, but raised in England from age eight until twenty-three, when he returned to the United States. Macdonald was born in San Jose but raised in Canada and educated in Michigan. Not surprisingly, both men find themselves

preoccupied with similar issues: exile, cultural duality and dislocation, class distinctions, wealth, success, and social responsibility.
Both are fascinated by the American voice and its particular accent
along the coast, and both equate that voice with a lively, independent point of view; in Macdonald's words:

> We shared . . . a powerful interest in the American
> colloquial language. Democracy is as much a language as
> it is a place. . . . American vernacular can serve [the
> detective] as a kind of passport to freedom and
> equality. . . . [A] rough-and-ready brand of democracy
> is still peculiarly rampant on this side of the
> Sierra Nevada.[10]

Finally, it is surely not coincidental that both, coming from broken
and unhappy childhoods, abandoned by their fathers, and raised
as poor relatives in class-conscious families, should project a California landscape littered with domestic strife and self-destructive
parental and sibling love.

But these interesting personal idiosyncrasies only go so far
in accounting for the new subjects and tones one begins to find in
works coming out of Los Angeles. The shift from saloons and
speakeasies to the suburbs mirrors significant shifts in the nature
of West Coast society. In the past sixty years, Los Angeles has
changed from a city of 576,673 residents to one with over three
million (approximately the population of the whole state in 1920).[11]
During the 1920s alone, the population of the city increased by
more than 100,000 each year. In their peculiar, even underhanded,
way, Chandler and Macdonald tell a corporate story in taking
advantage of their own semiexile, becoming chroniclers of this
migrant population. For all their differences, Chandler and Macdonald reveal similar assumptions about the essential ingredients
of the California story. They recognize that California, like the
rest of the American West, is both a new and an old territory. Its
Anglo story, at least, is an immigration history. Several cultures
have claimed, used, abused, possessed, and been absorbed into the
state. These civilizations layer each acre of land and often literally color the air we breathe. The narrative of this westward migration is the story of promise and possibility, the land of milk
and honey.

This myth of the New World has been immortalized in our

Western genre and, as John Cawelti and others have shown, the hard-boiled detective story borrows many of its strategies and formulas from this most American of literary forms.[12] Detective and Western stories appeared side by side in most of the pulp magazines of the 1920s like *Black Mask*, their gun-toting heroes spoke with a similarly informal, slangy populist iconoclasm, and both kinds of stories confirmed the power of the loner—the individual man of conviction like Sam Spade, the Virginian, Hopalong Cassidy, or Destry—to withstand and overcome the forces of social disruption and personal greed. In fact the identification of the genres was so complete that Hollywood was frequently referred to as the "new Wild West" in early detective fictions, and both Hammett and Chandler felt compelled to parody the Western in their work to try to establish their own claims to realism.[13]

But if the two genres have much in common, from the hero's knightly attitudes to women to his skeptical, democratic disregard for the power of law, they are exact opposites in their social asumptions. The Western replaces history with hope. It presents a dream of Eden on the verge either of destruction (ownership by the greedy, the self-serving, or the Eastern industrialists), or of renewed fecundity, in the labors of the new community of settlers. The land is redeemed and preserved by the strong, silent man of action, like the Virginian.

The Western characteristically preaches an anticivilization, proagrarian myth and proposes that our national fate has not yet been sealed. It offers hope that the old values and ideals, and the old links of character with nature, can still preserve us. It is a progressive, future-directed form. The nation is being made. The county can will its own destiny. Everything is possibility.

Like the characters in Westerns, the characters in California detective novels believe in the myth of a future, and they shape their lives by these beliefs. They turn their backs to the past and eagerly await the dawn of tomorrow. But this compulsive forward-looking must confront an ocean that turns people back on themselves, back into themselves. The unbounded territory of the imagined West, where the future might be enacted, is discovered to be bound by just those problems of everyday life and social resistance that the characters were so eager to escape from. The dream haven of ease and contentment and forever-afters is just another world of decay, corruption, and violence—perhaps even of more dread because of the frustrated ambitions condensed into the area. Hope gives way to memory; the promised new beginning becomes the despair of *déjà vu*.

Immigration and resettlement are as much a leaving behind as a going toward. Part legend, part land, California is to America as America once was to Europe, that mythological "world elsewhere," the territory of wishes attractive because it is where one is not. So the story of the West inevitably also becomes a story of the East, and of the complex interaction of the world left behind with the new life begun. California is the territory in which old cultural, and personal, battles are fought; it is not so much a new experience as a postponement, and finally a repetition, of old ones.

Seeking new beginnings, people reveal old dispositions. They dream in old frames, they think in learned categories, they act from habits confirmed over time, in other surroundings. Even rebellion apes the very power it denies. Yet entrenched in ways of being, they succumb to the necessities and assumptions and mores of their new environments. The interaction of person and place, past and present, new and old, always breeds hybrids. This is as true of individuals as of cultures: each bears the record of dual contexts.

This embedding of old in new is one of the central themes of the California detective story. The Los Angeles mystery plot maintains a double rhythm: moving inexorably forward in time while creeping slowly backward to resolve the disruptions and violence evident in the present. The detective in a family-centered environment does not "stir things up," like the Op; he digs them up. The family detective plot is a "buried treasure" narrative in which the solution to the crime is discovered in events that occurred long before the plot begins. The genre is directed to the past. It develops a legend of failure. High hopes have been corrupted, ideals have become hypocritical platitudes. Aspirations and dreams have decayed into violence.

The cities in these stories are dark, brooding places of old buildings and collapsing relationships. The stuffing is coming out of furniture and marriages. Shadows darken even the most well-lighted places and line the most innocent of faces. The characteristic story-telling voice is not so much hard-boiled as world-and-bone weary, having seen too much to expect any pleasant surprises, and so desiring no surprises at all.

These Los Angeles stories are curiously closer to the gothic novel in spirit than to the Western; or are, rather, a conjunction of the two genres, with Western dreams becoming gothic nightmares. There are few of the stereotypical gothic trappings, like chambers of horrors, hidden passages, heartbeats through the floorboards or messages received from the tomb. But the books are filled with what we might call gothic causality. The hard-boiled stories are about hauntings. Present circumstances make evident the powerful intervention of past experiences.

Both gothic and detective fiction reminds us that the past exerts a compelling moral force in the present. The two forms share common assumptions: that there is an undisclosed event, a secret from the past; that the secret represents an occurrence or desire antithetical to the principles and position of the house (or family); that to know the secret is to understand the inexplicable and seemingly irrational events that occur in the present. Both forms bring hidden experiences from shadow to light. The characters attempt to protect themselves by enclosing their secrets; disclosure in both threatens social status and family lineage. And both forms reverse time through regressive revelations.

Clients in Chandler and Macdonald often hire the detective to keep a secret from becoming known: to pay off a blackmailer in *The Big Sleep* (1939), to recover a "stolen" jade necklace in *Farewell, My Lovely* (1940), or a coin in *The High Window* (1942). Attempting to maintain secrecy, they unwittingly (and unconsciously) open the family vault. The discovery of one hidden indiscretion leads the detective to others, thwarting time itself until present and past merge in the concluding explanation. Disparate incidents only seem unconnected. They receive coherence and consistency with the revelation of the disjunctive secret: the misdeed, the sexual weakness, the earlier identity. Sometimes there is an actual skeleton in the closet (or at least beneath the floor, as in Macdonald's *The Ivory Grin*). In many cases the landscape itself is a chamber of horrors, enclosing the evidence of crime: a dead body rises to the water's surface amid an abandoned Hollywood set in *The Lady in the Lake* (1943); a body buried in a car is uncovered during a forest fire in Macdonald's *The Underground Man* (1971).[14]

One of the first, and most effective, explorations of this gothic framework is Chandler's *The Big Sleep*. The brilliant opening sequences of General Sternwood's hothouse of fleshy orchids ("like the newly washed fingers of dead men"), and Vivian Regan's white-on-white boudoir ("The white made the ivory look dirty and the ivory made the white look bled out") combine with the visual trappings of the huge old home, the family portraits, and the stained-glass depiction of knight and frightened damsel to enclose Marlowe in an imitative medievalism. Then Marlowe retreats to a more revealing landscape that ostensibly conflicts with all that has gone before. The white of Vivian's room is set against the black of the oil wells, the senseless banter in the house against the acrid smell, the impenetrable heights of wealth juxtaposed to their rank sources:

> I could just barely see some of the old wooden derricks of the oilfield from which the Sternwoods had made their money. . . . The Sternwoods, having moved up the hill, could no longer smell the stale sump water or the oil, but they could still look out of their front windows and see what had made them rich.[15]

The oil field represents the secret life of the Sternwoods, which is figured more immediately in the blackmail notes about Carmen, and in Rusty Regan's disappearance. It also symbolizes the right of the rich to deny accountability. The field supplies the money to protect Carmen, and it physically encloses the evidence of her killing: Regan's body lies in an abandoned well. It is a "daydream land," Marlowe tells us, where he and the "predatory," animal-like Carmen reenact her killing of Regan. By the end of the novel, the "stagnant and stinking" field symbolizes the sexual and violent sources of the family's pretensions. The estate's glistening, inviting beauty is thick with the sins and indiscretions of its citizens: "Outside the bright gardens had a haunted look, as though small wild eyes were watching me from behind the bushes, as though the sunshine itself had a mysterious something in its light" (p. 215).

The conflicting directions of the California detective plot—driving intensely forward to the future, turned by starts and jumps backward into the past—create the tension that gives social significance to the murder puzzles. The move a character makes to California—a classic Ross Macdonald situation—or into another social class or town in the state—the Raymond Chandler equivalent—is an attempt to declare personal amnesia. The California Myth grants magical, transformative power to alterations of place, and to the impulses of the individual will: "out of sight, out of mind." Geography is a pill that can make one well and whole once again. You are what you appear to be. Life becomes Hollywood: to act a part is to be a person. The American confidence in one's right to create a personal destiny free from social circumstance is encouraged by the new, migratory nature of the society, the open class structure, and the expanding opportunities for advancement that are found in and near Los Angeles.

Will, like a plastic surgeon, can alter the shape of one's face and so of one's future. A new identity replaces the old one; fate is denied power. The recreated self is represented in the alias, as character becomes synonymous with name. In *Farewell, My Lovely,* "Little Velma," a two-bit singer and moll, becomes Mrs. Lewin Lockridge Grayle, a woman of fashion. Velma sends a man to prison; Mrs. Grayle kills a man who knows about that earlier deed and previous incarnation. They are the same person, and different. In *The Lady in the Lake,* a woman is one man's nurse and lover, two men's wives, and a repeated murderer in different lives and different places. And through most of the story she is "dead," while Marlowe meets her in several disguises before he recognizes the actress in the characters.

California, as these novels represent it, places a premium on the present. The past that invariably intrudes suggests the unconscious self within the contemporary ego. The past is like a private "underworld"; hence it often reveals the connections that bind the rich to the criminal, or social, underworld elements, as in *Farewell, My Lovely* and *The Lady in the Lake.* '

The paradox of the personal alterations in these novels is that selfhood depends on one's neighbors. One is who one says one is only so long as others are convinced. Hence the problem of respectability—reputation—replaces morality. People live in mortal terror of their earlier lives or secret activities being discovered. Guilt is equated not with sins committed, but sins disclosed. It does not matter what one does; it only matters who knows it, and who else might be told.

Two people who share a secret in the tough-guy world are vulnerable to each other's knowledge, and intimate in their conspiracy. In James Cain's *The Postman Always Rings Twice* and *Double Indemnity*, the couples' profound knowledge of each other accounts for the intensity of their passion and the inevitability of their mutual destruction. In both cases, their dependence and complicity in the husband's death opens what Cain calls the "Pandora's Box." Together they have known and done everything they can imagine. The shared knowledge of these deepest and darkest ambitions is unendurable. They have revealed too much of themselves—about themselves—and their "cover" is blown.

In the classic Los Angeles detective plot, this intimacy almost always takes the form of blackmail. Blackmail is the intense relationship that develops from knowledge of someone else's secret self. To know something about someone is to "know" them in a Biblical, which is to say sexual, sense: you "have something on" someone and so possess the other. In the inevitably uneven and mismatched form that passion takes in the Los Angeles of these fictions, where eros has turned into struggles for power, blackmail replaces love relationships. The intensity of the tie is measured in the violence needed to break it.

Embedded in the specific knowledge the blackmailer has of, and "on," this self is the deeper sense of personal incapacity the discovered act comes to represent. Through his awareness of the victim's misdeed, the blackmailer triggers the mechanisms of regret. It seems as if one's deepest strains of inadequacy are vulnerable in each repressed act forced back into the memory and attention by the blackmailer; as if the discovered act is the entrance to primal and uncontrollable guilt. In psychoanalytic terms, the blackmailer functions as a punishing parental superego, a living memory that demands recognition from the new self. The victim tries to "pay off" the conscience, but the guilt is insatiable.

Proof, like a photographic negative, is the objective correlative of power, and of the abiding power of the past over the present.[16] The blackmailer parasitically eats of the host, consuming larger and larger payoffs until the new, California identity is all but swallowed by old debts. It is at this point that the victim almost invariably attempts to eliminate the blackmailer. The attempted murder is an admission of impotence, and an attempt to destroy the old self in the form of the person who knows of it and so mirrors that self. But the attempt to kill is actually a reversion in character, and often involves an almost literal reenactment of the original crime. This reenactment provides the detective with the "clue" that integrates past with present, name with person, in a neurotic cycle of repetition and compulsion.

Gothic (and detective) ghosts emerge from their graves to demand reparation and reform. This moral, revisionary task is handled by that seedy knight "not himself mean," walking "down these mean streets" of Chandler's and Macdonald's Los Angeles.

Chandler and Macdonald are both moralists. They look for, in Chandler's famous words, "a quality of redemption."[17] When Marlowe says that the world is corrupt, he means that it needn't be; when he rails against hypocrisy or irresponsibility, it's because he trusts his own honesty and sense of devotion, and he even manages to find spots of both dotting the landscape. To the end, he remains a romantic, worn down by but not conceding to a world whose reality resists his sentiments.

The detective sees life as a theme with variations, and instructs his clients in the circular, repetitive quality of experience. Memory is synonymous with the acceptance of limits in Chandler's and Macdonald's world. Marlowe and Archer stress the mediating controls of environment, time, and chance. Hence the re-membered and remembering self is one which accepts life as a social beast formed by and among others. The "discovery" one makes again and again in these stories is of the intricate symbiotic compact between person and person: the way each life not only replicates other lives, but blessedly and shamefully depends upon them.

There are temptations to power for the detective in this personal, familial environment parallel to the offers of political control one found in the gangster stories. When Marlowe or Archer know who is really who, they know who has done what, and why. They then replace the blackmailer as threat and intimate. The detective's morality is displayed in his refusal to maintain others' dependence on him. If the blackmailer functions as a punishing superego, the detective demonstrates the parent in an accepting, alternative form.

Refusing to consume those he "knows," the detective in his final gesture invariably sets them free. This act of liberation also, perhaps, reveals the private eye's deepest fears, in his persistent avoidance of any extended involvements and interdependencies. To love would mean that someone would know him as intimately as he knows others, and so alter the power balance. Knowing his shadow self, they would be able to shadow him.

In its understated kindness and evasiveness, Marlowe's last conversation with Vivian Regan in *The Big Sleep* is characteristic of this escape through letting go. The achievement Marlowe seeks is to reach the moment when "it all ties together—everything." And this binding of person to person and part to part, with the detective outside the package, also seems to be the only satisfactory way Marlowe can relate to anyone. He merges with the novelist in the aesthetic faith that the well-made plot somehow redeems the characters living within it:

> "You'll take her away," I said. "And do that damn quickly."
> She still had her back to me. She said softly now: "What about you?"
> "Nothing about me. I'm leaving. I'll give you three days. If you're gone by then—okey. If you're not, out it comes. And don't think I don't mean that."
> She turned suddenly. "I don't know what to say to you. I don't know how to begin."
> "Yeah. Get her out of here and see that she's watched every minute. Promise?"
> "I promise. . . ." (p. 215)

IV

> The dead require us to remember
> and write about them. . . . We
> reinvent them and ourselves out
> of memory and dream.
> Ross Macdonald, Foreword
> to *Archer in Jeopardy*

I have tried to demonstrate how the interweaving of old and new is not only a significant part of the California detective story, but also a notable fact in the history of the genre itself as it migrated from one coast to the other during the 1920s and 1930s. There were West Coast tough guys from the first days of the hard-boiled form, but by the mid-1930s, there was little else. The writers had moved to Hollywood, or at least to Los Angeles, and so had most of their detectives and villains. A few of these writers, like Paul Cain and James M. Cain and Raymond Chandler and Horace McCoy, found themselves writing a slightly different story under the pressure of the different times and different place. Gradually they began to reshape the assumptions and tone of the genre, shifting from issues of the underworld to tales in which gangsterism figured only as it touched individual lives. Not surprisingly, writers who were themselves exiles wrote stories of displacement, the hopes and disappointments of trying to begin again, and the disillusion, confusion, and despair that came with awakening from California dreams.

For reasons both historical and territorial, the California detective story has found its central theme in the dream of new beginnings, and its moral perspective in the detective's revelation of the power of a past that rises, ghostly, to cloud the sunny present. In the shift from East to West, and from the 1920s to the 1930s and after, the hard-boiled tough guy lost some of his starch and developed a weary tone of nostalgic disapproval that represents his distance from the surrounding society. And he has discovered, to no one's real surprise, that everyone is hiding something, and that keeping secrets is the real privilege and vice of the respectable. If murder remains the inevitable focus of these California tales, the more intimate relationship that binds rich to poor, over- to underworld, and criminal to victim is the power that comes from knowledge of someone else's private life. Old and new, past and future, and private and public are joined through financial and emotional blackmail—the tribute paid to the shadow self. The detective discovers and narrates the history of that dark soul, and thereby connects legendary Los Angeles to a real time.

At its best, the haunted detective plot discloses the unconscious life of both the person and the culture. Most of the villains in Chandler and Macdonald are not evil, but deranged. They exist in daydream worlds in which they have allowed themselves to enact their fantasies at the expense of others. The parallel cultural disease is the way public, contemporary Los Angeles society encourages, or at least does not discourage, such solipsism: through the disconnection of person from person; through the Hollywood myth of happy endings and glowing sunsets; or merely in the latitude provided by a place inhabited by newcomers.

As a corporate and personal fantasy, California is not so much a place as a symptom—a register of discomfort, an admission of failure, and a hope of escape. Its story is a magnified version of the dilemma of individualism: the right to make oneself up independent of obligations. Seeking to exclude social influences, people become exiles from themselves. The past suggests the determined (rather than free), fated (rather than willed) unconscious, the impulses, necessities, and compulsions that have been denied existence.

Beneath and behind California's promise is Poe's tell-tale heart, beating on as a reminder of the past, echoing in the characters' lives despite their best efforts to silence it, until the detective finally tells that tale. Like the novelist, the detective imposes form and causality on events, and makes the meaningless significant. The disorder and chaos take on the intricacy of his explanation, which literally relocates the characters in a binding human compact of narrative.

The detective's articulation of lost stories reveals not only the criminals, but also those willing and able to accept what they learn about themselves. It is these creatures, however often deceived and however evasive in pursuing answers, who elicit Marlowe's or Archer's sympathy and support. The detective's role for his clients is finally to serve as a variation of the Socratic figure, in dialogue against the trainings that have prevented clear insight. He demonstrates not so much that the unexamined life is not worth living as that the examined one is endurable.

The Los Angeles promise is of loss of memory in the Geographical Cure. The detective looks inward and backward, to the history of the disease. He returns the privilege of a past to clients who think they have bought exemption and forgetfulness, knowing that without that story of the territory behind, person and society have nowhere to begin. There is only one Genesis, again and again.

Notes

1. Raymond Chandler, Introduction to *The Simple Art of Murder* (Boston: Houghton Mifflin Co., 1950). Rpt. in Raymond Chandler, *Trouble Is My Business* (New York: Ballantine Books, 1972), p. viii.

2. Robert Wiebe, *The Search for Order, 1877–1920* (New York: Hill and Wang, 1967),p. vii and passim.

3. A different reading of this interest in murder is offered by John R. Brazil, "Murder Trials, Murder and Twenties America," *American Quarterly* 33 (1981):163–84.

4. Ibid., p. 167.

5. For comments on the gangster novel, see Robert Warshow, "The Gangster as Tragic Hero," in *The Immediate Experience* (Garden City, N.Y.: Doubleday & Co., 1962), and George Grella, "The Gangster Novel: The Urban Pastoral," in *Tough Guy Writers of the Thirties*, ed. David Madden (Carbondale: Southern Illinois Univ. Press, 1968), pp. 186–98.

6. *Red Harvest* (New York: Alfred A. Knopf, 1929); in *Dashiell Hammett Onmibus* (New York: Alfred A. Knopf, 1935), p. 255.

7. *The Glass Key* (1931; New York: Random House, Vintage Books, 1972), p. 203

8. Carolyn See, "The Hollywood Novel: The American Dream Cheat," in Madden, p. 203.

9. Paul Cain, *Fast One* (1932; New York: Fawcett Book Group, 1978), pp. 65–88. Further references to this work appear parenthetically in the text.

10. Ross Macdonald, Foreword, *Archer in Hollywood* (New York: Alfred A. Knopf, 1967), p. viii.

11. By contrast, San Francisco's population has increased from 506,676 in 1920 to 678,974 in 1980.

12. See, for example, John Cawelti, "The Gunfighter and the Hard-Boiled Dick: Some Ruminations on American Fantasies of Heroism," *American Studies* 16 (1975):49–64, and *Adventure, Mystery, Romance: Formula Stories in Art and Popular Culture* (Chicago: University of Chicago Press, 1976); Robert B. Parker, "The Violent Hero, Wilderness Heritage, and Urban Reality" (Ph. D. Diss., Boston University, 1971), and J. C. Porter, "End of the Trail: The American West of Dashiell Hammett and Raymond Chandler," *Western Historical Quarterly* (October 1975), pp. 411–24.

13. See, for example, Hammett's "Corkscrew," the many self-mocking comparisons Marlowe makes of his bumbling confusions and the Western hero's powerful authority, or the figure of the laconic sheriff in *The Lady in the Lake* (1943).

14.   The first, and most overtly, gothic of all tough-guy novels is *The Dain Curse* (1930), in which Dashiell Hammett takes advantage of San Francisco's Victorian homes and the Monterey Bay's coves and fog. As the title implies, the novel explores a family "curse," though it turns out to be less a hereditary problem of blood than of sexual passion, greed, and insanity. Somewhat disconnected in plot, the novel features everything from demonism to morphine, physical marks of derangement to Hollywood special-effects experts. Although unsatisfying in itself, it introduces the atmospheric gothic motifs, and the family focus in time, that would become central to Chandler and Macdonald.

15.   *The Big Sleep* (1939; New York: Ballantine Books, (1971), p. 18. Further references to the Ballantine edition of this work appear parenthetically in the text.

16.   Photographs replace the portrait of gothic fiction, which often revealed family relationships. Other evidence is occasionally used as well; in *The Lady in the Lake*, for example, a central clue is a lost slipper, in keeping with the mock-romantic title.

17.   "The Simple Art of Murder," rpt. in *The Simple Art of Murder* (New York: Ballantine Books, 1972), p. 20. Macdonald argues with this idealism of Chandler's in *On Crime Writing* (Santa Barbara, Calif., Capra Press, 1973) and "Down These Mean Streets a Mean Man Must Go," *Antaeus* 24/25 (1977):211–16. But despite his theoretical objections, and the real differences between Marlowe and Archer as detectives, both writers share the hope of a better day to come for some of the characters— and implicitly for the society—of their fiction.

Bibliographic Note

Many of the best stories from *Black Mask* and the other hard-boiled periodicals have been collected in three anthologies: Joseph T. Shaw's *The Hard-Boiled Omnibus* (New York: Simon and Schuster, 1946), Ron Goulart's *The Hardboiled Dicks: An Anthology and Study of Pulp Detective Fiction* (New York: Simon and Schuster, Pocket Books, 1967), and Herbert Ruhm's *The Hard-Boiled Detective: Stories from Black Mask Magazine (1920–1951)* (New York: Random House, Vintage Books, 1977). Works by Hammett, Chandler, and Macdonald are readily available in paperback, and occasional reprints of the fiction of Raoul Whitfield, George Harmon Coxe, Paul Cain (Peter Ruric), and Cornell Woolrich (William Irish) are worth looking for.

Any critical reading on the genre should begin with the comments of the writers themselves, such as those available in "The Simple Art of

Murder," Chandler's introduction to his collected stories (*The Simple Art of Murder* [Boston: Houghton Mifflin Co., 1950]), in *Raymond Chandler Speaking*, ed. Dorothy Gardiner and Katherine Sorley Walker (Boston: Houghton Mifflin Co., 1962), and in *Selected Letters of Raymond Chandler*, ed. Frank McShane (New York: Columbia University Press, 1981). Ross Macdonald (Kenneth Millar) has also written with intelligence about his own as well as his predecessors' work in several essays, most of which have been collected in *On Crime Writing* (Santa Barbara, Calif., Capra Press, 1973) and *Self-Portrait: Ceaselessly into the Past* (Santa Barbara, Calif.: Capra Press, 1981).

Among general books on the detective story, Howard Haycraft's *Murder for Pleasure: The Life and Times of the Detective Story* (New York: Biblo and Tannen, 1974), first published in 1941, remains standard, though it is by now somewhat outdated. An excellent recent overview is Julian Symons's *Mortal Consequences: A History—From the Detective Story to the Crime Novel* (New York: Harper and Row Publishers, 1972), and a helpful brief history of the genre can be found in *The Whodunit*, by Stefan Benvenuti and Gianni Rizzoni (New York: Macmillan Co., 1979).

John G. Cawelti's *Adventure, Mystery, Romance: Formula Stories as Art and Popular Culture* (Chicago: University of Chicago Press, 1976) is a highly intelligent reading of the importance of formula in literary artifacts. Among the more recent genre studies of the American tough-guy tradition, the most useful are William Ruehlmann's *Saint with a Gun: The Unlawful American Private Eye* (New York: New York University Press, 1974), Dennis Porter's *The Pursuit of Crime: Art and Ideology in Detective Fiction* (New Haven: Yale University Press, 1981), and an anthology, *Tough Guy Writers of the Thirties*, edited by David Madden (Carbondale: Southern Illinois University Press, 1968).

The generic approach tends to slight questions of social history, and so historical works on the 1920s and 1930s might usefully be read in conjunction. A good, painless introduction to the larger culture of the period might be Frederick Lewis Allen's lively contemporary volumes, *Only Yesterday* (1931), and *Since Yesterday* (1939), both available in Harper and Row Perennial paperbacks. Geoffrey O'Brien tries to integrate the historical and literary issues in *Hardboiled America* (New York: Van Nostrand Reinhold Co., 1981), a popular and breezy volume that gives a vivid sense of the era. And Walter Wells has offered useful readings of the tough-guy in a "Southland" context in *Tycoons and Locusts: A Regional Look at Hollywood Fiction of the 1930s* (Carbondale: Southern Illinois University Press, 1973).

A brief introduction to Hammett's and Chandler's work is Paul Skenazy's *The New Wild West: The Urban Mysteries of Dashiell Hammett and Raymond Chandler,* Boise State University Western Writers Series, No. 54 (Boise, Idaho: Boise State University 1982). Hammett's life is detailed in Diane Johnson's *Dashiell Hammett: A Life* (New York: Random House, 1983). Richard Layman's *Shadow Man: The Life of Dashiell Hammett* (New York: Harcourt Brace Jovanovich, 1981) and William F. Nolan's *Hammett: A Life at the Edge* (New York: Congdon and Weed, 1983) provide useful information and interesting anecdotes. Peter Wolfe's *Beams Falling: The Art of Dashiell Hammett* (Bowling Green, Ohio: Bowling Green University Popular Press, 1980) is a good introductory discussion of the fiction. Also of interest is Joe Gore's *Hammett* (New York: G. P. Putnam's Sons, 1975), a well researched hard-boiled mystery featuring the writer as a detective in 1920s San Francisco, and Lillian Hellman's memoirs of her years with Hammett, *An Unfinished Woman* (Boston: Little, Brown and Co., 1969), *Pentimento* (Boston: Little, Brown and Co., 1973), and *Scoundrel Time* (Boston: Little, Brown and Co. 1976).

FIVE

Raymond Chandler's City of Lies

Liahna K. Babener

Ever since its first chroniclers rhapsodized about the Arcadian terrain of Southern California, the region has borne the weight of hyperbole. Even before the movie industry enshrined Hollywood as the kingdom of illusion, local hucksters celebrated the Southland as a mecca of opportunity and abundance. Buoyed by slogans like "California or Bust" and "Eureka! I have found it," fortune hunters, homesteaders, health seekers, and others in the grip of the westering romance made their way to the Los Angeles basin, what they knew as "the fortunate coast."[1] Grandpa Joad in *The Grapes of Wrath* spoke for a whole company of misguided dreamers when he exulted, "Got a feelin' it'll make a new fella outa me."[2]

All too often, however, such expectations proved unfounded. The popular fable of easy living in Southern California was soon discredited, and the collective disappointment of the Joads and their fellow seekers has inspired several generations of writers to challenge and expose the duplicity behind it. Modern Los Angeles, steeped in the traditions of promotional ballyhoo and movie fantasy, has emerged in the works of its regional artists as the consummate symbol of cultural pretense, what Willaim Irwin Thompson has called an "imagi-nation."[3]

Such a vision—of an empire built on a spurious foundation, decked in tinsel, and beguiled by its own illusory promises—is central to the Los Angeles novels of Raymond Chandler. If ever a writer understood the metaphoric possibilities of his region, it was Chandler, who documented with a kind of morose glee the culture of flim-flam so pervasive in Southern California. While his critics have almost always felt the need to justify his penchant for the mystery form, it is hardly surprising that Chandler gravitated to the genre which by its very nature embodies the problem of deception at the heart of his fictional realm.

Chandler's Los Angeles is a metropolis of lies. Artifice is everywhere, a theme suggested by an insistent pattern of analogies to moviemaking and show business that informs virtually every novel. The verbal allusions to Hollywood are compounded by a dense matrix of images which augment the notion that fraudulence and deceit lie at the moral center of Chandler's city. The architecture of Los Angeles—often derivative, insubstantial, and tasteless—attests to the city's preoccupation with facade. Its buildings, roadways, and grid patterns have been perversely grafted onto an unreceptive landscape. Nature, in Chandler's vision, has been gilded and bastardized, recast as a tawdry imitation of itself. Rampant fakery governs human experience as well. Throughout the novels, the documents of daily life are seen to be false constructs; the business world is beset with quackery and double-dealing. Most important, personal identity is portrayed as unstable and uncertain. In a society of second chances and new beginnings, people are not what they seem or who they used to be. Virtually every one of Chandler's seven novels pivots on a case of mistaken, disguised, or altered identity. His characters discard their old selves and invent new ones. Sexuality, too, is illicit, ambivalent, and fraught with treachery.

Chandler maps a geography of sham to expose a commanding falsehood in western culture: that success, wealth, and personal betterment can nullify the past and bring contentment. The lesson of every novel undercuts such facile optimism. The past is irremediable, and money is the contagion, not the cure. The climactic irony is that, in such a culture, truth itself has been made impotent. For Chandler, falsity is so prevalent that the truth, if it surfaces at all, is neither redeeming nor ameliorative. More ominously, detective Philip Marlowe, thwarted in his mission to cleanse his world of cant, seems in the end to conform to the prevarication. Constrained to suppress or deny the knowledge he has uncovered, he thus fosters the very lies he has sought to expunge. When the saint defects to the sinners, it is clear that things are radically askew in Chandler's Los Angeles.

I

There is hardly a more appropriate metaphor for the fraudulence of Southern California life than Hollywood. Described variously as "Lotusland," "Glitter City," "Pasteboard Babylon," and "The Fabulous Empire of Oomph," Hollywood has long served the literary imagination as a symbol of artifice. As Oscar Levant is said to have remarked, "Under all the phony tinsel of Hollywood is real tinsel." In Chandler's city, where deception is ubiquitous, images drawn from the cinema and the theater are used repeatedly to stress the artificiality of the whole place. Marlowe must make his way through a profusion of false fronts, penetrating through appearances to the reality behind. No newcomer to the imposture of the world, Marlowe repeatedly likens his investigation to a drama where the principals play roles and speak from a script, the action is shaped into scenes, and, as he puts it in *The Big Sleep* (1939), "fate stage-managed the whole thing."[4]

As it turns out, many of the dissemblers whom Marlowe encounters actually are veterans of show business, where presumably they have been schooled in the art of fakery. Several in the criminal company of *Farewell, My Lovely* (1940) claim theatrical origins. Jules Amthor, a phony fortune teller, shows off a profile "as good . . . as Barrymore."[5] His henchman, named Second Planting, is an Indian who talks like an extra in a low-budget western: "Me Second Planting"; "Great White father say come quick"; "Gottum car." Chorus girls with exhibitionistic names like Linda Conquest and Lois Magic promote much of the mayhem in *The High Window* (1942). Retired screen idol Alex Morny now operates the Idle Valley Club, a hangout for the pampered rich with a lobby "that looked like a high-budget musical. A lot of light and glitter . . . an all-star cast," and, to cap the illusion, a ceiling of "soft lascivious stars that really twinkled."[6] The parade of poseurs is endless. Earl, a bodyguard in *The Long Goodbye* (1953), dresses like a movie cowboy in a skin-tight black gaucho suit and patent leather boots, a costume which Marlowe likens to "a Roy Rogers outfit."[7]

The triumph of movie-made sham, a recurrent motif in all the novels, becomes a central theme in *The Little Sister* (1949). The corrupt heart of the novel is the film business itself, portrayed as a sink of envy, vice, and duplicity. Power brokers and image makers preside over the "industry," cynically pandering make-believe to a credulous public. Marlowe reflects on the perversions of character and culture that result:

> Wonderful what Hollywood will do to a nobody. It will make a radiant glamour queen out of a drab little wench who ought to be ironing a truck driver's shirts, a he-man hero . . . reeking of sexual charm out of some overgrown kid who was meant to go to work with a lunchbox. Out of a Texas car hop with the literacy of a character in a comic strip it will make an international courtesan . . . so blasé and decadent at the end of it that her idea of a thrill is to seduce a furniture mover in a sweaty undershirt.[8]

Marlowe faults Hollywood for imposing a kind of movie vision of life that twists and corrupts those who fall under its spell. As Joan Didion has suggested in *Slouching Toward Bethlehem*, when movie fantasies begin to shape the ethos of a culture, when the dream begins to "[teach] the dreamers how to live," and "a belief in the literal interpretation of Genesis has slipped impercep-tibly into a belief in the literal interpretation of *Double Indem-nity*," the consequences may be homicide.[9] They certainly are in *The Little Sister*, where Orrin Quest, a refugee from middle Amer-ica caught up in the spurious promises of a movie-made world, acts out the very scenario Didion describes. Marlowe condemns the Hollywood trumpery that can "take a small-town prig like Orrin Quest and make an ice-pick murderer out of him in a mat-ter of months, elevating his simple meanness into the classic Sad-ism of the multiple killer."

The fusion of the real and the illusory permeates the novel. Marlowe conceives of the case as a cheap thriller with its melodramatic plot and backlot intrigue, its cast of posturing characters drawn from filmland, and its violent denouement.[10] He repeatedly calls our attention to his own cinematic paradigm, describing one client as a would-be tough guy who has forgotten his exit line and a house detective as "the wicked foreman of the Lazy Q." Conversations sound like screen dialogue with salty banter and hard-boiled clichés. The police address witnesses as "sweetheart" and complain about getting "the big razzoo" from uncooperative subjects. They speak in movie metaphors: a repeat interrogation is "a second show" and a suspect's retort is a "snappy comeback." Some exchanges read like parodies of matinee seduction scenes:

> "Did I hurt you?" she asked softly.
> I nodded.
> "That's fine." She hauled off and slapped me again, harder if anything. "I think you'd better kiss me," she breathed. (p.82)

Or:

> We went into my private thinking parlor and sat down.
> "You always wear black?" I asked.
> "But yes. It is more exciting when I take my clothes off." (p.176)

This is the parlance of self-conscious performers, actors who are so accustomed to impersonation that they live their parts. But the feigning in *The Little Sister* suffuses the whole Los Angeles culture. Marlowe describes an undertaker's contrived grief in histrionic terms: "The boss mortician fluttered around making elegant little gestures and body movements as graceful as a Chopin ending. His composed gray face was long enough to wrap around his neck" (p.152). A secretary at the film studio incarnates the studied glamor of the trade: "Her hair was a hot sunset. . . . Her fingernails matched her blouse exactly. She looked as if it would take a couple of weeks to get her dressed" (p.117). Behavior is dictated by established film conventions. The villains learn how to behave by watching gangster movies. Indeed, the dream has taught the dreamers how to live.

The show business model that informs *The Little Sister* underlies all Chandler's novels. Movies define the sensibility and inaugurate the standards of conduct. Acclaim means being "ranked . . . with Valentino." Generosity is to have "a heart as big as one of Mae West's hips." Even the clock bows to cinematic rules. In Los Angeles, time is organized in terms of early and late shows, rather than hours and minutes.

Again and again Marlowe likens the Los Angeles scene to a movie spectacle with a repertory company of liars, cheaters, and imposters. A recurring figure is the seductress who beguiles her way through a series of male dupes to position and power. Marlowe, always on guard against feminine treachery, exposes a lying woman behind almost every crime. In *The Big Sleep* Carmen Sternwood raises and lowers her eyelashes "like a theater curtain"; Vivian operates from a bedroom likened to "a screen star's boudoir, a place of charm and seduction, artificial as a wooden leg." Both women tease and dissemble to divert Marlowe: Carmen sucks her thumb like a cooing toddler and Vivian arranges herself in alluring poses. Ultimately the pretense is catastrophic, as play-acting is smplified into murder.

Helen Grayle of *The Big Sleep* and Mildred Haviland of *The Lady in the Lake* (1944) are more accomplished and more lethal femmes fatales. Helen is an ex-showgirl who has advanced her act from burlesque houses to upper-class bedrooms (appropriately she now resides on Aster Drive). Marlowe sees early on that virtually all her mannerisms are calculated for effect ("Her eyes got large and dark"; "She crossed her legs, a little carelessly"; "She put the smile back on her face"). Vigilance notwithstanding, he is taken in by the performance and it almost gets him killed. Mildred Haviland, another lady trickster, nearly evades detection by slipping into a new role at every turn of the plot. "You do this character very well," Marlowe allows when finally he penetrates the masquerade.

Repeatedly, Marlowe must contend with deceiving women. As Lieutenant Nulty warns him in *Farewell, My Lovely*, "Dames lie about anything." Mrs. Murdock in *The High Window* is an affluent dowager who cheats at cards, fakes an asthma condition so she can drink "medicinal" wine, fabricates a suicide to camouflage a murder, and passes the guilt off onto someone else. Eileen Wade, the blond princess of *The Long Goodbye*, is a female wolf in sheep's clothing. Who would suppose such a golden-haired girl with an "exquisitely pure" smile and a "voice like the stuff they used to line summer clouds with" to be capable of three brutal killings? She makes fools of her antagonists. And Orfamay Quest, the pious "little sister" from the plains, shows her true nature when she gets to Los Angeles. She sheds her spectacles (Marlowe calls them "cheaters"), her scruples, and her virtue, revealing the cunning self-seeker beneath. Marlowe perforates the innocent cover immediately, remarking that "nobody ever looked less like Lady Macbeth."

Underscoring the theatrical metaphor, Marlowe often portrays himself as a beleaguered film critic forced to view a tedious production. A grey-flanneled gangster in *The High Window* is said to have "B-picture mannerisms" and a cheating wife in the same novel is "early Lillian Gish." Sometimes he casts himself as a director, wryly exhorting "better dialogue" in one exchange or demanding a "retake" in another. A veteran observer of roleplaying, Marlowe employs it frequently himself, bluffing a rival with hard-boiled badinage or pretended naivete, or playing the fly to a temptress's spider. To survive in the Hollywood world of cozeners, he must in a sense become one of them. A cynical Marlowe sums it up in *The Long Goodbye:* "Life was just one big vaudeville show."

II

That artifice is everywhere present in Los Angeles is suggested not only by Marlowe's insistent use of movie motifs, but also by his geographic imagery. The detective's dark odysseys through the city carry him into the empty core of a pasteboard culture where fakery prevails in both the man-made and the natural landscape.

Regional commentators have almost uniformly characterized the city and its environs as a hodgepodge of townlets spreading across the semi-desert flatland. The old joke that Los Angeles was "six suburbs in search of a city" proliferated into forty and even 666 in one account; Westbrook Pegler once called Los Angeles a "big, sprawling, incoherent, shapeless, slobbering civic idiot in the family of American Communities."[12]

Chandler's portrait of Los Angeles stresses the idea of a city of surfaces without a nucleus, what other writers would call "the nowhere city" or "never-never land." The resulting montage of images suggests an apparitional place where gilding tricks the eye into accepting veneer for substance. Flimsy buildings are embellished in neon to give the illusion of solidity. Hamburger joints masquerade as palaces.

A survey of the names of streets and buildings that make up Marlowe's terrain corroborates the notion of an artificial city. In *Farewell, My Lovely*, Lindsay Marriott is bludgeoned to death in a glen ironically named Purissima Canyon, beneath the Belvedere Club where hoodlums mingle with the wealthy. Marlowe visits a flophouse in the ghetto absurdly called the Hotel Sans Souci ("carefree"). Again in *The High Window*, incongruous names reveal cultural pretense. Mrs. Murdock, a hardened killer, lives on Dresden Street. The Florence apartments are in the seediest part of town. Grisly murders take place at bucolic Little Fawn Lake in *The Lady in the Lake* and at streets with heartland names like Idaho and Wyoming in *The Little Sister.* Apartment buildings in *The Big Sleep* with exotic titles like La Baba and Casa de Oro house dispossessed dreamers.

The penchant for fakery cuts across all social strata and covers all geographic areas of the city. Writing in the 1930s and 1940s, Chandler pays particular note to the Art Deco vogue of the era. Most art historians have viewed the style as an imaginative celebration of futurism, a paean to the energy, velocity, and technology that promised to blast America out of the woes of the depression. As such, it serves as a kind of architectural mirage, covering over the afflictions of an age. The streamlined facades, glistening surfaces, and plastic ornamentation of Art Deco emphasize the structural contrivance of the style. But the deception goes further. As Peter Conrad has insightfully argued, writing about Chandler's fiction, "the purpose of Art Deco was to wish a personality on items as disposable and meretricious as paper cups, by merchandizing decoration [and] . . . punishing innocuous utensils into patterns of Aztec or Egyptian bizarrerie," thus making of "the detritus of industrial civilization" a city of "junky luxury."[13]

The Treolar Building in *The Lady in the Lake* is such an amalgam of opulence and tackiness. With its glittering lobby and glowing walls, it is an edifice designed to promote illusion. Appropriately, the building's main tenant is a manufacturer of beauty aids whose offices resemble a pagan temple with luminous icons. An elaborate display case with "tiers and steps and islands and promontories of shining mirror-glass" highlights a bottle of cologne hyped as "the Champagne of Perfumes." Conrad's point about Art Deco objects "punished" and pressed into unnatural forms seems apropos here. Stylized distortion is the essence of the mode. Violet light outlines the tower of Bullock's department store in *The Big Sleep* as a nimbus illuminates a sacred relic.

Architecture is used by Chandler to epitomize the city's preoccupation with make-believe.[14] In Marlowe's world, structures are designed to stage and embody fantasies, and the effect is often grotesque. Mavis Weld, an actress on the rise in *The Little Sister*, lives in the Chateau Bercy, a garish building with no French features. The apartment is a conjurer's quarters with a mock marble foyer, an aquatic garden made to look like the sea floor, and a false fireplace, the scene of many contrived seductions.

The Cypress Club in *The Big Sleep* embodies the region's typical violation of any natural relationship between form and function. The club, run by debonaire mobster Eddie Mars, is housed in a Victorian mansion with scrolled porches and "a general air of nostalgic decay." Inside, the gentry drink, gamble, and carouse, but the illusion of refinement is studiously preserved amidst the dissipation. The betting takes place in a formal drawing room with crystal chandeliers and rose-damask tapestries.

The houses of the rich are even more compelling testimony to the pretentiousness of Southern California life. Built above and away from the riffraff, they are tawdry monuments to the arrogance of wealth. The Sternwood mansion is a case in point. Everything is built to an exaggerated scale: rooms are oversized and the doors "would have let in a troop of elephants." Despite their millions, the Sternwoods have neither discernment nor originality. The trappings of the estate are pure kitsch: trees are trimmed to look like poodle dogs and the garagemen wear jodhpurs. The decor is an imbroglio of borrowed styles (French doors, baroque fireplaces, Turkish rugs)—what Carey McWilliams has described as "the wild debauch of eclecticism."[15] The decorative centerpiece at the entrance to the house, a stained-glass panel depicting a medieval knight rescuing a captive maiden, is a composite symbol of the hypocrisy within. The code of chivalry it celebrates is based upon

the sentimental ideal of lovers locked forever in fleshless passion—hardly an appropriate emblem for the sexually permissive
Sternwoods.

The Grayle house in *Farewell, My Lovely* is another model
of bad taste. Designed to flaunt the affluence of its inhabitants, it
features an imitation sunken garden "built to look like a ruin"
with stone water lilies and crouching griffins. Door chimes peal
like church bells, and flying cupids adorn the gateway of this loveless household. Like the Sternwoods, the Grayles are deceivers
whose conspicuous fortress shields them from the real ruins they
have fostered.

If phoniness and schlock denote the corruption of the mon-
eyed, they are also evident among the climbers who emulate
wealth. Lindsay Marriott, a small-time swindler in *Farewell, My
Lovely*, transforms his dwelling into a tacky version of a high society salon with an unused concert grand piano, pink velvet furniture, and rococo adornments. Arthur Geiger, the procurer posing
as a bookseller in *The Big Sleep*, and Chris Lavery, the womanizing
beach boy in *The Lady in the Lake*, are similar types whose dwell-
ings exhibit the same showy extravagance. Geiger's living room is
a simulated opium den, complete with Chinoiserie and carved
gargoyles. Lavery favors an apricot Chinese rug and a tan mohair
davenport. Chandler uses the decorative images, especially Oriental accoutrements and gratuitous embellishments, to suggest vanity and decadence.

Each of the three is in some sense a sexual misfit whose
aberrations are reflected in the irregular configurations of his dwelling. Marriott's is perched precariously at the brink of a cliff, one
of several houses "hanging by their teeth and eyebrows to a spur
of mountain and looking as if a good sneeze would drop them
down." Geiger's is an unnatural protuberance extending from the
side of a ravine. The Lavery house is also constructed on a sharp
embankment and appears to fold over the edge and slither down,
flouting gravity and the building codes in the process. The entire
building is topsy-turvy, with bedrooms underneath the sitting
room and a scrambled floor plan. These contorted structures beto-
ken the debased lives within.

In a larger sense they reflect Southern California's ethos of
trickery. Marlowe spots numerous instances of trespass against

nature in the place that Carey McWilliams has called "the land of upside down."[16] Edifices are makeshift and flimsy, though built to look solid and stable. As the detective notes, "about the only part of a California house you can't put your foot through is the front door." Neighborhoods are irrationally segregated from each other by concrete interstices, and expensive ones like Beverly Hills and Chandler's Montemar Vista and Idle Valley are made inaccessible to those without cars or credentials—"Paradise Incorporated and also Highly Restricted." Landscaping means wrenching the plant life from another ecosystem and grafting it onto the Southern California soil. Jessie Florian's poinsettias are lifeless in a climate of perennial summer. Whoever built the Loring house in *The Long Goodbye* "was trying to drag the Atlantic Seaboard over the Rockies."

Mechanization supplants the organic. Marlowe tells time in his hotel room by waiting for the glow of a neon sign to spread across the room. Auto horns and police sirens cancel out natural sounds. Manufactured objects set the standards for natural phenomena: "The fog had cleared off outside and the stars were as bright as artificial stars of chromium on a sky of black velvet." Los Angeles is a city of contrivances and therein lies both its curse and its charm. Ironically, the very meretriciousness of the place calls forth the writer's greatest imaginative resources. As Chandler himself acknowledged, "To write about a city you have to love it or hate it or both."[17]

III

For Chandler, the city's theatricality, its flimsy foundations, and its plastic veneer expose the mendacity of Southern California life. Institutions, too, are beset with fraudulence in his world: law enforcement is untrustworthy; business has become a sanctuary for deceivers; the professions are riddled with chicanery. "In our town quacks breed like guinea pigs," Marlowe complains. The pages of Chandler's fiction teem with charlatans—painless dentists, palm readers, faith healers—a category the author sums up as "fakeloo artist[s] and hoopla spreader[s]."

The line of demarcation between truth and falsehood is blurred and eventually obliterated. Even cameras cheat. Chandler employs the motif of the dissembling photograph insistently to demonstrate the prevalence of imposture. In *The Big Sleep,* Marlowe believes that the pornographic pictures used to blackmail Carmen Sternwood show her to be the victim of greedy exploiters. In fact, they are illusory clues, camouflaging the central fact that Carmen is not the prey but the predator. In *The High Window,* a counterfeit coin and an equivocating photograph together form the central enigma. Marlowe identifies the bogus doubloon early on, but the photograph, itself concealed behind a decoy, is a more perplexing sleight of hand. He finally fathoms the truth—that the arms in the snapshot which seem to be reaching out to prevent a suicide are actually extended to push a murder victim out of a window—but the damage done from the long-standing lie is irrevocable. Again in *The Little Sister* a blackmail photograph precipitates the violent denouement but turns out to be a red herring.

Ultimately, double-dealing escalates into double-being. In a culture founded on the lure of new beginnings and miracle makeovers, impersonation becomes the norm. As Lewis H. Lapham has written of Los Angeles:

> The ease with which the happy few become suddenly rich lends credence to the belief in magical transformations. People tell each other fabulous tales of El Dorado. They talk about scrawny girls found in drugstores and changed overnight into princesses, about second-rate actors made into statesmen. . . . Everybody is always in the process of becoming somebody else.[18]

Chandler's characters are obsessed with personal metamorphosis. Identity in his novels is inconstant and inscrutable. Reliable criteria for establishing character (age, sex, background, personality) become so many mirages. Almost every novel turns on a gripping moment of revelation where one person is unmasked as another or where a character's second self appears from behind a veil.

Perhaps the most dramatic example is Helen Grayle. She begins as Velma Valento, a chorus girl who trades dime-a-dozen promises for expensive favors. Her name calls up images of torrid matinee romance, and she signs her promotional glossies "Always yours." Velma's apparent transformation from trollop to socialite is the central lie in a convolution of frauds. The remade woman has spent eight years expurgating her promiscuous past. She disavows the dance-hall crowd, bribes and brutalizes into silence those who knew her former self, and hires a gangster to enforce the secret. Now married to a local impresario who finances her conversion to respectability, she has taken instruction in self-improvement, altering her speech patterns, appearance, dress, and demeanor.

Though he remarks that "all the society ladies talk like tramps nowadays," Marlowe nearly fails to recognize the masquerader behind the "full set of curves"—but the reader shouldn't. Cultivation has not refined out Velma's taste for the vulgar: though her dress is simple, her fingernails are painted a "jarring" magenta. The genteel finish falls away quickly to reveal the dime-store enchantress. Her allurements are corny and contrived ("She worked her eyelashes and made butterfly kisses on my cheeks"), and her steamy sexuality reminds us that old habits die hard. Apparently the distance from the gutter to the house on the hill is not as great as one might suspect.

A true product of Los Angeles, a city of resplendent surfaces without a center, Helen is a phantom who fluctuates from self to self, evading identification. On one occasion she announces herself to Marlowe as "the Duchess of Windsor"; another time she leaves him "with the curious feeling of having talked to somebody that didn't exist." Indeed, there is no such person. "Helen" is a figment, inspired by a culture that glorifies illusion and turns the notion of the fresh start into dogma.

The malcontent who refashions herself into another person as a means of advancement is commonplace in Chandler's city of seekers. *The Little Sister* is virtually peopled with make-overs. Leila Quest lives out the local fable of the small-town girl who comes to Hollywood and is reincarnated as a movie queen. The same tale is represented by another pilgrim from Mid-America who recasts herself for the screen as a Mexican spitfire named Dolores Gonzales who likes her men "con cojones." Mildred Haviland in *The Lady in the Lake* escapes a criminal past by adopting a new persona, Muriel Chess, who becomes Crystal Kingsley, who mutates into Mrs. Fallbrook. Each character shift provokes a murder and another transmutation. Only in death is her identity fixed. Eleanor King, in *Playback,* can't decide whether to be Betty Cumberland, a wronged wife who has run away from a false accusation to a fresh start in California, or Betty Mayfield, a woman of the world who dallies with racketeers. She vacillates between the two, and her final designation is left uncertain at novel's end.

The mobster who doffs his underworld associations, joins the *beau monde*, and becomes a man about town appears in several of the novels and serves as a consistent reminder of the vacuous and ephemeral Southern California way of life. East Coast syndicate boss Weepy Moyer of *The Little Sister* transplants himself to Los Angeles and turns into a chic capitalist named Steelgrave who escorts starlets, runs a nightclub for the smart set, and moves up the hill to the affluent part of town. His pattern is repeated by Laird Brunette in *Farewell, My Lovely* and Mendy Menendez in *The Long Goodbye*, both gunmen gone respectable who mingle with the genteel until they are mistaken for one of them. Ultimately, there are no meaningful distinctions between gangsters and gentlemen.

The transpositions work both ways. For every criminal listed on the social register, there is a first family with a wayward daughter or a black-sheep husband. General Sternwood in *The Big Sleep* and Harlan Potter in *The Long Goodbye* are both moguls whose privileged offspring have gone bad—Carmen Sternwood poses for sex magazines and Sylvia Potter Lennox spurns her refined breeding for a life of debauchery. Leslie Murdock in *The High Window* extends the dictum of *noblesse oblige* to include *nostalgie de la boue*, hankering after the low life and marrying a showgirl.

All of these themes coalesce in the portrait of Terry Lennox in *The Long Goodbye*, who is driven by compulsion and a supportive culture to eradicate his past and to assume a succession of fictitious identities that become progressively more alien. Each guise is invented to rescue him from some casualty or menace, often of his own making. This parade of alter egos begins with Paul Marston, who had served as a British commando in World War II, remolds himself through plastic surgery into Terry Lennox to erase the vestiges of Nazi torture. Lennox now has a new name and face, and an empty slate. He moves to California, marries again, and so reinforces the pattern of sloughing his past and starting over as a different person.

As troubles accelerate, Lennox, who has found disguise a painless nostrum, alters himself again, forcing others to bear the consequences of each personal extinction. The tiers of duplicity multiply until the separate impersonations merge into one composite masquerade, and Marston/Lennox/Rodriguez/deCerva becomes Cisco Maioranos, a deliberate parody of all his former selves. In the final scene, Marlowe confronts the disguised Lennox with his treachery:

> "I'm not judging you. I never did. It's just that you're not here anymore. You're long gone. You've got nice clothes and perfume and you're as elegant as a fifty-dollar whore."
> "That's just an act," he said almost desperately. . . . "An act is all there is. There isn't anything else. In here—" he tapped his chest with the lighter— "there isn't anything." (p. 311)

This is the central fact about Chandler's city: pare away the layers of pretense and you find only more delusion. Marlowe calls Lennox a "moral defeatist" who prates on about honor and integrity while he betrays his only friend, but he stops short of reviling the man because he understands that Lennox is as much a product of a theatrical culture as he is a born cad.[19]

Perhaps, too, Marlowe refrains from full condemnation of his devious friend because he is himself a pretender. Who could not be and still survive in such a mendacious world? Detection has become the process of sifting through lies, of decoding finesse, of outwitting an adversary through artful circumvention. Marlowe readily allows that trickery is part of his craft. "The game I play is not spillikins. There's always a large element of bluff connected with it," he admits in *The Big Sleep* (p. 199). A man of many faces, he plays the tough guy or the pushover, the sharper or the dimwit as circumstances dictate. He invents aliases to broaden his range of action. So he conjures up Doghouse Reilly, the cynical sleuth who can ward off Carmen Sternwood's nymphet act with wisecracks.

These pretenses amount to more than mere contrivance. In fact Marlowe sometimes identifies so strongly with the objects of his search that he relives their plights.[20] Detection, of course, involves retracing others' steps, but Marlowe carries the affinity further. In *The Big Sleep*, he takes over for the missing Rusty Regan as confidant to General Sternwood and as target for Carmen's psychosexual pathology, almost to the point of reenacting Regan's death scene at the oil sump. In *Farewell, My Lovely* he becomes

Helen's dupe just as Moose Malloy and Lindsay Marriott have before him. His own actions ironically mimic those of his fellow victims, and he unwittingly appears at the scene of each man's demise, barely escaping slaughter himself. The similarity of the names Malloy, Marriott, and Marlowe underlines the linkage.

The double motif is strongest in *The Long Goodbye,* where Marlowe becomes a surrogate of Roger Wade and of Terry Lennox, both husbands of Eileen Wade and both finally destroyed by her blighted passion. In one especially telling scene, Eileen, who has slipped into a sick fantasy, involuntarily commandeers Marlowe to play Lennox's former role as her lover. In spite of his distaste for the psychotic melodrama at hand, Marlowe is drawn into the revery and for a moment actively becomes Terry Lennox. He cannot censure Lennox for impersonation since he becomes an imposter himself; there is no simple blame to disburse. In Marlowe's domain, falsehood underlies the cultural traditions, defines the environment, and infuses all human contact. Those who endure must adapt and exploit the mode in their own behalf—Marlowe as well as his adversaries.

IV

Chandler's Los Angeles is finally more than a portrait of a depraved regional society. The many falsehoods merge into a larger one and the city becomes a graphic symbol of The Big Lie—the cardinal deception of American civilization—that prosperity brings personal contentment and deliverance from the past. Chandler demonstrates with a relentless consistency that money and privilege are traps and that the past is inescapable.

Virtually every novel documents this vision and accentuates the point that life at the top is neither blissful nor free. Wealth does not buy contentment—it only brings more costly afflictions. This is the lesson that Marlowe learns from Helen Grayle in *Farewell, My Lovely,* who has bought a new life but must be cordoned off from the rest of the world in her solitary castle on a hill, fortified against the intrusion of the past. The Sternwoods, too, in *The Big Sleep* are cursed by their wealth—in fact, the family is racked with calamity, a cruel irony since its pedigree and capital are coveted by everyone, including those who murder their way into the inner circle. Mrs. Murdock, the hardened dowager in *The High*

Window, festers in her Pasadena mansion, living by proxy in indulging her hypochondria. Roger Wade, the writer in *The Long Goodbye*, loathes himself progressively more with each new bestseller; Terry Lennox marries a rich woman believing that all his troubles are over, but wealth only assures him a more extravagant decline.

All these cases—and others too numerous to cite—invalidate the facile myth of money. Broadly speaking, Chandler's stories are powerful counterfables that expose unremittingly the fraudulence at the heart of the culture. Images of artifice are heaped layer upon layer like a Babel of deceit, culminating in the supreme falsehood that equates fortune with bliss. But the foundation is insubstantial and the colossal mass topples. Indeed, Chandler's particular vision of the apocalypse is the avalanche of the dream dump.

There is a further and final point to be made, however. In Chandler's city of rampant illusion, truth has been so denatured that it has lost its power to redeem. When Marlowe burrows through the cant, he only finds another deception. When at last he clutches at a fact or lays bare a truth, the knowledge is too late and too feeble. Time and again he is forced to suppress or repudiate the information he has imperiled himself to uncover. Nominally on the side of truth, the detective becomes in effect an agent of deceit. He gives consent to the lies because in the end they are both pervasive and invincible.

Sometimes Marlowe rationalizes his concealment with the sophistry that lies can be told in the service of truth, as he does at the end of *The Big Sleep*. When he declines to inform Sternwood of the grisly deeds of his daughters, and again when he agrees to withhold the fact of Carmen's culpability for the murder of Rusty Regan, Marlowe is himself complicitous in the world's hypocrisy. As the detective admits when he reflects upon his silence, "Me, I was part of the nastiness now. Far more a part of it than Rusty Regan was" (p.216). His motives are mixed: he wishes to spare the old man the travail of recognition, and he knows that even if it surfaced, the truth would be an ineffectual force. But the first reason is misplaced compassion, since it was the father's permissiveness that precipitated his daughters' crimes. The second reason is more creditable. The Sternwoods' birthright and resources will buy them immunity from the law.

Moreover, as Peter Rabinowitz has persuasively argued about *The Big Sleep,* "the perpetrator of evil is not the cause of evil. . . . Evil is fundamentally tied to an overwhelming sickness in the society at large; the capture and punishment of deranged individuals has only a minimal effect."[21] Marlowe understands that the corruption inheres so deeply it cannot be healed by candor. When he gives in to the subterfuge, the taint upon him is visible. At the novel's opening, he is "clean, shaved, and sober," ready to champion honor and veracity. At the end, he is gulping double scotches, bemoaning the world's dishonesty, and half-yearning for death.

The pattern is reiterated in novel after novel. Marlowe struggles to separate reality from delusion, then is forced to discredit or suppress his own revelations. At the end of *Farewell, My Lovely,* Velma walks out the door a fugitive from a career "dark and full of blood." Marlowe knows there will be no remedy in law for Velma's crimes, and no palliative for the deeper social infirmity which produced them. She is an inveterate trickster and a killer. Still, he adjusts the grim truth at the end to a more palatable rendition, casting Velma as a deliberate martyr who dies to save her husband's dignity. Appropriately, the cop on the case rebukes Marlowe for his sentimental misconstruction.

In *The High Window,* the original transgression from which all others derive, Mrs. Murdock's murder of her first husband, remains undisclosed and unavenged. Marlowe knows she is responsible for a homicide, but he accuses her only of cheating at solitaire, preserving for her and for the world the myth that she is the victim rather than the wrongdoer. The detective laments his vain quest for "the justice we dream of but don't find," but the failure of justice here is partly of his own making. Similarly, though Marlowe's detection eventually lays bare the source of the contamination in both *The Little Sister* and *The Lady in the Lake,* his discoveries do not lead to a sanitizing resolution of the crimes in either case. Rather, the revelation of the truth provokes a pageant of bloodshed as the principals destroy each other while Marlowe stands powerless in the wings.

Even more vexing is the end of *The Long Goodbye,* where Marlowe sits impassively as a masked Terry Lennox disappears forever into a world of unreality, leaving a trail of carnage behind him. Marlowe allows his friend to exit through the looking glass and even endorses the bogus identity by saying "So long, Señor Maioranos." The last remembrance of Lennox is the sound of his footsteps receding "down the imitation marble corridor" as the fake man is swallowed up into the fake city.

In Los Angeles, where pretense holds dominion over all facets of experience, truth is no longer a viable means of cultural regeneration. Marlowe cannot wield the truth like an avenging saber—he is neither disposed to, because he is something of a pretender himself, nor able to, since the cutting edge of the weapon has been dulled. At best he can survive in a perverse world with unfixed foundations and hallucinatory surfaces, but it ought not to surprise us that to do so he must finally surrender to falsehood himself. Perhaps this is why Raymond Chandler eventually wrenched himself from Los Angeles and moved south, to escape the beguiling but corruptive illusions of Hollywood. He once wrote to explain his leavetaking: Here in Los Angeles, "I have a sense of exile from thought, a nostalgia of the quiet room and the balanced mind."[22] Whether Chandler found solace away from the city is another question, but we know that Marlowe is left there to founder among the lies.

Notes

1. Hamlin Garland coined the phrase, which is quoted in Carey McWilliams, *Southern California: An Island on the Land* (Santa Barbara, Calif. Peregine Smith, 1973), p. 5.

2. John Steinbeck, *The Grapes of Wrath* (1939; New York: Penguin Books, 1977), p.100.

3. Thompson's phrase is cited in John Gregory Dunne, "Eureka! A Celebration of California," *New West*, 1 January 1979, p.32.

4. Raymond Chandler, *The Big Sleep* (1939; New York: Random House, Vintage Books, 1976), p. 170. The first quotation from each of the seven novels will be cited in a note. Subsequent quotations will be cited parenthetically in the text.

5. Chandler, *Farewell, My Lovely* (1940; New York: Random House, Vintage Books, 1976), p. 125.

6. Chandler, *The High Window* (1942; New York: Random House, Vintage Books, 1976), p.103.

7. Chandler, *The Long Goodbye* (1954; New York: Ballantine Books, 1977), p. 117. The Earl character may have been inspired by Earle

Shoop in Nathanael West's *The Day of the Locust.* Shoop is another western movie extra whose only cowboy credentials are that he looks good in buckskin.

8. Chandler, *The Little Sister* (1949; New York: Ballantine Books, 1971), p. 175.

9. Joan Didion, "Some Dreamers of the Golden Dream," in *Slouching Toward Bethlehem* (New York: Delta, 1968), pp. 17, 4.

10. An especially thoughtful discussion of the Hollywood motifs in *The Little Sister* may be found in a doctoral dissertation by James Whitfield Thomson, "The Slumming Angel: The Voice and Vision of Raymond Chandler" (Ann Arbor, Mich.: University Microfilms International, 1977), pp. 191–212.

11. Chandler, *The Lady in the Lake* (1943; New York: Random House, Vintage Books, 1976), p. 168.

12. In a syndicated column, "Fair Enough," 22 November 1938, quoted in W. W. Robinson, ed., *What They Say About Los Angeles* (Pasadena, Calif.: Val Trefz Press, 1942), p. 59.

13. Peter Conrad, "The Private Dick as Dandy," *London Times Literary Supplement,* 20 January 1978, p. 60.

14. A survey of the titles of recently published books on Los Angeles architecture suggests that the perception of the city as a place of make-believe continues. See Charles Jencks, *Daydream Houses of Los Angeles* (New York: Rizzoli International Publications, 1978); Charles Lockwood, *Dream Palaces: Hollywood at Home* (New York: Viking Press, 1981); Brendan Gill and Derry Moore, *The Dream Come True: Great Houses of Los Angeles* (London: Thames and Hudson, 1980); John Halpern, *Los Angeles: Improbable City* (New York: E. P. Dutton & Co., 1979); Jim Heimann and Rip Georges, *California Crazy: Roadside Vernacular Architecture* (San Francisco: Chronicle Books, 1980).

15. McWilliams, p. 360.

16. Ibid., p. 104.

17. In an unpublished letter to William Campbell Gault, dated "Bastile Day, 1956," in the Chandler memorabilia of the Special Collections at the UCLA Research Library.

18. Lewis H. Lapham, "Lost Horizon: Intimations of Immortality in California,: *Harper's,* February 1979, p. 16.

19. Curiously, the casting for the 1973 film version of *The Long Goodbye,* directed by Robert Altman, underscores the make-over theme pervasive in Chandler. Terry Lennox was played by Jim Bouton, heretofore a baseball player; Eileen Wade by Nina Van Pallandt, previously known as the erstwhile companion of writer Clifford Irving who wrote the fabricated biography of Howard Hughes; the slimy Dr. Verringer was

played by Henry Gibson, a veteran of television's "Laugh-In" where he specialized as a homespun poet; Roger Wade was played by Sterling Hayden, an actor turned novelist.

20.   An excellent discussion of Marlowe as double, with a focus different from mine, may be found in Chapter 5 of Stephen Knight's *Form and Ideology in Crime Fiction* (Bloomington: Indiana University Press, 1980), pp. 135–67.

21.   Peter Rabinowitz, "Rats Behind the Wainscoting: Politics, Convention, and Chandler's *The Big Sleep,*" *Texas Studies in Literature and Language* 22 (Summer 1980): 240.

22.   "Farewell, My Hollywood," *Antaeus* 21–22 (1976): 33.

Bibliographic Note

The fiction of Raymond Chandler has received ample attention; his work has been critically examined almost from the beginning of his publishing career. Most of the literary analysis has concentrated on Chandler's particular version of the hard-boiled tradition, with emphasis on the character, methodology, and moral vision of detective Philip Marlowe. Another prevalent concern has been the relationship between author Chandler and character Marlowe. My study for this collection focuses primarily on the writer's portrait of Los Angeles. While relatively few critical treatments of Chandlers's work take precisely this approach, a number are especially useful for characterizing aspects of Chandler's city and for offering penetrating insights into the criminal domain in which Marlowe operates.

Several basic sources are indispensable: Frank MacShane's 1976 biography, *The Life of Raymond Chandler* (New York: E. P. Dutton & Co.) provides a richly detailed tableau of Chandler in his Southern California milieu. A collection of essays, *The World of Raymond Chandler*, edited by Miriam Gross (New York: A & W Publishers, 1977) tilts primarily toward biographical reminiscences, but contains several essays that address questions of place. These include pieces by Eric Homberger, Julian Symonds, Russell Davies, Philip French, and T. J. Binyon. The essay by Michael Mason, "Marlowe, Men and Women," looks peripherally at the city, but offers an incisive analysis of Marlowe and the aberrant sexuality of his world. Jerry Speir's recent monograph, *Raymond Chandler* (New York: Frederick Ungar Publishing Co., 1981), a basic introduction to the writer, is intelligent and observant. Discussions of individual novels are very useful and furnish a composite image of Chandler's fictional territory. I found Speir's discussion of *Playback*, a novel almost always dismissed by critics as the product of a writer in decline, to be most discerning.

James T. Whitfield's unpublished dissertation, "The Slumming Angel: The Voice and Vision of Raymond Chandler" (Ann Arbor: University Microfilms International, 1977) is thorough and informative. The treatment of Hollywood in the chapter on *The Little Sister* is especially effective. Walter Wells's book about literary portrayals of Hollywood, *Tycoons and Locusts* (Carbondale: Southern Illinois University Press, 1973) is obligatory reading for any study in literary regionalism, particularly the chapter on Chandler, "Grey Knight in the Great Wrong Place," which treats *Farewell, My Lovely*. Gavin Lambert's *The Dangerous Edge* (London: Barrie & Jenkins, 1975) also explores the relationship between setting and art and contains a useful chapter on Chandler.

There are far too many critical articles on Chandler to mention, but several address to some extent the question of Chandler's vision of Los Angeles. David Smith, in "The Public Eye of Raymond Chandler," *Journal of American Studies* 14 (1980):423 41, presents an astute discussion of the criminal culture of Marlowe's Southern California. Thomas S. Reck's invaluable piece, "Raymond Chandler's Los Angeles,: *The Nation*, 20 December 1975, pp. 661 63, examines Chandler's use of landscape, architecture, and local ambience. Two articles consider the symbolic uses of California in the works of Chandler and other hard-boiled writers. One is Joseph C. Porter's fine essay, "The End of the Trail: The American West of Dashiell Hammett and Raymond Chandler," *Western Historical Quarterly* (October, 1975):411–24. The other is my own, "California Babylon: The World of American Detective Fiction," *Clues: A Journal of Detection* 1 (1980):77–89. A number of "Raymond Chandler Tours of Los Angeles," based on Ruth Windfeldt's Scene of the Crime Bookstore tour, have been published. The most substantial is Maurice Zolotow's "The Big Schlep," *Los Angeles*, September 1978, pp. 168 ff. Though amply detailed, the piece is riddled with errors (fictional buildings are placed in the wrong novels and addresses are incorrectly transcribed from the texts; Chief of Police John Wax in *Farewell, My Lovely* is misnamed "Henry Wax" after a local politician).

Several essays on various aspects of Chandler's fiction deserve special note. Peter Conrad's flamboyant review of the MacShane biography and Chandler's *Notebooks*, "The Private Dick as Dandy," *TLS*, 20 January 1978, p. 60, offers thoughtful observations about the relationship between Marlowe's language and his world. R. W. Lid, in "Philip Marlow Speaking" *Kenyon Review* 31 (1969): 153–78; E. M. Beekman, in "Raymond Chandler & An American Genre," *Massachusetts Review* 14 (1973): 149–73; George P. Elliott, in "Country Full of Blondes," *The Nation*, 20 April 1963, pp. 354 ff.; Paul Jensen in "Raymond Chandler: The World You Live in," *Film Comment* (November 1974):18–26; Howard Kaye,

"Raymond Chandler's Sentimental Novel," *Western America Literature*, 10 (1975):135–45; and James Monaco, "Notes on 'The Big Sleep'/Thirty Years After," *Sight and Sound* 5 (Winter 1966): 34–38, all bring acuity and a rich sensibility to their portraits of Chandler territory.

Three recent pieces offer sophisticated textual analysis and advance provocative and persuasive theses: Peter J. Rabinowitz, in "Rats Behind the Wainscoting: Politics, Convention, and Chandler's *The Big Sleep*," *Texas Studies in Literature and Language* 22 (Summer 1980):222–44, offers an original and probing discussion of Marlowe's sense of defeat at the end of *The Big Sleep*. Stephen Knight's "'A Hard-boiled Gentlemen': Raymond Chandler's Hero," a chapter in *Form and Ideology in Crime Fiction* (Bloomington: Indiana University Press, 1980) is a fascinating treatment of Marlowe as sympathetic surrogate of the male victims of female duplicity in several of the novels. Jonathan Holden takes a more traditional approach but with a wealth of detail in "The Case for Raymond Chandler's Fiction as Romance," *Kansas Quarterly* 10 (1979): 41–47.

Finally, useful sources also include a battery of works—essays, monographs, anthologies, and oddities about Los Angeles and California, and a number of studies of Southern California architecture and urban layout, too extensive to enumerate.

SIX

The Ultimate Seacoast: Ross Macdonald's California

Jerry Speir

In the novels of Ross Macdonald, Southern California is the embodiment of the American dream defiled. Lew Archer lies floating in the Pacific one afternoon in *The Drowning Pool* (1950), contemplating the California landscape, and observes:

> They had jerrybuilt the beaches from San Diego to the Golden Gate, bulldozed superhighways through the mountains, cut down a thousand years of redwood growth, and built an urban wilderness in the desert. They couldn't touch the ocean. They poured their sewage into it, but it couldn't be tainted.
> There was nothing wrong with Southern California that a rise in the ocean level wouldn't cure.

The comment is emblematic of Macdonald's thematic vision. In its headlong, rapacious rush west, modern civilization has reached a final barrier in California. Naively and egoistically, it has created not "a shining city on a hill" but, in the words of *Meet Me at the Morgue* (1953), a "Bohemia on its last legs, driven back to the ultimate seacoast."

To comprehend the overall structure toward which such statements point requires some understanding of the author's background and education and of the literary and political concerns that grew out of them. Ross Macdonald (pseudonym of Kenneth Millar) was born near San Francisco in 1915 but was moved as a small child to Canada, where, after his parent's separation, he was shunted from relative to relative until his late adolescence. This experience instilled in him a "feeling of exile, which my mother had cultivated by teaching me from early childhood that California was my birthplace and natural home."[1] This bicultural background provided him, he has said, with "the fresh suspicious eye of a semi-outsider who is fascinated but not completely taken in by the customs of the natives."[2] And that "suspicious eye" is, no doubt, responsible for Archer's distanced, objective tone.

During his Canadian youth, Macdonald was also forced by the economic necessities of the depression into work as a farm laborer, and he recalled from that experience the "moral pain inflicted . . . by the doctrine . . . that poverty is always deserved."[3] His resulting concern for all those who fall at the lower extreme of the socioeconomic scale is apparent throughout the novels. In the course of his education, which culminated in graduate school at the University of Michigan, he became fascinated by modern psychology and, ultimately, completed a dissertation on S. T. Coleridge and his psychological criticism. Of Sigmund Freud, another major influence from this period, he has claimed that he "made myth into psychiatry, and I've been trying to turn it back into myth again in my own small way."[4]

All these experiences influenced Macdonald's fiction generally and his use of the California landscape specifically. California is the Promised Land, both for Macdonald personally (the "home" from which he was "exiled" as a child) and within the American myth he is constructing (the logical extension of the doctrine of "manifest destiny"). It functions both literally and figuratively as the end of the West, the end of five centuries of European movement westward, where man is finally halted, where he can no longer avoid the implications of his economic and social systems by simply moving on, and where the injustices of those systems manifest themselves at every turn.

One of the most apparent of these manifestations is the obvious social stratification of Southern California, a stratification that isolates the wealthy in regal, absurd splendor and that is reinforced by the landscape itself and by its inhabitants' appropriation of that landscape. *The Moving Target* (1949), for example, the first Archer novel and the first of Macdonald's works in which California is essential to the plot, opens with the detective reflecting on the differences between the classes that populate the high ground of Cabrillo Canyon and those relegated to the "mile of slums . . . at the bottom of the town near the sea." The former is a landscape of "lawns effervescent with sprinklers, deep white porches, roofs of red tile and green copper" while the latter is a vision of "collapsing shacks and storefront tabernacles, dirt paths where sidewalks should have been, black and brown children playing in the dust." Such pointed social comment is often a part of Macdonald's work—but always behind it are "the mountains . . . making them all look silly."

There is, in fact, throughout the novels a developing tension between nature and man, between the eternal landscape and its temporal inhabitants. In *The Zebra-Striped Hearse* (1962), for instance, Archer describes "a small isolated settlement north of Malibu. Far down below the highway under the slanting brown bluffs, twelve or fifteen houses huddled together as if for protection against the sea. It was calm enough this morning, at low tide, but the overcast made it grey and menacing." The menace is also apparent in *The Chill* (1964), where Archer tells us that he "could hear the surf roaring up under the cottages and sucking at their pilings." Later in the same novel, the fog threatens to turn Pacific Point "into a kind of suburb of the sea."

And it is not only the sea and fog that threaten. The sun frequently seems on the verge of setting the whole world ablaze. In *The Instant Enemy* the hot wind from the desert hisses of mysterious, unseen forces, and the very light can shine with "a cruel clarity." By the late novels, this implicit tension erupts into explicit conflict.

The Underground Man (1971), in fact, chronicles an explosion of natural forces in direct, explicit response to the moral outrage fostered by humans. In this book, one man, Stanley Broad-hurst, is seeking "the truth" about his father, but for the very self-ish purpose of fixing blame while denying personal responsibility for the declining spiral of his own life. While digging in the spot where he suspects his father is buried, Stanley is himself killed. He ends up buried in a hole he dug himself at the very site where his father was murdered and buried years earlier following his own protracted moral obtuseness. Almost magically, mystically, a fire erupts at the exact spot, and by the time Archer arrives, it has taken on mythical proportions.

Approaching the scene, he tells us:

> Before we reached Santa Teresa I could smell smoke. Then I could see it dragging like a veil across the face of the mountain behind the city.
> Under and through the smoke I caught glimpses of fire like the flashes of heavy guns too far away to be heard. The illusion of war was completed by an old two-engine bomber which flew in low over the mountain's shoulder. The plane was lost in the smoke for a long instant, then climbed out trailing a pastel red cloud of fire retardant.[5]

This war imagery is sustained throughout the novel. The fire is said to resemble the flashes of artillery and at night it glows in the hills around the city "like the bivouacs of a besieging army." And the athletic field which serves as headquarters for the firefighting equipment "resembled a staging area just back of the lines in a major battle."

The Underground Man marks a major advance in this theme of tension between Man and Nature that has been evident at least since the "urban wilderness in the desert" speech of *The Drowning Pool*. The new effect of this concern is to underscore the alien-ation that Macdonald perceives as the essential flaw in the brave new world of California. In all fairness to California, though, it should be pointed out that Macdonald found similar alienation in Detroit in his first novel, *The Dark Tunnel* (1944), and invariably finds it in Reno or Mexico or Bridgeton, Illinois, or wherever else Archer's various travels take him. The novelist's critique is of the modern world, generally; California is simply the most obvious microcosm of that world and the specific subject of that critique.

Consistently in the novels, modern evil is a product of the egoism with which characters approach their fellow humans and the world. It is an avaricious and aggrandizing egoism that treats Nature as raw material for human exploitation and that is countered in the later novels by an almost personified reaction on the part of Nature.

Sleeping Beauty (1973) carries the theme a step further and finds corporate, as well as personal, greed at the root of the society's ills. Archer's first glimpse of the oil spill that serves as the thematic focus of this novel comes as he is flying back into Los Angeles from Mazatlán: "It lay on the blue water off Pacific Point in a freeform slick that seemed miles wide and many miles long. An offshore oil platform stood up out of its windward end like the metal handle of a dagger that had stabbed the world and made it spill black blood." The accident happened, we are told by a young fisherman, because the drillers failed to acknowledge the fragility of the natural order—because "there's something the matter with the structures down there. They're all broken up. It's like trying to make a clean hole in a piece of cake and hold water in it. They should never have tried to drill out there." We can see here that the optimism of *The Drowning Pool*—"they couldn't touch the ocean. . . . it couldn't be tainted"—has been dramatically modified. Even the ocean is now endangered by the greed and thoughtless exploitation of humans.

The oil spill in *Sleeping Beauty* establishes an apocalyptic vision that is sustained throughout the novel. Along the public beach, "a few people, mostly women and girls, were standing at the edge of the water, facing out to sea. They looked as if they were watching for the end of the world, or as if the end had come and they would never move again." The surfers, the next generation, "looked as if they had given up on civilization and were ready for anything or nothing." Since one of Macdonald's central thematic concerns is with the effect of his plots on the society's youth, these are significant statements of the pessimistic side of the author's vision.

Archer is similarly capable of such pessimism. When he has a moment in *Sleeping Beauty* to sit and relax in a chair, to "let my mind go loose," he tells us: "Black waves washed over it [his mind], carrying me in to a black shore. I sat up with a start." Such interiorized landscapes are not uncommon in Macdonald. In fact, they are a primary vehicle for expressing the personal alienation at the root of the larger alienation of the society. Frequently, the mind's interiors are reflected in the interiors in which characters choose to confine themselves—like Sampson's red bedroom with a ceiling mirror in *The Moving Target* that looked "like the inside of a sick brain, with no eyes to see out of, nothing to look at but the upside-down reflection of itself." But they can also take on their own landscape quality and perform much the same thematic function as the author's use of landscape *per se*. Of Alicia Hallman's "doomsters," for example, Archer says, "If they didn't exist in the actual world, they rose from the depths of every man's inner sea, gentle as night dreams, with the backbreaking force of tidal waves."

The sea, particularly, is an important feature of Macdonald's landscape, functioning both externally—as a part of the whole of Nature against which the human race appears in endless conflict—and internally—as an image of all the amorphous forces repressed, sublimated, and striving for attention. In the external world, the sea may provide "a continual sound of grief running under the morning";[6] it may be "coughing in its sleep";[7] or its nighttime whitecaps may rise up "like ghosts . . . quickly swept backward into darkness."[8] In describing characters, Macdonald often uses sea imagery to probe beneath the psychological surface. Archer may say, for example, "I looked for irony in her eyes, which were green and cool as the sea, and saw it flickering deep down near the sea floor";[9] or he may speak of "the shifting play of hidden currents"[10] in the eyes of another; or say of yet another, "Our eyes met. Hers were dark ocean blue. Discontent flicked a fin in their depths."[11]

The personification of the external and naturalization of the internal invites us as readers to see the subjective projected onto the objective and the objective collapsed within the subjective, with the ultimate effect of insinuating a profound sympathy between the two. When we then read of "the surf thundering in like doom"[12] or of the sea "surging among the pilings like the blithe mindless forces of dissolution,"[13] we are led to perceive a psychological as well as a sociological fragility within the human enterprise—and a fragility that is sympathetically objectified in the "real" world. *The Underground Man* and *Sleeping Beauty* expound the theme on the grandest scale. Such deft conflation of the psychic and natural worlds is a trademark of Macdonald's work and one that is essential to his concern for a society up against limits which are both physical and psychological.

In many specifics, the author's vision is indeed pessimistic, particularly in his depiction of the man-made additions to the Southern California landscape. Los Angeles is described succinctly in *The Moving Target* as a "white smudge . . . [of] rubbish lots and fields and half-built suburbs." The beach cities appear in *The Barbarous Coast* as having been "washed up on shore." And Hollywood, we are told in the same novel, "started as a meaningless dream, invented for money. But its colors ran, out through the holes in people's heads, spread across the landscape and solidified . . . . Now we were stuck with the dream without a meaning. It had become the nightmare that we lived in."[14] Persistently, the images are of the insubstantial, the decaying, and the tasteless.

The novels exhibit a particular bias against California architecture. In *The Way Some People Die* (1951), Archer avoids the front entrance of the local morgue/mortuary with its "white pseudo-Colonial columns lit by a pink neon sign" and enters through the back. In the same novel, Dr. Benning's house stands "flimsily against the dark red sky like a stage set propped by scantlings from behind," and Archer drives up into the terraced hills of the wealthy, describing them as a "manmade purgatory . . . of glass-and-aluminum living-machines. . . . It was the earthly paradise where money begot plants upon property. People were irrelevant." And back in Santa Monica, Archer reflects sadly on the demise of formerly proud houses broken up into apartments and tourist rooms. "Even the palms that lined the street," he says, "looked as if they had seen their best days and were starting to lose their hair." Again, there is an almost mysterious sympathy between the natural and the manmade.

The small coastal and valley towns to which Archer's cases invariably lead him are no less afflicted by the modern blight than is the great formless maze of Los Angeles. Frequently their problem is that they have been transformed by riches. After a lengthy description of haphazard sprawl in *The Drowning Pool*, Archer comments simply, "A quiet town in a sunny valley had hit the jackpot hard, and didn't know what to do with itself at all." But, he adds, "More had changed than the face of the buildings, or the number and make of the cars. The people were different and there were too many of them." Always the real problem is in people. And, always, a primary concern is for the youth and for their ability (or inability) to cope and continue in the modern world created by the follies and foibles of their elders. In his bleaker passages, Macdonald gives us characters like those on the beach near the beginning of *Sleeping Beauty* who seem to be "waiting for the end of the world" or the young surfers "waiting on the water for a final big one" who seem to have "given up on civilization."

But as powerful as all these images of apocalypse and dissolution are, they are not Ross Macdonald's final statements on the human condition. Indeed, Macdonald is, with rare exception, a novelist of hope. "Only an optimist," he has argued, "could go through the mental pain of writing such pessimistic books."[15] Frequently, nature and the California landscape support a kind of redemption.

It is important to recall that Macdonald viewed California as a microcosm of a world in transition, as the raw material from which "it was possible for the new world to create itself" and said, explicitly, "That's what I'm writing about." He described his detective, Archer, as "modern man in a technological society, who is, in effect, homeless, virtually friendless, and who tries to behave as if there is some hope in society, which there is."[16] He finds that hope in the people and the relationships among them—despite the egocentricity that is the fatal flaw in many of his characters, and he reinforces that hope with paeans to the idyllic beauty of California—despite the exploitation to which the land has been subjected by avaricious generations.

Against all the doom-saying pessimism of the foregoing must be counterpoised such passages as the opening of *Meet Me at the Morgue:* "It was a bright and blowing day. The wind was fresh from the sea, and the piled white cubes of the city sparkled under a swept blue sky. I had to force myself to go to work." And in *The Ivory Grin* (1952), Archer describes the landscape, as he often does, from his car:

> Below me the road meandered among brown September
> hills spattered with the inkblot shadows of oaks.
> Between these hills and the further mountains the valley
> floor was covered with orchards like vivid green chenille,

brown corduroy ploughed fields, the thrifty patchwork of truck gardens. Bella City stood among them, a sprawling dusty town miniatured and tidied by clear space.

Though the town may be "sprawling" and "dusty," such flaws are tempered by the beauty of its setting and, certainly in comparison to such settings as Quinto and Nopal Valley of *The Drowning Pool*, it is a place of considerable appeal. Even so, on closer inspection, we find the same ugly buildings and the same social stratification that hinted at the underlying flaws of other towns. Macdonald seldom allows us optimism without qualification.

Significantly, though, his most optimistic passages come at the end of several of the novels. At the end of *The Underground Man*, for example, after the moral outrage of the human plot and the physical threat of the great fire, families are restored and a steady rain quenches the fire and promises a new beginning. *The Blue Hammer* (1976), his last novel, likewise ends with a restoration of family and the promise of a healthier future. *The Galton Case* (1959) concludes with a similar reunion and the singing of birds, which Macdonald said are "there as reminders of a world which encloses and outlasts the merely human."[17] Nature is capable of redemption as well as dissolution; but even Archer frequently finds it difficult to be optimistic. Always there is the perversity of the "merely human" to bring one up short. In *The Instant Enemy*, for example, Archer is being driven through an area "remote and untouched as back-country," and is commenting on the splendid simplicity of its birds, fields, foliage, and lake when, suddenly, "My escort drew his revolver and, without stopping his jeep, shot the nearest mud hen. I think he was showing off to me. All the ducks flew up, and all the mud hens but one ran like hell into the water, like little animated cartoons of terrified people." The lunacy of just one alienated individual is sufficient to threaten the idyllic with terror and destruction.

Macdonald, of course, was well-schooled in the American literary tradition and was very conscious of his own place in that tradition. Historically, the American literary "hero" has been a figure of colossal innocence adrift in a new world, "an individual emancipated from history," as R. W. B. Lewis has argued in *The American Adam*, "happily bereft of ancestry, untouched and undefiled by the usual inheritances of family and race; an individual standing alone, self-reliant and self-propelling, ready to confront whatever awaited him with the aid of his own unique and inherent resources."[18] In California, Ross Macdonald found a metaphor for extending that notion to its logical and often catastrophic end. With no values beyond "sex and money: the forked root of evil," he tells us in *The Drowning Pool*, our wildly individualistic society is doomed to self-destruction—to the total alienation of its children and the crass consumption of its natural resources and native beauty.[19] He has created a mythical world at the very limit of Man's westward advance that holds out the possibility of redemption even while demonstrating our overpowering drive toward dissolution and destruction. Macdonald shows us our civilization trapped between the soaring mountains and shimmering ocean of California and turned back upon itself for the realization of its dreams. His most pessimistic characters are all-consuming and self-destructive; his most optimistic achieve insight—at a great price—and face their world with a new humility, a new humanity.

His purpose in writing, he said, was to "heal the schizophrenic pain"[20]—both on the personal level of his own divided life and on the communal level of our alienated society torn between the poles of ego and compassion. Throughout his body of work, Southern California, that "instant megalopolis superimposed on . . . raw nature, . . . the twentieth century right up against the primitive,"[21] serves as the central image of the contemporary human condition. Though there is danger and fragility, wickedness and evil, here in this land of cantilevered houses and illusion, there is also hope, and Macdonald's fiction at its best points us toward the brighter possibilities of paradise.

Notes

1. Ross Macdonald, "Writing *The Galton Case*," in *On Crime Writing* (Santa Barbara, Calif.: Capra Press, 1973), p. 33.

2. Macdonald, "Foreword to *Archer in Hollywood* (New York: Alfred A. Knopf, 1967), p. viii.

3. "Writing *The Galton Case*," pp. 32–33.

4. Quoted by Raymond A. Sokolov in "The Art of Murder," *Newsweek*, 22 March 1971, p. 108.

5. Macdonald, *The Underground Man* (1971; New York: Bantam Books, 1972), p. 26.

6. Macdonald, *The Ferguson Affair* (1960; New York: Bantam Books 1971), p. 63.

7. Macdonald, *The Blue Hammer* (New York: Alfred A. Knopf, 1976), p. 174.

8. Macdonald, *Black Money* (New York: Alfred A Knopf, 1966), p. 82.

9. Macdonald, *The Dark Tunnel* (1944; New York: Bantam Books, 1972), p. 20.

10. Macdonald, *Blue City* (1947; New York: Bantam Books 1974), p. 34.

11. Macdonald, *The Galton Case* (1959; New York: Bantam Books, 1960) p. 19.

12. *The Ferguson Affair*, p. 213.

13. Macdonald, *The Chill* (1964; New York: Bantam Books, 1965), p. 39.

14. Macdonald, *The Barbarous Coast* (1956; New York: Bantam Books, 1957), p. 79.

15. Quoted by Jon Carroll in "Ross Macdonald in Raw California," *Esquire*, June 1972, p. 188.

16. Quoted in Sokolov, p. 108.

17. "Writing *The Galton Case*," p. 29.

18. R. W. B. Lewis, *The American Adam: Innocence, Tragedy and Tradition in the Nineteenth Century* (Chicago: University of Chicago Press, 1955), p. 5.

19. Macdonald, *The Drowning Pool* (1950; New York: Bantam Books, 1970), p. 8.

20. Macdonald, "Foreword" to *Archer in Jeopardy* (New York: Alfred A. Knopf, 1979), p. vi.

21. Carroll, p. 149.

Bibliographic Note

Aside from the novels themselves, the best material on Macdonald's ideas and intentions appears in the articles based on interviews with the author: Jon Carroll's "Ross Macdonald in Raw California," *Esquire*, June 1972, pp. 148–49ff.; Sam Grogg, Jr.'s "Ross Macdonald: At the Edge," *Journal of Popular Culture*[7] (Summer 1973); John Leonard's "Ross Macdonald: His Lew Archer and Other Secret Selves," *New York Times Book Review*, 1 June 1967; and Raymond A. Sokolov's "The Art of Murder," *Newsweek*, 22 March 1971, pp. 101–108.

The author also provides much useful information in his essays in *On Crime Writing* (Santa Barbara, Calif.:Capra Press, 1973) and in "The Writer's Sense of Place," *South Dakota Review* 40 (August 1975). And he drops a few clues in his forewords to the omnibus reprints *Archer in Hollywood* (New York: Alfred A. Knopf, 1967), *Archer at Large* (New York: Alfred A. Knopf, 1970), and *Archer in Jeopardy* (New York: Alfred A. Knopf, 1979). Many of these essays, and a few others, are collected in Macdonald's *Self-Portrait: Ceaselessly into the Past* (Santa Barbara: Capra Press, 1981), edited by Ralph B. Sipper.

Of the secondary sources Judith Holtan and I. Orley's "The Time-Space Dimension in the Lew Archer Detective Novels," *North Dakota Quarterly* (Autumn 1972) provides some interesting facts and speculation on California's importance to the novels. My own *Ross Macdonald* (New York: Frederick Ungar Publishing Co., 1978) attempts an overall survey and assessment of the writer's canon, as does Peter Wolfe's *"Dreamers Who Live Their Dreams: The World of Ross Macdonald's Novels* (Bowling Green, Ohio: Bowling Green University Popular Press, 1976). Matthew Bruccoli's *Ross Macdonald* (New York and San Diego: Harcourt Brace Jovanovich) was published as this book went to press.

PART THREE

Perspectives

SEVEN

Fantasy Seen: Hollywood Fiction Since West[1]

Mark Royden Winchell

For millions of Americans, Hollywood is a far-off enchanted city where a lucky few can rise not only from rags to riches, but from osbcurity to fame. The movies gave Tom Wingfield a rich vicarious dream life in Tennessee Williams' *The Glass Menagerie*. For Binx Bolling in Walker Percy's *The Moviegoer*, they provided a means of "certifying" the mundane reality of his life. In a sense, the image of the movie capital is the mythic culmination of the American Dream. As Norman Mailer writes: "When the West was filled, the expansion turned inward, became part of an agitated, overexcited, superheated dream life. The film studios threw up their searchlights as the frontier was finally sealed, and the romantic possibilities of the old conquest of land turned into a vertical myth, trapped within the skull."[2]

Just as every thesis produces its antitheses, so too does every myth generate an antimyth.[3] Simply because of its location in

147

Southern California, Hollywood—like the rest of Los Angeles—has been viewed as the end of the yellow brick road. This is the region where the pioneer spirit runs up against the unbreachable boundary of the Pacific Ocean. In Joan Didion's words, Californians realize that "things had better work here, because here, beneath that immense bleached sky, is where we run out of continent."[4] And yet, for far too many people, the dream of an earthly paradise has not come true. For them, Jonas Spatz writes, "The westward movement, once symbolic of rebirth out of Old World privilege, oppression, and poverty, becomes a journey into despair. The American is betrayed not by the brutalities of the city but by the image of his own salvation."[5]

Of course, Hollywood is not just another part of California, but the dream factory itself. As such, it is a place where both the hope of success and the potential for disillusionment are greater than elsewhere. For this reason, those who denigrate Hollywood depict it as a cruel scam, a town where beneath the false tinsel one finds only real tinsel.[6] Among those who succumbed to the siren allure of Hollywood during that national era of disillusionment known as the Great Depression were some of the finest writers of the twentieth century. These men came west to supply the additional dialogue that was required by the introduction of sound in motion pictures. Originally drawn to Hollywood by the promise of easy money and some time in the sun, they stayed long enough to feel artistically traduced and to vent their spleen in nihilistic novels which have made the Hollywood antimyth a permanent part of our national folklore.

The purveyors of the antimyth have succeeded so well that when we think of the Hollywood novel, we think of a narrative in which the film capital is revealed as the old Gomorrah in the guise of a new Eden. However, when we begin to examine individual novels that are set in Hollywood, we find that there is no monolithic genre, no single party line. Indeed, if Hollywood is in many ways an exaggerated metonymy of America, then there are as many possible responses to that metonymy as there are versions of the American experience itself. What Hollywood fiction gives us is not so much a definitive picture as a suggestive mosaic. This essay will focus on five fragments of that mosaic: F. Scott Fitzgerald's *The Last Tycoon* (1941), Budd Schulberg's *What Makes Sammy*

Run? (1941) and *The Disenchanted* (1950), Norman Mailer's *The Deer Park* (1955), and Joan Didion's *Play It as It Lays* (1970).

There is probably no more pathetic image in recent literary mythology than that of F. Scott Fitzgerald in Hollywood. To think of the author of *The Great Gatsby* "dying at Malibu, attended only by Sheilah Graham, while he ground out college-weekend movies,'"[7] is enough to confirm forever one's notion of Hollywood the Destroyer, epitome of everything that is meretricious in American life. For devotees of the antimyth, "Fitzgerald in Hollywood" is what "The Rape of Belgium" was for opponents of the Kaiser—a vivid if somewhat contrived rationale for taking arms against the forces of darkness. It is not my purpose here to authenticate or debunk the popular conception of Fitzgerald's final years (revisionists like Tom Dardis and the indefatigable Matthew J. Bruccoli already have gone a long way toward setting the record straight); however, no assessment of Hollywood as mythic locale can fail to deal with Fitzgerald's problematic relationship with that locale. It is significant that in his unfinished novel, *The Last Tycoon*, Fitzgerald left a final, fragmentary statement about his attitude toward Hollywood—one that is at sharp variance with the statement that others have made from the sad events of its author's own time in the sun.

Judging from *The Last Tycoon*, we might well conclude that Fitzgerald believed much of the original Hollywood myth to be true; that for him the place was not a fraud exposed, but a once great society in decline. Indeed, in Virgil Lokke's opinion, Fitzgerald's view was as follows:

> Hollywood at its best stands for an earlier period in our national development. It represents an island of the past in the present—an isolated province which provides the opportunity for the late survival of a once more numerous and now outmoded breed of men who have been largely supplanted by uncultured, irreverent, prosaic and impersonal creatures whose society leaves little room for the play of individual power of character.[8]

Hollywood, thus conceived, is not entirely dissimilar from the American South as it is depicted in the works of the great writers of the Southern Renaissance. Indeed, in his discussion of *The Last Tycoon*, Robert Roulston sees Fitzgerald's life-long fascination with the South reflected in his fictional treatment of Hollywood. Speaking of Southern California, Roulston writes: "Although hardly an ancient society, it comes to seem a place that has seen its grandest days. Cecilia, daughter of a producer, recalls Rudolph Valentino's appearance at her fifth birthday party with that blend of matter-of-factness and nostalgia with which a Georgia Belle in 1870 might have remembered a ball in her family's pre-Civil War mansion."[9] Viewed from the outside, Hollywood may appear to be tinsel town. Viewed from the inside, it can sometimes be mistaken for "the last extant stable society."[10]

In choosing Cecilia as his narrator, Fitzgerald gives us an insider's perspective on Hollywood. Unlike Nathanael West's characters, who are pathetic victims come west to die, Cecilia is able to see Hollywood as neither Eden nor Gomorrah, but as an insular and provincial community in which real people live and work. Indeed, Joan Didion argues that "to the extent that *The Last Tycoon* is 'about' Hollywood it is about not Monroe Stahr but Cecilia Brady . . . [the inheritor] of a community as intricate, rigid, and deceptive in its mores as any devised on this continent."[11]

At the outset of Fitzgerald's novel, Cecilia makes a deliberate attempt to demystify Hollywood. "My father was in the picture business," she tells us, "as another man might be in cotton or steel, and I took it tranquilly. At the worst I accepted Hollywood with the resignation of a ghost assigned to a haunted house. I knew what you were supposed to think about it but I was obstinately unhorrified." In addition to establishing the novel's perspective on Hollywood, Cecilia also shows us how the film community responds to the condescension of outsiders. Referring to what one might have regarded as Fitzgerald's natural constituency, she remarks: "When I was at Bennington some of the English teachers who pretended an indifference to Hollywood or its products really *hated* it. Hated it way down deep as a threat to their existence." In contrasting their attitude with hers, she continues: "You can take Hollywood for granted like I did, or you can dismiss it with the contempt we reserve for what we don't understand."[12]

That Fitzgerald should take such a benign view of Hollywood is surprising when one considers his own experience as a screenwriter. It would have been relatively easy for him to have dramatized his conflict with Joseph Mankiewicz (whom he frequently referred to as "Monkeybitch") over the script of *Three*

Comrades as a classic tale of Hollywood the Destroyer. Instead, he resisted the impulse to self-justification and self-pity in order to be fair to an industry about which he must have had mixed emotions. As he indicated in an undelivered letter to Norma Shearer: "I invented a tragic story. . . . [N]o one has ever written a tragedy about Hollywood. *A Star is Born* was a pathetic and often beautiful story but not a tragedy and doomed and heroic things do happen here."[13]

Although Fitzgerald never finished *The Last Tycoon,* it is clear from what he did write and from the notes that he left that his Hollywood tragedy was, at least in part, to be an admiring fictional portrait of Norma Shearer's late husband, the legendary producer Irving G. Thalberg. Fitzgerald owed Thalberg no personal gratitude and even considered him a professional enemy; however, he correctly intuited that in the collaborative medium of film a strong producer like Thalberg was the principal artistic consciousness, what a later generation of critics would call the *auteur.* "Thalberg has always fascinated me," Fitzgerald wrote in a letter to *Collier's* editor Kenneth Littauer. "His peculiar charm, his extraordinary good looks, his bountiful success, the tragic end of his great adventure."[14]

The parallels between Thalberg and Fitzgerald's protagonist Monroe Stahr are so well known that there is no point in belaboring them here. Instead, we should keep in mind that Fitzgerald was inspired more by a fictive image of Thalberg than by the producer himself (Thalberg's widow Norma Shearer and close friends Anita Loos and Albert Lewin said that they did not recognize the man they knew in the figure of Monroe Stahr). Indeed, by the time Fitzgerald began his final stint in Hollywood in 1937, Thalberg had been dead for a year and was already a folk hero. Bruccoli suggests that at this time Fitzgerald had "ambitions of winning elevation to producer or even director status" and that he "saw Thalberg as a model for what could be done in the movies."[15] That model is further delineated by Cecilia when she says of Stahr: "He was a marker in industry like Edison and Lumière and Griffith and Chaplin. He led pictures way up past the range of power of the theatre, reaching a sort of golden age, before the censorship" (p. 28).

If Stahr is meant to be regarded as a serious artist, we might well ask why Fitzgerald's novel is called *The Last Tycoon* (Actually, the choice of title was Edmund Wilson's doing, but the phrase "last tycoon" is found several times in Fitzgerald's notes). The point would seem to be that the art of motion picture making is to a large extent organizational. Stahr is really quite serious when he tells his girl friend Kathleen that he has achieved his boyhood ambition to be chief clerk. "That's my gift, if I have one," he tells her. "Only when I got to be it, I found out that you had to know why it was where it was, and whether it should be left there. They began throwing it all at me, and it was a very complex office. Pretty soon I had all the keys. And they wouldn't have remembered what locks they fitted if I'd given them back" (p. 79). It has been frequently remarked that *The Last Tycoon* is one of the few American novels to deal seriously and positively with any form of business. To imagine Dreiser, Sinclair Lewis, or the early Dos Passos writing a novel called *The Last Tycoon* is to imagine a very different book from the one that Fitzgerald was writing at his death.

We must remember, however, that the term "tycoon" refers only in a colloquial sense to a successful businessman. In its primary meaning, it was the title which foreigners applied to the Japanese shogun. Clearly, Monroe Stahr was meant to be seen as a tycoon in this older and grander sense of the term. He is an absolute but benevolent despot, a man who can act with seemingly ruthless decisiveness in removing an ineffective director from a picture and yet go out of his way to restore the confidence of an impotent matinee idol and to reinstate an unjustly fired cameraman. And he is the *last* tycoon in representing the end of an old order. This sense of Stahr as a magnificent and revered anachronism is movingly conveyed at the end of Chapter 2:

> He spoke and waved back as the people streamed by in the darkness, looking, I suppose, a little like the Emperor and the Old Guard. There is no world so but it has its heroes, and Stahr was the hero. Most of these men had been here a long time—through the beginnings and the great upset, when sound came, and the three years of depression, he had seen that no harm came to them. The old loyalties were trembling now, there were clay feet everywhere; but still he was their man, the last of the princes. And their greeting was a sort of low cheer as they went by. (p. 27)

Among Fitzgerald's notes for *The Last Tycoon,* we find the following statement: "I look out at it—and I think it is the most beautiful history in the world. It is the history of me and my people. And if I came here yesterday like Sheilah I should still think so. It is the history of all aspiration—not just the American dream but the human dream and if I came at the end of it that too is a place in the line of the pioneers."[16] In Fitzgerald's Hollywood we find not a dream factory but a dream attic, one which preserves an earlier, nobler vision of our culture. When Cecilia wanders through the back lot of Stahr's studio, the reader is reminded of Tod Hackett's sojourn through a similar Hollywood studio in West's *The Day of the Locust.* The difference in tone, however, is crucial. Whereas Tod sees a "Sargasso of the imagination," a history of civilization "in the form of a dream dump,"[17] Cecilia sees "the torn picture books of childhood, like fragments of stories dancing in an open fire" (p. 25).

At the same time that Fitzgerald was writing his last novel, a Hollywood native named Budd Schulberg was writing his first. It is a noteworthy irony that Fitzgerald the outsider seemed to have greater affection and respect for the film capital than did Schulberg the hometown boy. *"What Makes Sammy Run?* (published in the same year as *The Last Tycoon*) is a cynic's version of the decline of Hollywood, a theme Fitzgerald had approached as tragedy.

Not only were Fitzgerald and Schulberg writing at the same time, but each was aware of the other's work in progress. (Indeed, in creating the character of Cecilia Brady, Fitzgerald relied greatly on Schulberg's inside knowledge of Hollywood.) In both novels, an old-guard producer with the taste and integrity of Irving Thalberg fights a losing battle against a sleazy opportunist. The main difference is that Fitzgerald's focus is on the fall of the producer, whereas Schulberg's is on the rise of the opportunist. The contrast between these two novels becomes even more pronounced when we consider that both Monroe Stahr and Sammy Glick rose from poverty and obscurity in the Jewish ghetto of New York to achieve fortune and fame in Hollywood. Stahr did so as an Horatio Alger figure, Glick as a Flem Snopes.

In *What Makes Sammy Run?* Schulberg employs a first-person narrator whose primary function in the novel is to try to understand its protagonist (a function emphasized by the question that serves as the novel's title). In this regard, *Sammy* is similar to *The Last Tycoon, The Great Gatsby*, and quite a few other major works of twentieth-century fiction. In the hands of a Fitzgerald or a Conrad such a technique can result in a subtle tale of moral education. Schulberg's narrator Al Manheim is, however, an essentially static character who serves as a fairly unambiguous surrogate for the author.

Like Fitzgerald, West, Faulkner, and so many other lesser lights, Al Manheim and Sammy Glick are eastern writers who move to Hollywood during the depression (actually, Sammy is less a writer than a con man who is adept at stealing the ideas and exploiting the talents of others). As a newcomer to Southern California, Al makes all the obligatory local-color observations about the strangeness of the landscape and the people. However, he also delivers a comment unconventional enough to have been the view of an insider like Cecilia Brady or Budd Schulberg. "You have to stay up till two o'clock to realize what a small town Hollywood is," Al tells us. "It goes to sleep at twelve o'clock like any decent Middle Western village."[18]

There are also a few places in *Sammy* where Al Manheim is genuinely excited by the aesthetic possibilities of the motion picture medium. Like Fitzgerald and quite a few others, Manheim is essentially a writer of words who must learn how to tell stories in pictures. At one point, the Thalberg-type producer Sidney Fineman tells Al of the time he brought a famous Broadway playwright out to Hollywood. Given the assignment of writing an opening scene which would establish that a husband was tiring of his wife, the playwright came back fifteen thousand dollars later with a twenty-page scene filled with brilliant dialogue but way over the length for the start of the picture.

Fineman gave the scene to his director, Ray MacKenna, a veteran of the Mack Sennett days. MacKenna reduced the scene to half a page of wordless action in an elevator. The husband and wife are in evening clothes, when a "classy dame" enters. The husband removes his hat with a flourish, as his wife glares at him. "Mac couldn't write a complete sentence," Fineman says. "But that was great writing—for the screen" (p. 142).[19] Inspired by this story, Al "couldn't wait to get out of Fineman's office and start writing the greatest screenplay of all time." He then remembers something

his girl friend Kit has told him: "The most exciting way ever invented to tell a story is with a moving picture camera" (p. 142).

Such paeans to the magic of movies, however, are few and
far between in Schulberg's novel. As the wheel of fortune turns,
the Finemans are on their way down and the Glicks are on their
way up. In the process, men with real talent experience Hollywood
as Destroyer. This is true of Sammy's ghostwriter Julian Blumberg
and, on a grander scale, of the lyric poet Henry Powell Turner, a
former Pulitzer Prize winner who has degenerated into an alco-
holic hack.

Of course, what makes this novel memorable is not Al Manheim, Sidney Fineman, or Henry Powell Turner, but the obnox-
ious social climber Sammy Glick. If Sammy is in many ways the
obverse image of Monroe Stahr, he is also a cynical perversion of
other Fitzgerald heroes. In his maniacal pursuit of social prominence, he vaguely resembles Jay Gatsby—even to the point of
changing his name. The main difference is that Gatsby seeks to
rise in the world in order to win the golden girl, whereas Sammy
seeks the girl as confirmation that he has already risen. Sammy's
bride, the blue-blood Laurette Harrington, is a variation of the Fitzgerald coquette—kin to Daisy Buchanan, Nicole Warren, and Judy
Jones. Indeed, the only time that Sammy is not in control of his
life is when Laurette cuckolds him on their wedding night. The
one thing that his gall and his money cannot buy him is entrance
into the aristocracy. To achieve that level of decadence requires several generations. Instead, he simply ends up as Gatsby with horns.

If Sammy represents the wave of the future in Hollywood,
then vulgarity has indeed triumphed. (In a prophetic exchange early
in the novel, Al says jokingly to Sammy: "I'll bet you got Irving
Thalberg plenty worried"; to which Sammy replies: "If he's not
he oughta be. . . . I've got a hunch Hollywood is my meat" [p. 30]).
Unfortunately, Schulberg's liberal social philosophy will not allow
him to present Sammy as a culpable villain. Toward the end of
the novel Al discovers that it is Sammy's ghetto background that
has made him into an aggressive little punk who runs over everyone who stands in his way. Thus, what is ostensibly an anti-Holly-
wood novel turns out to be an indictment of the New York slums.

Midway between the extremes defined by Monroe Stahr and
Sammy Glick is Victor Milgrim, the producer in Schulberg's 1950

novel *The Disenchanted.* Lacking the genuine taste and integrity of Thalberg or Stahr, Milgrim is essentially a more sophisticated and benign version of Glick. Although he is a man of intellectual pretensions who lusts after an honorary Doctor of Humanities degree, he is capable of referring to himself as an "omnipotent reader."[20] He hires the once-great writer Manley Halliday not because he wants to elevate the literary quality of the cinema, but because he wants to promote his own image as a man of culture. Basically an opportunist and a hypocrite, "Milgrim was nominally a Republican, just as he was nominally a monogamist, but his first loyalty was to success" (p. 79).

Milgrim, however, is at best a peripheral figure in *The Disenchanted.* The focus of the novel is on two of his screenwriters, the youthful Shep Stearns and the aging Manley Halliday. Because Stearns and Halliday are so obviously fictionalized versions of Budd Schulberg and Scott Fitzgerald, much criticism of *The Disenchanted* has concentrated on the book's biographical veracity. This is understandable when one considers that Schulberg is probably more responsible than any other individual for our popular image of Fitzgerald in Hollywood. As Tom Dardis has demonstrated, the figure of Manley Halliday reappears not only in Schulberg's 1960 *Esquire* piece "Old Scott," but also in the biographical writings of Fitzgerald scholars Arthur Mizener, Andrew Turnbull, and Aaron Latham. Mizener and Turnbull even seem to have paraphrased bits of dialogue from *The Disenchanted.*[21]

And yet to read Schulberg's novel solely as *roman à clef* is to miss the point. Like Monroe Stahr, Manley Halliday is a fictional character inspired by a real-life prototype. Just as Fitzgerald was responding to the mythic Thalberg in *The Last Tycoon,* so too was Schulberg more concerned with symbolic reality than with biographical verisimilitude in *The Disenchanted.* By giving us an alternative to Schulberg's image of Fitzgerald in Hollywood, Dardis and Bruccoli have made it possible to read *The Disenchanted* for what it is—a powerful and touching work of fiction.

Manley Halliday and Shep Stearns represent different generations. Halliday is still living in the carefree 1920s, while Stearns is an earnest, socially conscious product of the 1930s. These different perspectives are reflected in their contrasting attitudes toward Hollywood: Halliday sees screenwriting as a quick means of getting out of debt so that he can return to serious fiction, whereas Stearns sees the motion picture medium as potentially a folk art. The conflict of generations provides a social context for the action of the novel; however, Schulberg does not simply stack the deck so that his own alter ego emerges as morally superior to Fitzgerald's. Instead, the novel traces the development of Shep's understanding of the older writer.

At first, Stearns stands in awe of Halliday's literary legend, but he gradually comes to see behind that legend only an irresponsible drunk. Then, at the end of the novel, he reads the beginning of Manley Halliday's new work-in-progress, and his opinion changes again:

> Shep knew why Manley Halliday hadn't published in nearly a decade: because he was defeatist, an escapist, cut off from "vital issues," from "The People," a disillusioned amanuensis of a dying order—oh, Shep hadn't read his *New Masses* for nothing! Yet here were these eighty-three pages. My God, this was alive, while the writers who were not defeatist, not escapist, not bourgeois apologists and not "cut off from the main stream of humanity" were wooden and lifeless. . . . Maybe ideology wasn't the literary shibboleth he had believed in so dogmatically. (p. 368)

Although he does not use the precise terminology, Jonas Spatz believes the paradigm figure of the Hollywood myth to be "Irving Thalberg" and that of the antimyth to be "Scott Fitzgerald."[22] But, as Spatz himself admits, even these literary paradigms, not to mention the historical realities behind them, contain internal complexities. Monroe Stahr, for example, can momentarily stoop to the level of his nemesis Pat Brady in an effort to save his studio. And Manley Halliday, despite his contempt for the commercialism of present-day Hollywood, is able to regard the old Hollywood with an elegiac fondness. "Hollywood was—a lot crazier then than it is now," he tells Shep, "—more of a factory town now. But in those days it was—it had the quality of a vulgar fairy land. There were wonderful parties that lasted for days and there was a nice sense of sin that's only found in worlds of true innocence" (p. 214).

Another inheritor of the Fitzgerald tradition is Norman Mailer.[23] Unlike Schulberg, however, Mailer appears more inter-

ested in absorbing the influence of Fitzgerald's art than in mytholo-
gizing the tragedy of his life. As Michael Millgate observes: "In
The Deer Park (1955), Norman Mailer seems to have tried to take
over where Fitzgerald left off [in *The Last Tycoon*] and bring us
up-to-date on Hollywood." Millgate proceeds to note that both
Fitzgerald and Mailer employ peripheral first-person narrators.
Also, each author places his protagonist in a similar dilemma: "he
wants to make good pictures but everyone, in the name of commercialism, is against him and he is further distracted from his
proper business of making pictures by the intrusion of politics into
his life."[24]

Although Millgate is correct in his comparisons, he begs the
larger question of whether Mailer has written a Hollywood novel
at all. Most of the action of *The Deer Park* takes place not in
Hollywood, but in Desert D'Or (a fictionalized Palm Springs), and,
as Robert Merrill points out, the relationship of Mailer's protagonist to Hollywood "is resolved before the novel is half over."[25]
Nevertheless, I would argue that Hollywood as metonymy for
America is the essential backdrop against which Mailer tells his
story. Each of the three principal characters in *The Deer Park*—
Sergius O'Shaugnessy, Marion Faye, and Charles Francis Eitel—
reveals much of his basic nature through his stance toward the
film capital.

A young veteran of the Korean War who has become psy-
chosomatically impotent because of guilt over the mass death he
has inflicted as a bomber pilot, Sergius is a sort of updated Jake
Barnes. However, unlike the physically wounded Barnes, Sergius
regains his virility—in the bed of a hot-blooded Hollywood sex
symbol named Lulu Meyers. Sergius's description of his coupling
with Lulu is vintage Mailer:

> Like a squad of worn-out infantrymen who are fixed for
> the night in a museum, my pleasure was to slash
> tapestries, poke my fingers through nude paintings, and
> drop marble busts on the floor. . . . To the pride of having
> so beautiful a girl was added the bigger pride of knowing
> that I took her with the cheers of millions behind me.
> Poor millions with their low roar! They would never
> have what I had now. They could shiver outside, make a
> shrine in their office desk or on the shelf of their

olive-drab lockers, they could look at the pin-up picture
of Lulu Meyers. I knew I was good when I carried a
million men on my shoulder.[26]

Not only is Sergius enjoying the favors of a nubile young
woman, but he is also possessing, even desecrating, the erotic fantasies of millions of moviegoers. To bed the reigning sex goddess
of Hollywood is to achieve a conquest that, in the age of push-
button warfare, is no longer to be had on the conventional field of
battle. As the novel progresses, however, it becomes apparent that
the only way that Sergius can keep his prize is by becoming the
movie queen's prince consort. He eventually rejects Hollywood
by turning down the chance to sell his life story to the movies
and, in turn, loses Lulu to a young actor named Tony Tanner. Having resisted the temptations of Hollywood, Sergius moves on, a
picaresque hero, to further experiences and further conquests.

Marion Faye is Mailer's fictionalized portrait of the hipster—
the psychopath as hero. He is presented as a kind of existential
saint who carries his war against hypocrisy to perverse lengths.
As such, he is the antithesis of Hollywood. Hollywood preaches
chastity while practicing debauchery; Faye is quite openly a pimp.
Hollywood projects an image of compassion and humanity while
actually destroying the lives and talent of its most creative people;
Faye gratuitously torments a heroin addict and deliberately seeks
to drive his mistress to suicide. Contemplating the sham and cu-
pidity of Desert D'Or from a hilltop one morning, Marion thinks
in apocalyptic terms reminiscent of Nathanael West:

> So let it come, Faye thought, let this explosion come, and
> then another, and all the others, until the Sun God
> burned the earth. . . . Let it come, Faye begged, like a man
> praying for rain, let it come and clear the rot and the
> stench and the stink, let it come for all of everywhere,
> just so it comes and the world stands clear in the white
> dead dawn. (p. 161)

If Sergius and Marion, each in his own way, avoid falling
prey to Hollywood the Destroyer, Charles Francis Eitel is not so
fortunate. A brilliant director who has achieved success with a
series of slick commercial films, Eitel falls out of favor with the
Hollywood establishment when he proves to be an uncooperative

witness before a congressional investigating committee. Out of work, he retreats to Desert D'Or, where he works on an original film script and begins an affair with Elena Esposito, the cast-off mistress of a studio executive.

Some critics have assumed that because the relationship between Eitel and Elena is the central action of Mailer's novel the essential story would have remained unchanged had Eitel been something other than a motion picture director. Yet Hollywood functions as something of a hidden presence in this love affair. Eitel begins his life with Elena at the same time that he is fired from Hollywood; he starts to drift away from her when he makes plans to sell a sentimentalized version of his new script to his old studio, with Elena's former lover serving as front man. Quite appropriately, Elena's own ardor begins to cool when she sees Eitel compromising his artistic integrity. Eventually, Eitel agrees to testify before the congressional committee and regains his earlier prominence in the film capital. Meanwhile, Elena has left him for Marion Faye.

If we carry the idea of Hollywood as character one step further and personify it as a woman, then what we have is a love triangle. Eitel, who has been married to what William James called the bitch-goddess success, becomes estranged from that fair-haired wife and takes up with a dark and brooding earth mother, only to return at last to his original spouse. This interpretation seems less extravagant when we consider that at the end of the novel Eitel is having an illicit affair with his ex-wife, the Hollywood bitch-goddess Lulu Meyers. To add to the irony, he is legally united in a loveless marriage to Elena.

Eitel is finally a more interesting character than either Sergius or Marion. His personality is more complex and ambiguous than theirs; and if they seem all too often to be stock figures in an existentialist morality play, Eitel is more like a tragic antihero. All three individuals have something of Mailer in them. Sergius is the all-American war hero who, like Mailer, often seems intent on living out the role of a Hemingway protagonist. Marion is the sort of "psychic outlaw" whom Mailer describes in "The White Negro," depicts in *An American Dream*, and emulates in the more psychotic moments of his own life. Finally, the middle-aged Charley Eitel comes closest to being the young Norman Mailer's projection of what he feared he himself might become.

Like Eitel, Mailer is an artist who came from a working-class background to achieve early fame and success. For each man, love of the bitch-goddess wars against a sense of artistic integrity. Perhaps the most obvious similarity between Mailer and Eitel, however, is in the script on which Eitel works while exiled in Desert D'Or. Several critics have remarked on the resemblance of this script to Nathanael West's novel *Miss Lonelyhearts*. What few people seem to realize is that Mailer and Jean Malaquais tried to sell just such a script to Sam Goldwyn in 1949 and withdrew it when it became evident that Goldwyn would bring in some hack writers and sentimentalize it.[27] Had Mailer given in to Goldwyn, he might have ended up—twenty years later—another Charles Francis Eitel. In contrast to Schulberg's conventional naturalism, Mailer offers us a radical vision of free will. If Hollywood is the destroyer, it can claim none but the willing victim.

As different as their views may be, both the advocates of the myth and the purveyors of the antimyth share the tendency to depict Hollywood as larger than life. In recent years, however, a third force has emerged, one that seems intent on *demythologizing* Hollywood—of seeing it in much the same light as Cecilia Brady did. For lack of a better term, we can refer to this third point of view as the "anti-antimyth." Its principal spoksmen are Joan Didion and John Gregory Dunne.

Because the focus of this volume is Los Angeles in fiction, it would be inappropriate to concentrate too heavily on the outspoken and controversial essays of Didion and Dunne. I mention them only to suggest a context for discussion of Didion's 1970 Hollywood novel *Play It as It Lays*. If we look at this novel in isolation, we might hastily conclude that it is a rather extreme rendering of the antimyth. However, if we attempt to reconcile *Play It as It Lays* with Didion's nonfiction writings on Hollywood, a more interesting and complex interpretation recommends itself.

Upon first reading *Play It as It Lays*, one is likely to be struck by its spare, bleak nihilistic tone. What becomes evident with successive readings, however, is the crucial function that irony and humor serve in this novel. For me, one of the most hid-

eously black comic scenes in *Play It as It Lays*, the contact between Didion's protagonist, Maria, and the man who is to take
her to an abortionist—is also one of the most memorable in contemporary fiction.

Maria meets her contact, a moral zombie in white duck
pants, under the big red T at the local Thriftimart. To pass the
time, he hums "I Get a Kick Out of You" and begins to make inane
small talk. Speaking of the neighborhood through which they are
passing, he says: "Nice homes here. Nice for kids."[28] He then asks
Maria whether she gets good mileage on her car and proceeds to
compare the merits of his Cadillac with those of a Camaro he is
contemplating buying: "Maybe that sounds like a step down, a Cad
to a Camaro, but I've got my eye on this particular Camaro, exact
model of the pace car in the Indianapolis 500" (p. 79).

Because Maria has strong maternal instincts, her abortion
is the cause of much guilt and anxiety. It can also be seen as a
symbol of the breakdown of the family and of traditional standards of morality. But what makes the episode of the abortion un-
forgetably grotesque is the image of that cretin in white duck pants
babbling about the mileage that Maria gets on her car. Throughout *Play It as It Lays*, Didion employs just such comic touches
to undercut the sentimental, self-pitying nihilism inherent in
Maria's story.

Nowhere is this ironic distance between Didion as author
and Maria as character more important than in the novel's climactic scene. Here, Maria's friend, a movie producer and homosexual
named BZ, climbs into bed with Maria, swallows a handful of
Seconal, and dies in her comforting arms. (In a bar across the way,
the juke box is playing "King of the Road," Roger Miller's country-
western formulation of the play-it-as-it-lays philosophy.) If, as
Albert Camus argues, the only serious philosophical problem is
"judging whether life is or is not worth living,"[29] BZ, in doing away
with himself, resolves that problem in the negative. He tells Maria:
"You're still playing. . . . Some day you'll wake up and you just
won't feel like playing any more" (p. 212). BZ sees suicide as a last
significant act of defiance, a ritual of self-annihilation. If life cannot be improved, he seems to say, then at least it can be ended.
But for Maria such an attitude amounts to a pathetic kind of pose;
or, as she says to BZ, "a queen's way of doing it" (p. 212).

Unlike BZ, Maria is averse to examining life, philosophically or otherwise. (At the outset of the novel, she says: "What makes Iago evil? some people ask. I never ask" [p.13].) She tells us that she keeps on living only because she hopes some day to get back her brain-damaged daughter Kate and go some place where they can live simply. Maria will do some canning and be a mother to her child. This "hope" is encouraging, however, only if there is a chance of its being realized, and by the end of the novel, we understand that Maria's dream is, in fact, hopeless. Viewed in this light, the closing lines of *Play It as It Lays* seem ironic indeed. Maria tells us:

> *I know something Carter never knew, or Helene, or maybe you. I know what 'nothing' means, and keep on playing.*
> *Why, BZ would say.*
> *Why not, I say.* (p. 214)

Maria may actually believe that she is living for Kate; however, the truth, as Didion's narrative perspective forces us to see it, is that Maria continues to live because she does not even share BZ's faith in the meaningfulness of death.

In examining Didion's writings about the movie capital, we must finally wonder whether to give greater credence to the relatively sanguine view of that place which we find in her essays or to the nightmare vision of her Hollywood novel. To resolve this dilemma, however, we need to understand the difference between Didion's respective approaches to journalism and to fiction. In her journalism, she is trying to tell us what she knows about a particular subject. But in her fiction, she is trying to tell the stories that certain mental images suggest to her. Let us, then, consider the image that served as the basis for *Play It as It Lays*.

In her 1976 essay "Why I Write," Didion recalls having seen "a young woman with long hair and a short white halter dress . . . [walk] through the casino at the Riviera in Las Vegas at one in the morning. She crosses the casino alone and picks up a house telephone." The author watches this woman "because I have heard her paged, and recognize her name. . . . [But] I know nothing about her. Who is paging her? Why is she here to be paged? How exactly did she come to this?" "It was precisely this moment in Las Vegas,"

Didion concludes, "that made *Play It as It Lays* begin to tell itself to me."[30]

It is important for us as readers to keep this image in mind, not only to see the young actress as Didion sees her, but also to see Didion looking *at* her. In short, to lose sight of the ironic perspective in this novel is inevitably to misread its author's intentions. At one level, Maria's story is one of genuine suffering and despair. Yet, at another level, Didion seems to be writing a parody of the novel of despair. She does this not by minimizing or ridiculing Maria's plight, but by undercutting the kinds of philosophical responses to that plight which romantic-existentialist writers might invoke.

Perhaps we can better understand Didion's attitude here if we consider the treatment of "nothingness," or *nada*, in one of the most famous works of romantic-existentialist fiction, Ernest Hemingway's "A Clean Well-Lighted Place." According to Carlos Baker, Hemingway's greatest achievement in this story lies in his "development, through the most carefully controlled understatement, of the young waiter's mere *nothing* into the old waiter's Something—a Something called Nothing which is so huge, terrible, overbearing, inevitable, and omnipresent that, once experienced, it can never be forgotten."[31] BZ and Maria have both experienced something very similar to the *nada* of Hemingway's story. BZ responds to that experience by allowing it to become for him a Something called Nothing. Maria, however, is living testament to the fact that Nothing is actually *no thing*.

In contrast to many other Hollywood novelists, Joan Didion is obviously not writing *about* the movie capital. The city can hardly even be described as the "setting" of *Play It as It Lays.* Rather one thinks of the action of this novel as occurring in the void. (Didion claims that she set out to write a book "in which anything that happened would happen off the page, a 'white' book to which the reader would have to bring his or her own bad dreams.")[32] In this regard, *Play It as It Lays* would seem to be very much in the absurdist tradition of Nathanael West's *The Day of the Locust.* If anything, Didion has pushed deeper than West into the abyss of nihilism. In the process, she has extended the Hollywood antimyth to the point of self-parody.

The five novels we have considered here suggest something of the heterogeneity of Hollywood fiction. Indeed, the Hollywood novel appears to be less a monolithic than a dialectical genre.This is because the myth and the antimyth articulate mutually dependent images of the film capital. To the extent that the literature of the antimyth is one of disillusionment, it requires that the original illusions remain at least vivid memories. Similarly, the vision of the myth is tragic and elegiac only if it is challenged by an equally powerful countervision. In recent years, however, the Hollywood novel has met the same fate as the Southern novel: it has become passé because it depicts a mythic conflict which has ceased to exist. (It is no accident that the most recent version of *A Star is Born*—written by Joan Didion and John Gregory Dunne—dealt with the music industry, not with motion pictures.) Because Hollywood is no longer seen as the embodiment of the American Dream, it can no longer be portrayed as the realization of the American Nightmare.

Notes

1. Allan Seager has characterized Nathanael West's *The Day of the Locust* as "not fantasy imagined, but fantasy seen." This seems to me a fairly apt description of Hollywood fiction in general. Because West is discussed extensively elsewhere in this volume, I have chosen not to deal with *The Day of the Locust* here. For the Seager quote see James F. Light, *Nathanael West: an Interpretive Study* (Evanston, Ill.: Northwestern University Press, 1971), p. 168.

2. Norman Mailer, "Superman Comes to the Supermarket," in *Smiling Through the Apocalypse*, ed. Harold Hayes (New York: McCall Publishing Co., 1969), p. 13.

3. The term "anti-myth" is applied to Los Angeles by J. U. Peters in his essay "The Los Angeles Anti-Myth," *Itinerary Seven: Essays on California Writers*, ed. Charles L. Crow (Bowling Green, Ohio: Bowling Green State University Press, 1978), pp. 21–34.

4. Joan Didion, *Slouching Towards Bethlehem* (New York: Farrar, Straus & Giroux, 1968), p. 172.

5. Jonas Spatz, *Hollywood in Fiction: Some Versions of the American Myth* (The Hague: Mouton, 1969), p. 114.

6.   Although I have not been able to track down the source of this aphorism, it is attributed to Oscar Levant.

7.   Didion, *Slouching Towards Bethlehem*, p. 150. Here Didion is challenging what she calls the myth of "Hollywood the Destroyer."

8.   Quoted in Spatz. pp. 61–62.

9.   Robert Roulston, "Whistling 'Dixie' in Encino: *The Last Tycoon* and F. Scott Fitzgerald's Two Souths," *South Atlantic Quarterly* 79(1980):357.

10.   This characterization of Hollywood is Didion's. See *The White Album* (New York: Simon and Schuster, 1979). p. 155.

11.   Ibid., p. 153.

12.   F. Scott Fitzgerald, *The Last Tycoon* (New York: Charles Scribner's sons, 1941), p. 3. Subsequent quotations are cited parenthetically in the text.

13.   See Matthew J. Bruccoli, *Some Sort of Epic Grandeur* (New York: Harcourt Brace Jovanovich, 1981), p. 466.

14.   Ibid., p. 462.

15.   Ibid., p. 467.

16.   See Bruccoli, *The Last of the Novelists: F. Scott Fitzgerald and the Last Tycoon* (Carbondale: Southern Illinois University Press, 1977), p. vii.

17.   Nathanael West, *The Complete Works* (New York: Farrar, Straus & Giroux, 1957), p. 353.

18.   Budd Schulberg, *What Makes Sammy Run?* (1941; Harmondsworth, Middlesex, England: Penguin Books, 1978), p. 46. Subsequent quotations are cited parenthetically in the text.

19.   There is a similar scene in *The Last Tycoon* when Monroe Stahr gives the British writer George Boxley a lesson in screenwriting.

20.   Schulberg, *The Disenchanted* (New York: Random House, 1950), p. 73. Subsequent quotations are cited parenthetically in the text.

21.   See Tom Dardis, *Some Time in the Sun* (New York: Charles Scribner's Sons, 1976), p. 62.

22.   Spatz, pp. 87–88.

23.   For a fuller discussion of the affinities between Mailer and Fitzgerald, see Richard Foster, "Mailer and the Fitzgerald Tradition," *Novel* 1 (1968):219–30.

24.   Michael Millgate, *American Social Fiction: James to Cozzens* (New York: Barnes and Noble, 1964), p. 159.

25.   Robert Merrill, *Norman Mailer* (Boston: Twayne Publishers 1978), p. 57.

26.   Mailer, *The Deer Park* (New York: G. P. Putnam's Sons, 1955), p. 130. Subsequent quotations are cited parenthetically in the text.

27. See Hilary Mills, *Mailer: A Biography* (New York: Empire Books, 1982), pp. 118–19.

28. Didion, *Play It as It Lays* (New York: Farrar, Straus & Giroux, 1970), p. 78. Subsequent quotations are cited parenthetically in the text.

29. Albert Camus, *The Myth of Sisyphus*, trans. Justin O'Brien (London: Hamish Hamilton, 1955), p. 11.

30. Didion, "Why I Write," *New York Times Book Review*, 5 December 1976, p. 98.

31. Carlos Baker, *Hemingway: The Writer as Artist* (Princeton, N. J.: Princeton University Press, 1952), p. 124.

32. Didion, "Why I Write," p. 98.

Bibliographic Note

I am familiar with two book-length studies of the Hollywood novel: Jonas Spatz's *Hollywood in Fiction: Some Versions of the American Myth* (The Hague: Mouton, 1969) and Walter Wells's *Tycoons and Locusts: A Regional Look at Hollywood Fiction of the 1930s* (Carbondale: Southern Illinois University Press, 1973). The Wells book should be of particular interest to readers of Los Angeles fiction, in that it includes discussions of such non-Hollywood writers as Raymond Chandler and James M. Cain. Spatz is more narrowly focused on Hollywood; however, unlike Wells, he carries his study up to the 1960s. Michael Millgate's *American Social Fiction: James to Cozzens* (New York: Barnes and Noble, 1964) also deals in part with the Hollywood novel.

Almost all of the many critical studies of F. Scott Fitzgerald contain some discussion of *The Last Tycoon*. An absolutely indispensable textual and bibliographical study is Matthew J. Bruccoli's *The Last of the Novelists: F. Scott Fitzgerald and the Last Tycoon* (Carbondale: Southern Illinois University Press, 1977). Among the most interesting recent essays on Fitzgerald's unfinished novel is Robert Roulston's "Whistling 'Dixie' in Encino: *The Last Tycoon* and F. Scott Fitzgerald's Two Souths," *South Atlantic Quarterly* 79 (1980):355–63. For information on Fitzgerald's years in Hollywood, see Tom Dardis, *Some Time in the Sun* (New York: Charles Scribner's Sons, 1976) and Matthew J. Bruccoli, *Some Sort of Epic Grandeur* (New York: Harcourt Brace Jovanovich 1981).

Thus far, Budd Schulberg has received scant critical attention. The most extended treatment of *What Makes Sammy Run?* is found in Wells's *Tycoons and Locusts*. Spatz looks more briefly at both *Sammy* and *The Disenchanted*, while Millgate does little more than mention the two books.

In the past fifteen years, Norman Mailer has been the subject of at least twenty books. Consequently, much has been written on *The Deer Park*. Robert Merrill's *Norman Mailer* (Boston: Twayne Publishers, 1978) is particularly good. For background on the novel, see Mailer's *Advertisements for Myself* (New York: G. P. Putnam's Sons, 1959) and Hilary Mills's *Mailer: A Biography* (New York: Empire Books, 1982).

Joan Didion is beginning to receive increasing critical attention. The two books devoted to her works are my own *Joan Didion* (Boston: Twayne Publishers 1980) and Katherine Usher Henderson's *Joan Didion* (New York: Frederick Ungar Publishing Co., 1981). Among journal articles, the most provocative discussion of *Play It as It Lays* is David J. Geherin's "Nothingness and Beyond: Joan Didion's *Play It as It Lays*," *Critique: Studies in Modern Fiction* 16 (1974): 64–78. This essay discusses Didion's novel within the context of Camus' philosophy. It sees Maria as having pushed beyond nothingness to a limited affirmation of meaning.

EIGHT

Between Two Worlds: Aldous Huxley and Evelyn Waugh in Hollywood

Walter Wells

The Hollywood Novel, *sui generis*, was born in the depression 1930s, the artchild of American writers possessed by visions of American decline. Whether set in the studios, or elsewhere in the palmy half-city that surrounded them, the fictions of James M. Cain, Horace McCoy, John O'Hara, Raymond Chandler, Nathanael West, and Scott Fitzgerald were each, in their own way, metaphors for a dying American Dream—an insider's lament.[1] But like Coca Cola, the two-reeler, and other uniquely American artifacts, the Hollywood Novel was soon taken up by Europeans—most notably Aldous Huxley and Evelyn Waugh—foreigners to whom America, and Hollywood, meant things very different, and far less moribund.

Huxley came first. By vague design, his journey to America in the spring of 1937 was intended to last only nine or ten weeks. But a deepening fear of war in Europe, a desire to protect wife and son from its easily imagined horrors, and his failure (along with that of his fellow pacifists) to alter British foreign policy turned that journey, in stages, toward permanent expatriation. The Huxleys toured much of America that spring, from New York to California. They stayed the summer at Frieda Lawrence's ranch near Taos, where Huxley finished *Ends and Means*. Then, in spite of earlier resolutions to the contrary, he went with Gerald Heard on an extended lecture tour across the country. The following February, at Anita Loos's instigation and with the prospect of lucrative assignment from MGM, Huxley returned to Los Angeles, joining the growing colony of European expatriates there.

Like the earlier novels of the place into which he was settling, Huxley had about him an aura of despair. His health was poor. Immediately upon returning he came down with bronchial pneumonia. He was also, by this time, almost blind, the consequence of earlier illness. Though instinctively sanguine, he had become disheartened over "the curious rigidity and opacity of most human beings. There's something," he wrote his brother Julian, "dismally fixed, stony, sclerotic about most of them. . . ."[2]

Conditions abroad worsened, but Huxley overcame the more immediate of his maladies. He rationalized that Europe might be understood more clearly from afar; while Germany agitated, Spain burned, and the English dug defensive trenches in Hyde Park, he struggled in Los Angeles to work out the economic and social justifications for a system of philosophical anarchism. He also went to work for MGM on a script for the projected *Madame Curie*, and he gave unfailingly and generously of the money he earned to help family and friends to endure, or escape, the growing hardships abroad. During that first year in California, Huxley also found treatment for his eyes in the controversial Bates Method of "visual re-education"—a regimen that worked a virtual miracle for him. With steady work, frequent periods of rest, and some occasional socializing, it was (as Sybille Bedford wrote) "a divided existence," a life once "resigned to uncertainty, now aware of danger, now getting on with things, looking the other way. . . ."[3]

By October 1938, eight months after settling in Los Angeles, Huxley put aside a larger work-in-progress and began "a short phantasy" with lots of California in it: "a wild extravaganza," he wrote Harold Raymond at Chatto and Windus, "but built up of solidly realistic psychological elements . . . a most serious parable."[4] Twelve months later, Chatto's published that phantasy, *After Many a Summer Dies the Swan.*

The California that Huxley brings to this novel consists of the Los Angeles landscape (as encountered by a visiting English scholar), the city's sybaritic youthfulness and its congeniality to Utopian communities and experimenters, a handful of Dust Bowl migrants (who'd landed south of Steinbeck country), a vast and pretentious cemetery (like the Forest Lawn to which Huxley took his visitors before all else), and most of all the living legend of William Randolph Hearst (at whose mountaintop castle the Huxleys had spent a weekend). The parable into which he turned it all is an updated version of the myth of Tithonus. It was Tithonus, the Trojan prince, to whom the Gods had granted immortality—but neglected to throw everlasting youth into the bargain. As time passes, the prince withers, then decays. In Tennyson's version (whence Huxley's title), he spends his days bitterly roaming "the quiet limits of the world," envying those "happy men who have the power to die." Like Tithonus, and Hearst himself, Jo Stoyte craves immortality. We meet Jo sequestered in his great hilltop castle with his little "bit of yum-yum," Virginia Maunciple. (In early draft her last name was Dowlas, but Huxley chose to make Marion Davies an iota less evident as model and changed it.) Surrounded by the artifacts of the past he has hoarded, owner of a hundred profit-squeezing enterprises below—and the fabled Beverly Pantheon, the "Personality Cemetery" across the valley—Jo Stoyte fears nothing. Except death. He is immune, of course, to his own commercial propaganda. Beverly Pantheon, like the castle itself, is but a monument to his own hubris. The promise of stingless passage through Elysian meadows filled with ersatz statuary and "the tremolo of the Perpetual Wurlitzer" might be good enough for the slobs who buy into the Pantheon. But Jo's wealth would buy him better.

As he often does, Huxley sets up a dialectic around his focal character—albeit a loaded one. Having listened to two advisers, Jo defers, in his mortal anxiety, to the amoral Dr. Obispo (his resident scientist-*cum*-bishop), who points Jo toward the mysterious Fifth Earl of Gonister, an English nobleman known—a century before—to have found longevity in a diet of carp guts. Obispo's adversary, Jo's old college chum, William Propter, warns Jo against

Obispo's scientific pretensions. A voluble humanist, solar-power advocate, and prophet of decentralized cottage-economics, Propter embodies the theories of Ralph Borsodi, whose School for Living in Suffern, New York, Huxley had visited shortly before returning to Los Angeles. "Time and craving . . . craving and time," laments Propter. "The longer you live, the more evil you automatically come into contact with."

But Science (like European belligerence) has its way. Jo is undeterred by Propter's warnings. As the incarnation of all the values hawked on billboards in the valley below (EATS, COCKTAILS, MILE HIGH CONES, JESUS SAVES, DRIVE-IN NUTBURGERS, BEVERLY PANTHEON, PSYCHIC READINGS, ABIDING YOUTH IN THRILL-PHORM BRAS . . .), Jo craves more time. With Virginia and Dr. Obispo, he travels to England, where they discover the Fifth Earl of Gonister still alive in a stinking cave beneath his manor house. Over two centuries old, bedecked in his rotting ribbons, the Earl has done a Darwinian about-face and become a filthy anthropoid, grunting, urinating, defiling his equally ill-preserved and ape-like housekeeper while his uninvited guests look on.

The nauseating spectacle gives pause to Jo's yearning. He is stunned into silence (for the first time in his life, one assumes). But after a moment, he turns to Obispo and says, "you know . . . once you get over the first shock—well, they look like they were having a pretty good time . . . don't you think so?" Beyond Obispo's laughter, the resolution seems clear. Bring on the carp guts.

Within a month of the novel's publication, war began. Huxley's mood darkened, his long-shot hope that individual Propters on the margins of society would somehow rescue mankind at the brink now faded. When in mid-1940 he heard that Paris had fallen, his face, Anita Loos recalled, took on the look of someone peering into Hell.[5] To Sybille Bedford, he seemed drawn and strained, excessively so, even in light of events, as though "almost deliberately . . . putting [himself] under the greatest possible strain, submitting . . . to some rigorous process of repression."[6] Hostilities abroad, the resulting uncertainties in America, and Huxley's generally fragile health (like that of his wife) kept him in Southern California for the duration, his only move the one in 1942 from Pacific Palisades to the desert dryness of Llano. Publicly, he stayed aloof from politics, writing no pamphlets, taking to no platforms, signing no manifestos. "[T]he situation of the world," he wrote Julian that summer, "make[s] all political or social speculation look silly and irrelevant before the ink is dry. . . ."[7] Coming to town intermittently to work at MGM, he sent frequent parcels abroad and maintained a personal living standard of frayed upper-class asceticism. Under treatment, his eyes continued to improve. "Yesterday for the first time," he reported to Julian, "I succeeded, for short stretches, in getting a single fixed image from both eyes together—a thing I have never had."[8] Between the studio and his study, he wrote constantly.

Completed during the early stages of the war, his *Grey Eminence* (1941), a life of the Bourbon Father Joseph of Paris, lamented the corruptibility of even the saintliest intentions when allied to the power of the state. And like Father Joseph, Huxley saw himself caught between visions of salvation and nightmares of politics. Quoting Matthew Arnold, his great uncle, he complained to Sybille Bedford that he'd been "born between two worlds, one dead, the other powerless to be born, and . . . made, in a curious way, the worst of both." Each world demanded commitment, "requir[ed] that one . . . be whole-heartedly *there*, at the moment," he said. "Whereas I have always tended to be somewhere else, in a world of analysis, unfavourable equally to Micawberish living, Tolstoyan art and contemplative spirituality. The title of my first book of stories, *Limbo*, was, I now see, oddly prophetic!"[9]

The Art of Seeing (1942) defended the unorthodox Bates Method and chastised medical science for ignoring the arts of prevention and restoration. Huxley's only wartime novel, *Time Must Have a Stop* (1944, its title an allusion to Hotspur's dying words), renewed William Propter's condemnation of those clock-bound obsessions that dominate people's lives. In its final scene (which hasn't aged a day in almost forty years), Sebastian Barnack runs his fingernail across the radio speaker and says: "One can either go on listening to the news—and of course the news is always bad, even when it sounds good. Or alternatively one can make up one's mind to listen to something else"—a theme that Huxley kept at the forefront of *The Perennial Philosophy* (1945), his anthology of the "Highest Common Factor" in the world's religions, which warned (among other things) against our addiction to newscasters and commentators. "St. John of the Cross would have called it indulgence," he wrote, "and the cultivation of disquietude for disquietude's sake." The clouds were beginning to lift, the darkness diminishing.

Within weeks of Huxley's completing *The Perennial Philosophy*, armistice in Europe was declared. Then the revelations of Auschwitz. And Hiroshima. (With an eerie prescience, he had written to Frieda Lawrence eighteen months earlier: "Of course one never knows; the [collapse] may go suddenly, with a bang.")[10] The day after Nagasaki's barely more credible destruction, Huxley wrote privately, "Thank God, we are to have peace very soon. But peace with atomic bombs hanging overhead." States armed by science with superhuman powers reminded him, he said, "of Gulliver being carried up to the roof by the King of Brobdingnag's palace by a gigantic monkey: reason, human decency and spirituality, which are strictly individual matters, find themselves in the clutches of the collective will, which has the mentality of a delinquent boy . . . [and] the physical power of a god."[11]

By war's end, his health and spiritual well-being needed more of mountain than desert; the Huxleys moved an hour away, to Wrightwood, whence they journeyed frequently to Los Angeles (Maria always driving) to the studio work Huxley found necessary to sustain them. The end of war had also liberated the polemicist in him. He began his pamphlet *Science, Liberty and Peace* (1946) by quoting Tolstoy to the effect that every so-called victory over Nature only increases the power of the state to oppress people's lives. Moreover, Nature itself would resist. "Treat Nature aggressively, with greed and violence and incomprehension," he wrote in a lengthy article called "The Double Crisis," and "wounded Nature will turn and destroy you."[12] He was also contemplating two novels, one set in fourteenth-century Siena around the life of St. Catherine, the other a futuristic society after atomic war.

Whether in the desert, the mountains, or the city (to which the Huxleys would return for good in 1949), California had become—with time, if not in the deepest sense—home. Europe had declined and fallen. New French writing was, it seemed to Huxley, "half heroism, half unutterable moral squalor."[13] "Aldous has no wish to go to England any more," said Maria. "He loved Italy, he loved France, but his home-sickness was only for England. That has gone now. It's dried up."[14] Almost ten years passed before the Huxleys set foot outside of Southern California, driving to New York in the fall of 1947—much more than halfway, culturally, back to the Europe of their past—for a family reunion. In New York, Huxley seemed to his wife reinvigorated, stimulated by the eastern climate and the people. She realized there how little she liked California; but for him Los Angeles kept its hold. "Unlike Dr. Johnson," he had earlier confided to Julian, "I prefer climate to conversation."[15] During the trip east, he abandoned work on the St. Catherine novel and began the other, this one set for the most part in twenty-second-century Los Angeles. By December they were back home. Huxley was writing scenarios, seeing his doctor daily (the major problems again bronchial), and getting well along with *Ape and Essence*—which by February was complete.

The heart of this second of Huxley's two Los Angeles novels is an ostensible film script dropped, in the twentieth century, from a studio trash wagon on its way to the incinerator. It is a strange scenario of a Satan-worshiping civilization inhabiting the radioactive ruins of Los Angeles in the year 2108, a century after World War Three. The metaphor of the transformed landscape had been with Huxley for several years. He had even "succeeded," he wrote privately, "in planting it in the *Bulletin of the Atomic Scientists.*" The question was this: "will the politicians go on with their lunatic game . . . ignoring the fact that the world they are squabbling over will shortly cease to exist in its old familiar form, but will be transformed, unless they mobilize all available intelligence and . . . good will, into one huge dust bowl . . . ?"[16]

In 2108, a boatload of scientists from New Zealand (whose grandfathers had been spared annihilation) poke their way past the ruins of coastal oil derricks, across a treeless, sand-covered plain of concrete, and into—inevitably—a large cemetery, desolate but for its weeds and statuary, and a motley band of Graverobbers. The Great Hollywood Necropolis of the twentieth century remains the only resource worth plundering.

The scientists are driven off by the ghouls, who capture the expedition's chief botanist, Dr. Poole. He is dragged into the local heart of darkness where the populace, lapsed into sullen barbarism, are presided over by hierarchies of devil chieftains and a priesthood of eunuchs. The people, it turns out, are atomic mutants who live without love in enforced celibacy—except for two weeks of annually sanctioned licentiousness. Men are valued only as laborers; women are damned as mere "vessels"; and any child more than slightly deformed—four out of five in these radioactive times—is sacrificed during torchlit ceremonies in the Los Angeles Coliseum, ritually disemboweled on an altar by the three-horned Patriarch of Pasadena. Anyone caught "in love," or practicing sex out of season, is arrested as a "Hot" and slaughtered.

Huxley had become convinced by war's end that world hunger was the future's greatest imperative; as a consequence, Dr. Poole, whose training makes him a potential adviser to the chieftains on food cultivation, is spared by His Eminence the Arch-Vicar (Lord of the Earth, Primate of California, Bishop of Hollywood). Echoing "The Double Crisis," the Arch-Vicar lectures Poole on the historic functions of "Progress" and "Nationalism," those two great ideas put into men's heads by the Devil: "Bigger and bigger," he sermonizes Poole, "richer and more powerful—and then, almost suddenly, hungrier and hungrier. . . . Conquerors of Nature, indeed! . . . Fouling the rivers, killing the wild animals, destroying the forests, washing the topsoil into the sea, burning up an ocean of petroleum, squandering the minerals it had taken the whole of geological time to deposit. An orgy of criminal imbecility. . . ." As enticement, Poole is given offices in the ruins of the University of Southern California, and offered priesthood—at the "eusual" price.

Unbeknownst to his patron, however, Poole has fallen in love during the annual two-week saturnalia. He has lost his innocence to Loola, a closet "Hot" with four nipples but otherwise quite a lovely throwback to Hollywood's twentieth century. He chooses escape. As the script closes, Poole and Loola make their way out of the nightmare of twenty-second-century Los Angeles, across the rugged San Gabriel Mountains, toward a colony of renegade "Hots" known to be thriving in the wilderness north of Fresno.

"I am choosing a Shakespearean title," Huxley wrote Cass Canfield as the novel neared completion. From Isabella's plea to the cruel Angelo in *Measure for Measure*, that title also illuminates both the continuity between Huxley's pre- and postwar visions of Los Angeles, and the shift. In contrast to merciful heaven,

. . . man, proud man,
Drest in a little brief authority—
Most ignorant of what he is most assured,
His glassy essence, like an angry ape,
Plays such fantastic tricks before high heaven
As make the angels weep . . . .

Angelo's little brief authority asserts itself in sexual tyranny; Jo Stoyte's in egomaniacal folly. But Jo's striving for immortality is so exuberant, and played out with such extravagant determination, that it is hard not to see in his portrayal at least a modicum of tainted admiration on the part of Huxley, for whom Hollywood and its folkways in the late 1930s provided an odd but comforting sanctuary. Overtly, of course, it is William Propter who speaks for Huxley, insisting that it is man's duty—and Jo's—to escape the tyranny of time, not by struggling with it (for such struggle is doomed to fail) but by rendering its passage inconsequential. Yet Huxley's devils are often more interesting than his philosophers and idealists; and Jo's crude vitality—especially as played against the static grayness of Propter's wisdom—invites a choice between their contrasting means for vanquishing time and death.

Nine years and another world war later, the tone has changed, and the choices have narrowed. In place of Jo Stoyte's bumptious acceptance of apehood over death against the advice of a down-home Jeffersonian philosopher "sitting on a bench under the largest of his eucalyptus trees," we are given an unwilled and apparently irrevocable mass descent into anthropoid barbarity, played out in a poisonous landscape and maintained by a cadre of philosopher priests whose cruelties Angelo or Jo could not have imagined. But Huxley could never quite resign himself to doom; peering into Hell would always pale and sicken him. So the horror of twenty-second-century Los Angeles is admittedly only a fabrication, a tale told in filmscript by a misanthrope, now dead, and found serendipitously on its way to the trash furnace. It is, moreover, a script whose "voice-over" narrator, like William Propter, reminds us, when all seems bleakest, that hate, unceasing restlessness, and chronic misery are the ape in us; that the essences most assured us, if only we will have them, are Love and Joy and Peace. That narrator's message, quite consistent with Huxley's enduring belief in the individual's potential for overcoming tyranny, imposes on the story a burden of hope that its scenes won't bear. Correspondingly, the awful sights and sounds and furies of the twenty-second century signify less than they might have as cautionary tale had Huxley not been so constitutionally bound to what he could call, near the end of his life fifteen years later, a "sense of the world's fundamental All-Rightness."[17] Evelyn Waugh's Los Angeles would bear no such ambivalence.

In February 1947, as Huxley contemplated images of both St. Catherine and postatomic society, and wrestled with the more immediate problems of bringing his "Gioconda Smile" to the screen, MGM was extending elaborate welcome to Waugh, who had come to Los Angeles to arrange adaptation of his recent *Brideshead Revisited.* Waugh, whose novels Huxley usually ignored, had not been to California before. The weary peace in Europe, and its political realignments, had deepened his already profound social pessimism.Arch Tory, ex–commando captain, and ardent Catholic convert, Waugh had returned from the war to his cherished country-squiredom, and at forty-three (nine years younger than Huxley) was already England's ranking literary curmudgeon. His diaries suggest that he hoped, in planning his visit to California, to exploit the place for another novel—in some as-yet-indefinite way that would combine America and death.Within the previous twelve months, Waugh had traveled to Nuremburg to observe the war trials. He had also gone to Spain, somewhat frivolously, for a conference commemorating a sixteenth-century Dominican jurist. The trials proved tedious, but the Spanish trip inspired a trenchant little satire on the postwar condition: *Scott-King's Modern Europe.* By that autumn, he was also contemplating a permanent move to Ireland, where several agents were searching out a suitable country estate. He was counting on the tidings the MGM offer would bring.

The Irish move was to be a retreat from an England that increasingly disenchanted him. His estate at Stinchcombe lay in the path of planned urban expansion. The British working class had become, in his eyes, increasingly slothful. Foreign policy was pure appeasement of the Soviet. Atlee's Labour government—"the grey lice," he called them—were making sure "that England as a great power is done for."[18]

In mid-November, with "*Scott-King* bowling effortlessly along to its end," Waugh received the cable to come to Hollywood. After a quick trip to Ireland, a distracted Christmas at Stinchcombe, and a painful operation on his hemorrhoids, he embarked, "full of cocaine, opium and brandy, feeble and low spirited," aboard the S.S. *America* for the States. Among his few diary notes on the crossing was an observation that "the only English on board . . . are traveling second class . . . while a curious proletarian colony of G.I. brides travels first class, another sign of the times."[19] After four days in New York, Waugh and his wife boarded the 20th Century Limited for Los Angeles, and a six-week stay there.

The place seemed to him, during the first few days, more like an outpost of empire than the center of an industry: "a city quarter-built. . . . full of vacant lots and filling stations and nondescript buildings and palm trees with a warm hazy light. . . . more like Egypt—the suburbs of Cairo or Alexandria—than anything in Europe."[20] The emphasis on youth (both real and feigned) and the disdain of age, reminded Waugh,as it had Huxley, of Tennyson's "Tithonus." "Here at the quiet limit of the world," in this barbarous region of rusty palm-leaf, music, and scrubby foothills, roamed many a white-haired shadow "wither[ing] slowly in[its] arms." Waugh quickly judged the film community "a people apart . . . like monks in a desert oasis, their lives revolving about a few shrines—half a dozen studios, two hotels, one restaurant; their sacred texts their own publicity and the local gossip columns. The only strangers they ever meet," he wrote, "are refugees from central Europe for whom the ease and affability of the place, seen against the background of the concentration camp, appear as supreme gods."[21] There was clear connection in Waugh's mind between expatriates from the shattered Old World and this subtropical City of Refuge in the New.

While *Gioconda Smile* reached completion under the guidance of Zoltan Korda,[22] the adaptation of *Brideshead* never got beyond story conference. Waugh insisted on retaining the novel's theological implications, while the studio wished to see it simply as a love story. Waugh haggled contemptuously through the conferences, despising the "trance" his scenarist seemed to be in, and the "ignorance" of the others about anything approximating art. He seemed as relieved as they when problems over the story's adulterous theme gave MGM an excuse to abandon the project.

The remainder of his six-week stay thus became a subsidized holiday. "Andrea Cowdin appointed herself our hostess," Waugh noted in his diary. "We lunched or dined there every day, went with her to parties and met all the most agreeable people at her house." One of the less agreeable was an old friend, Randolph Churchill, briefly in town, with whom he spent "a rather disgusting two days." Waugh also called upon the Archbishop of Los Angeles, and passed the morning with him arranging food parcels for Europe. Except for a Mount St. Mary's College colloquium, and dinner at Loyola University, there was no academic lionizing—a fact for which Waugh claimed to be grateful. Still intermittently in pain, he felt, with some pride, that he had antagonized most of the expatriate Englishmen he encountered, seeing them as "guiltily sensitive of criticism."[23] He did some lionizing of his own at "a highly secret first performance" of Chaplin's *Monsieur Verdoux*. Politics aside, Waugh respected Chaplin's "artistic conservatism" and felt a strong affinity between Chaplin's comic vision and his own. Whereas Huxley thought *Verdoux* an intolerable pastiche of murder, farce, and psychology, Waugh called it brilliant. He thought of Chaplin as one of Hollywood's only two artists. "We also went over to Walt Disney's studios," he wrote, and thereby paid his homage to the other.

Among Mrs. Cowdin's other dinner guests that winter was Sheila Milbanke, Lady Milbanke to others but an old friend of Waugh's, who expressed delight at having visited an extraordinary cemetery in Glendale, northeast of town, a place that fused religion and art in a way surpassing anything she had seen. Waugh went to Forest Lawn and was no less captivated. He told others he'd discovered "a Tivoli garden for the dead."[24] Frequently during the days that remained (an MGM limousine still at his disposal), he returned to Forest Lawn, combing the grounds, the chapels, and the mortuaries, coaxing the entrée due a visiting notable, getting "on easy terms with the chief embalmer," seeing "dozens of loved ones half painted," having lunch with Hubert Eaton, the founder. "It is wonderful literary raw material," he wrote his agent. "Aldous flirted with it in *After Many a Summer* but only with the superficialities. I am at the heart of it."[25] The juxtaposition that Waugh had earlier mused upon—between death and America—took form before his eyes in Forest Lawn. In unique and surprising ways, the place was giving him the metaphor he had hoped to find. His diary, which he'd put aside when *Brideshead* fizzled, was almost empty of usable detail; but from Forest Lawn he took away masses of printed material, from promotional pamphlets to training manuals explicit enough to explain techniques for removing the ghastly expressions from the faces of strangulated suicides. They were like deeds to the "deep mine of literary gold" he boasted of finding there.

Back at Stinchcombe (and still moving painfully with "the irksome consequences of my operation"), Waugh began to exercise his recollections and his materials. First he dashed off a humdrum article on Hollywood studios, "Why Hollywood is a Term of Disparagement," for the *Daily Telegraph*.[26] Then, for *Life Magazine*, he began a richer, more evocative comic essay on Forest Lawn, called "Death in Hollywood."[27] Still intent on Ireland, he made another, futile, trip to look at houses there. After returning in May, he finished the Forest Lawn essay and began work on *The Loved One*. He felt the writing went slowly, thought in fact that its pace reflected his own physical deterioration. One element in the novel's genesis, he admitted, was simply *memento mori*. Still, by early July the first draft was finished; and during a socially hectic summer, capped by a two-week trip to Scandinavia, Waugh completed the book. Feeling much aged and in waning health, he consoled himself on his forty-fourth birthday in October with having "written two good stories—*Scott-King's Modern Europe* and *The Loved One*—in the course of the year . . ." and having decided to remain in England.

Waugh was right. *Scott-King* remains a lively period piece, and *The Loved One* one of the most incisive and far-reaching satires of the twentieth century. The latter also internationalized the Hollywood Novel. Set in the film capital, centered on Whispering Glades (Waugh's mock-Whitmanian alias for Forest Lawn), *The Loved One* is not—except as metaphor—primarily about either. The studios and the cemetery took direct assaults in the earlier articles. The novel has a broader target. Where Hollywood novels by Americans—Fitzgerald, West, McCoy, O'Hara, Schulberg, and others— had all been microcosms of American decline; and Huxley's had

been parables of human nature that universalized their local settings; *The Loved One* explicitly makes Hollywood a metaphor for
the fate of western civilization in the mid-twentieth century. Less
than two years after revelation of the Holocaust, Waugh's Los
Angeles—with Whispering Glades and a satellite pet cemetery at
its center—has become the place to which the torch of European
barbarism has been passed, from a defeated Germany to an ascendant America, over the moribund body of English culture.

The design was clear. *The Loved One* was the first deliberately preplotted novel Waugh had written, "the conclusion firmly
in my mind when I c[a]me to give definite form to the beginning."[28]
The novel both opens and closes on its Englishmen. Sir Francis
Hinsley, Sir Ambrose Abercrombie, and the young poet Dennis
Barlow are three generations of English artist abroad in Hollywood.
The eldest, Sir Francis, has slipped down the greased pole of studio favor, and hangs himself. Sir Ambrose, more resilient in his
decline, upholds the great tradition by crisscrossing Hollywood
in his deerstalker cap and Inverness cape raising funds for the
respect he says "we limeys have to keep up." Dennis, an ex-officer
and "young man . . . of a generation which enjoys a vicarious intimacy with death," comes to Hollywood to write the life of Shel-
ley for the movies. Lassitude overcomes him, though, and he quits
the studio for a job in the pet cemetery. A victim of his time, Dennis still imagines himself the product "of an earlier civilization
with sharper needs." So he pursues Miss Aimée Thanatogenos, the
sleek but vacant cosmetician at Whispering Glades. Aimée speaks

> the tongue of Los Angeles; the sparse furniture of her mind
> . . . had been acquired at the local High School and
> University; she presented herself to the world dressed
> and scented in obedience to the advertisements; brain
> and body were scarcely distinguishable from the standard
> product, but the spirit—ah, the spirit was something
> apart; it had to be sought afar; not here in the musky
> orchards . . . but in the mountain air of the dawn, in the
> eagle-haunted passes of Hellas.

Aimée represents what the classical tradition has become, and
what Dennis can only apathetically pursue. When Aimée, torn
between her own attractions to Dennis and the chief mortician,
kills herself, Dennis burns the body, shakes down his rival, and

absconds with the money—something that Waugh himself hadn't the stomach to do.

Alongside English decline in the novel is the symbolic residue of the Third Reich, page after page of it. A bare two years after Hitler's destruction, the teeth of dead murder victims, as at Auschwitz, disappear from the police morgue in Los Angeles. Mr. Schultz, the surviving voice of German character, has become an American— and found(ed) in Hollywood a "Happier Hunting Ground," another cemetery and crematorium, this one for animals. Among the creatures consigned to its flames is a run-over dog owned by a family named Heinkel (after the German warplane). Upon its death, the Heinkels refuse to look at the body, or even to speak of the animal's fate. When Dennis picks up the carcass, Mr. Heinkel thanks him for "relieving me of a great responsibility." "This," Dennis replies, "is what the Happier Hunting Ground aims to do."

Schultz is Waugh's quintessential barbarian; Dennis the barbarian's cynical and calculating lieutenant. Schultz boasts that he has no time for reading. When Dennis tells him that most stories are "tragedies" anyway, Schultz replies, "I ain't got time for tragedies neither. Take an end of this casket"—a response that more than vaguely echoes Hermann Goering's quip, "Whenever I hear the word 'culture' I reach for my pistol." (Goering, whom Waugh had watched at the dock at Nuremburg, had recently cheated the hangman by destroying himself.)

Like Huxley, Waugh had long before predicted barbarian ascendancy. To Waugh, however, blame belonged not to our enthrallment with brief authority, but to the specific decline of the British upper class, and its brief authority. Where Huxley lamented man's surrender to politics, Waugh despised political and cultural surrender. By 1948, the year both *Ape and Essence* and *The Loved One* were published, the prophecy (whatever its source) had been fulfilled; but for Waugh its malignant spirit had passed over to America, to California, to Hollywood. What was more, the place was proving irresistible to a new generation of Englishmen like Dennis Barlow—as well as many of Waugh's and Huxley's own.

Hollywood, for Waugh, was the final resting place of a twenty-five-hundred-year-old civilization—a conception which (much more than Huxley's) invited the leitmotifs of earlier Hollywood novels. Though Waugh shifted the fictional center from the studios to the graveyard, the studio's characteristics—those details of moviemaking so vividly exploited by West and Fitzgerald and Schulberg—persist in Whispering Glades. Its grounds and "slumber rooms" abound with images of mask and facade. Electronic sound effects imitate the chirping of birds and buzzing of bees. In its parlors, the standards of costuming and makeup rival those at MGM. The jumble of stage sets in *The Day of the Locust, The Last Tycoon,* and *What Makes Sammy Run?* become, in Whispering Glades, an eclectic hodgepodge of architectures, landscapes, and statuary. The chief mortician, Mr. Joyboy, is as much a figure of awe within the gates as Monroe Stahr or Sammy Glick: a master director creating true-to-life roles with a cast of inert but compliant actors. The founder's dream, however, is not to create new cultural artifact, new life, but rather to plunder, through imitation, the treasures of other cultures so as to vitiate death. The dream, which in earlier Hollywood novels had been American and dying, became to Waugh the living death of western civilization.

The reach of Waugh's Hollywood metaphor is even clearer when looked at alongside *Scott-King's Modern Europe,* the other book of his discomfited forty-fourth year. The two books represent flip sides of the postwar western condition. Persistent confusions between illusion and reality—a convention of Hollywood novels—are equally evident in "modern Europe." Misleading facades and discordant identities, fusions of life with death, of the real with the ersatz, all these characteristics of the Hollywood necropolis have their counterparts in Neutralia, the skulking "modern European" country to which Scott-King travels. The international flavor of Whispering Glades—which Waugh makes much of in *The Loved One*—is paralleled by the ethnic conglomerate of Neutralia, much of it expatriate.

Even the "dimmest" of English intellectuals, Professor Scott-King, after a single encounter with modern Europe in its new totalitarian motley wants nothing more to do with it. But the younger, surer Dennis Barlow is drawn to Hollywood, where there are no bloody partisanships or political terror, but instead an alluring pseudo-melting-pot democracy where Europeans are decultured by choice, not intimidation. While the moribund Neutralia has only one, third-rate piece of cultural heritage—the seventeenth century poet Bellorius—Whispering Glades overflows with bogus copies of the treasures of western art. Anyone—even "good style Jews" willing to pay higher prices—can be buried near them and partake of their spurious spirit of regeneration.

The connection goes even further. Waugh expressly links the European past to the Hollywood present by revealing that Bellorius (whom Scott-King has gone to Neutralia to commemorate) devoted his best known poem to "an imaginary island of the New World where in primitive simplicity, untainted by tyranny or dogma, there subsisted a virtuous, chaste and reasonable community." The echo is clear here of the early-sixteenth-century Spanish poet, Montalvo, who conjured a misty, half-mythical island in the western sea, a terrestrial paradise populated by Amazons, griffins, and other exotica, and called the place California.

Scott-King's Neutralia and the bizarre yet easily recognizable Hollywood of *The Loved One* were indeed sister metaphors, forged by the same dyspeptic but deeply committed imagination—an imagination which, no less than Huxley's, wandered between two worlds, one dead, the other powerless to be born. *Scott-King* came directly out of Waugh's brief encounter with Franco's Spain in 1946, to which he grafted bitter impressions of Yugoslavia under Tito. *The Loved One* was created out of what he called his "overexcitement with the scene" in Los Angeles, a city that seemed, in early 1947, to be destiny's loved one. Neither book has any of the ambivalence that characterized Huxley's two "Hollywood" parables, nor pallor over staring into Hell. To Waugh, after the war, Los Angeles and Neutralia were as opposite sides of the same coin of the realm—a realm destroyed. There was no refuge north of Fresno.

Notes

1. I have examined the genesis of the Hollywood Novel, and the consistencies of style and theme that unify that genre, in my *Tycoons and Locusts: A Regional Look at Hollywood Fiction of the 1930s* (Carbondale: Southern Illinois University Press, 1973).

2. *Letters of Aldous Huxley*, ed. Grover Smith (New York: Harper & Row, Publishers, 1969), p. 428.

3. Sybille Bedford, *Aldous Huxley: A Biography* (New York: Alfred A. Knopf/Harper & Row, 1974), p. 372.

4. *Letters of Aldous Huxley*, p. 440.

5. *Aldous Huxley: 1894–1963, A Memorial Volume*, ed. Julian Huxley (London: Chatto & Windus, 1965), p. 94.

6. Bedford, p. 393.

7. *Letters of Aldous Huxley*, p. 454.

8. Ibid., p. 450.

9. Ibid., p. 476.

10. Ibid., p. 501.

11. Ibid., p. 532.

12. Aldous Huxley, "The Double Crisis," *Themes and Variations* (London: Chatto & Windus, 1950), p. 271.

13. *Letters of Aldous Huxley*, p. 541.

14. Bedford, p. 449.

15. *Letters of Aldous Huxley*, p. 554.

16. *Letters of Aldous Huxley*, p. 578.

17. Laura Huxley, *This Timeless Moment: A Personal View of Aldous Huxley* (New York: Farrar, Straus & Giroux, 1968), p. 312.

18. *The Diaries of Evelyn Waugh*, ed. Michael Davie (London: Weidenfeld & Nicolson, 1976), p. 663.

19. Ibid., p. 669.

20. Ibid., p. 672.

21. Evelyn Waugh, "Why Hollywood is a Term of Disparagement," *New Directions in Prose and Poetry*, no. 10 (New York: New Directions, 1948), pp. 34–35.

22. The film, directed by Korda and starring Charles Boyer, was released the following year with a different title. Huxley wrote his cousin Gervas: "The all-powerful Jewish gentlemen in charge of distribution have elected to call the thing *A Woman's Vengeance*, and there is nothing to be done about it" (*Letters of Aldous Huxley*, p. 576).

23. *The Diaries of Evelyn Waugh*, p. 675.

24. Harold Acton, *Memoirs of an Aesthete: 1939–1969* (New York: Viking Press, 1970), p. 224.

25. *The Letters of Evelyn Waugh*, ed. Mark Amory (New Haven and New York: Ticknor & Fields, 1980), p. 247.

26. Evelyn Waugh, "Why Hollywood is a Term of Disparagement," *Daily Telegraph and Morning Post* (London) 30 April 1947.

27. Evelyn Waugh, "Death in Hollywood," *Life*, 29 September 1947, pp. 73–84.

28. *The Diaries of Evelyn Waugh*, p. 680.

Bibliographic Note

The three novels primarily in question are, of course, Aldous Huxley, *After Many a Summer Dies the Swan* (New York: Harper & Row Publishers, 1939) and *Ape and Essence* (New York: Harper & Row, Publishers, 1948); and Evelyn Waugh, *The Loved One* (Boston: Little, Brown and Co., 1948), the revised edition of which was published by Chapman and Hall (London, 1965). Of the three novels, only *The Loved One* is presently in print in the United States. Waugh's "Death in Hollywood" was published, and illustrated, in *Life* (29 September 1947). "Why Hollywood is a Term of Disparagement," published originally in the *Daily Telegraph and Morning Post* (London), 30 April 1947, is reprinted in Evelyn Waugh, *A Little Order*, ed. Donat O'Donnell (London: Eyre Methuen, 1977). Also interesting to read alongside *The Loved One* is Waugh's earlier satire on the motion picture business in London: "Excursion in Reality" in Waugh's *Tactical Exercise* (Boston: Little, Brown and Co., 1954).

Since Huxley lived for a quarter-century in Southern California, substantial portions of the *Letters of Aldous Huxley*, ed. Grover Smith (New York: Harper & Row, Publishers 1969) are grist for readers interested in Los Angeles as a literary vantage point. Smaller portions of *The Diaries of Evelyn Waugh*, ed. Michael Davie (London: Weidenfeld & Nicolson, 1976) and *The Letters of Evelyn Waugh*, ed. Mark Amory (New Haven and New York: Ticknor & Fields, 1980) focus upon the region. Huxley's views are largely those of an insider, views of California as an adopted home. Waugh's, on the other hand, are, like his earlier portraits of Latin America and Ethiopia, those of a cynical, short-term alien. Indeed, those views reflect perfectly Waugh's spiritual notion of man as a displaced person, "by nature an exile . . . never self-sufficient or complete on this earth" (Waugh, *Robbery Under the Law, The Mexican Object Lesson* [London: Chapman and Hall, 1939]. p. 17).

The biographies of both writers—Sybille Bedford, *Aldous Huxley: A Biography* (New York: Alfred A. Knopf/Harper & Row, 1974), and Christopher Sykes, *Evelyn Waugh* (Boston: Little, Brown and Co. 1975)—are indispensable, though frustrating in their limitations. Huxley's early days in Los Angeles are entertainingly recalled by Anita Loos in *Aldous Huxley: 1894–1963, A Memorial Volume*, ed. Julian Huxley (London: Chatto & Windus, 1965); his latter years there are remembered by his second wife, Laura Huxley, *This Timeless Moment:A Personal View of Aldous Huxley* (New York: Farrar, Straus & Giroux, 1968). Several interesting vignettes of Waugh in Los Angeles are told by Frances Donaldson, *Evelyn Waugh: Portrait of a Country Neighbor* (London: Weidenfeld and Nicolson, 1968), and by Harold Acton, *Memoirs of an Aesthete: 1939–1969* (New York: Viking Press 1970).

My own views of the "Hollywood novel"—as American genre—are spelled out in Walter Wells, *Tycoons and Locusts: A Regional Look at Hollywood Fiction of the 1930s* (Carbondale: Southern Illinois University Press, 1973). *After Many a Summer, Ape and Essence,* and *The Loved One* are, I think, more fully appreciable as adjuncts to the genre when read alongside the Los Angeles novels of James M. Cain, Nathanael West, Raymond Chandler, Scott Fitzgerald, and the rest.

NINE

Home and Transcendence in Los Angeles Fiction

Charles L. Crow

Facing west from California's shores,
Inquiring, tireless, seeking what is yet unfound,
I, a child, very old, over waves, towards the house of
    maternity, the land of migrations, look afar,
Look off the shores of my Western sea, the circle almost circled;
For starting westward from Hindustan, from the vales of Kashmere,
From Asia, from the north, from the God, the sage, and the hero,
From the south, from the flowery peninsulas and the spice islands,
Now I face home again, very pleas'd and joyous,
(But where is what I started for so long ago?
And why is it yet unfound?)
—Walt Whitman, "Facing West from California's Shores"

What has Whitman's speaker been seeking? "Gold and adventure" might seem the obvious response, yet I suggest that "home and

transcendence" are the enduring answers in the American imagination. Home is not just *a* home, but *the* home, the place of wholeness which the wanderer has imagined, and the transcendence of
the individual or of society which must occur when this resting
place is found and the seeker is worthy of it. These themes are
found of course elsewhere in American literature, but are re-
stated here with distinguishing intensity in California, for reasons
clear in Whitman's poem. Though the speaker faces the old home
of Asia he will not reach it. The main thrust of American migration ends on California's shores. "What is yet unfound" must be
found here, or not at all. The western landscape, with its incredi-
ble variety representing infinite choices and opportunities, holds
out a promise of success. Yet Whitman's poem is guarded. Joyous
yet puzzled, old and young, the wanderer awaits either renaissance
or cultural collapse. These are precisely the extremes explored in
literature about California.

These issues focus most insistently on Los Angeles.[1] Since
the completion of the rail lines into Southern California in the
1880s, it has been Los Angeles which has drawn the greatest number of immigrants and their dreams. As the perceptive British
scholar Reyner Banham observes, "San Francisco was plugged into
California from the sea," but "Southern Californians came, pre-
dominantly, overland to Los Angeles, slowly transversing the
whole North American land-mass and its evolving history."[2] Arriving in the Los Angeles basin, they found a landscape which, unlike
most of the rest of California and the American West, did not dominate its inhabitants with awesome spaces, looming mountains, or
craggy seaside cliffs. Indeed, the landscape of the basin still seems
composed of light and weather. The transverse range often is in-
visible in mist or, now, smog, and the hills and sandy washes are
subdued easily to human will or whimsy. Only occasionally, in
earthquake, flood, or fiery Santa Ana wind is human frailty revealed.[3] Set in motion upon this landscape to seek their own versions of home and transcendence, fictional characters succeed or
fail according to the artist's imaginative response to this ambiguous place.

These generalizations can be supported by dozens of historical, journalistic, and literary texts. In a short study only a hand-

ful of suggestive and, I hope, evocative examples can be given, the beginning of a structure upon which the reader can build. My illustrations are Evelyn Waugh's *The Loved One*, Joan Didion's *Play It as It Lays*, Marc Norman's *Bike Riding in Los Angeles*, and Hisaye Yamamoto's "Yoneko's Earthquake": two well-known novels, an obscure one, and a recently rediscovered short story. The authors are a distinguished literary tourist, two native Southern Californians of different ethnic backgrounds, and a Sacramento-born writer who has adopted Los Angeles as a second home. The search for common themes, then, is made among writers and works as varied as possible.

I

The case against Los Angeles is a litany told by hostile, bewildered tourists as a spell against seduction: the city is an alienating, mindless place, which drives its inhabitants to "werewolf" freeway speeding, despair, drugs, divorce, and violence. As Marc Norman's narrator Bike Rider observes, journalists from the east always "say the same thing: Los Angeles is the Unreal City."[4] The native Angeleno is likely to respond with statistics comparing rates of crime and automobile accidents to those of other cities. But such objections are merely logical and miss the cultural symbolism of the case against Los Angeles. For its critics, the "stuff" of Southern California, "split-level ranch houses and bloated shopping centers and drive-in banks" are opposed to "humanity."[5] To attack Los Angeles is to participate in a debate over the direction of our culture, to objectify our nightmares of chaos and collapse. Misguided souls may lodge there, but the Unreal City can never be "home," a place of peace and stable tradition. In its hubris, Los Angeles deserves the purifying flames which will ensure that this twisted future will not appear elsewhere. The rhetoric of apocalypse has become one of the literary traditions of Los Angeles, a convention treated with sophistication in *The Loved One* and *Play It as It Lays.*

The Loved One is a story of alienation, or, to put it slightly differently, of home and transcendence. The novel begins by introducing a tropical landscape, two Englishmen on a veranda, and a dry water hole—and forces the reader to register an amused double-take. We realize, first, that this is not a desolate jungle outpost, but a house by an empty swimming pool in Los Angeles. Then we acknowledge Waugh's satirical jab: Los Angeles is *exactly* a desolate outpost, and nothing else. The novel echoes the tradition—nurtured by Conrad, Maugham, and Greene—of Englishmen gone to seed at the antipodes. One of the Englishmen on the veranda hangs himself, while the other, the novel's protagonist Dennis Barlow, ignores warnings against "going native." He pursues a local priestess, Aimée, who is perfumed with "Jungle Venom," and the resulting love affair leads to the suicide of this unfortunate native girl.

The novel stresses the impossibility of making a home in this inhospitable place. Dennis Barlow's attempt to find a home in Los Angeles is of course foredoomed; the natives themselves have no sense of home. Aimée lives in a concrete cell, and her boss Joyboy's tract house is a horror where his mother's malevolent screeches are indistinguishable from those of the parrot. Waugh's implications, however, go beyond local satire. The whole country, not just Los Angeles, is a "land of waifs and strays."[6] Waugh once observed that there is "no such thing as an American"; that is, America is a land without a people, merely filled with confused refugees who have failed to produce a civilization of their own.[7] They are easy targets for satire because they engage in unconscious parody of real civilization. They only manipulate broken symbols, the meaning of which they have forgotten.

Yet, strangely enough, Los Angeles does create a homecoming and a transcendence for Dennis Barlow.

Throughout the novel, Waugh has delighted in parodying, within the Los Angeles setting, not only American popular culture, but the patterns that American artists and scholars have found central to American experience: manifest destiny, the frontier, the Garden of Eden, and the Henry Jamesian pattern of American innocence versus European sophistication. It is subtly appropriate that an American poem, Poe's "To Helen," is used by Waugh in the book's last pages to knit together the strands of theme and plot. As Aimée's body burns in the crematorium of the Happier Hunting Ground pet cemetery, Dennis quotes from the poem, inserting his beloved's name for Helen's, and changing tense:

Aimée, thy beauty was to me,
Like those Nicean barks of yore,
That gently, o'er a perfumed sea
The weary way-worn wanderer bore
To his own native shore.

"It's really remarkably apposite, is it not?" Dennis cruelly asks of his rival, the mortician Mr. Joyboy (pp. 162–63).

The appositeness only superficially concerns Dennis's planned return to his own native shore, England, with money coerced from Mr. Joyboy and the local cricket club. Poe's poem, after all, is about the transcendence of the artist, a theme that parallels Dennis's own painful transformation. Helen begins the poem as a real woman, but is metamorphosed to Helen of Troy, leading the poet to contemplate the perfect forms of antiquity. He is brought "home," not literally, but in his imagination, "To the glory that was Greece,/ And the Grandeur that was Rome." Finally, seen "statue-like in "yon brilliant window-niche" (as Aimée is seen through the window in the crematorium door), Helen become a goddess or icon, then is identified with Psyche, or the poet's own soul.[8]

The Loved One reflects Waugh's own belief that the artist is created by the savage destruction of innocence, the "heart" which Dennis must leave behind:

He was carrying back instead a great, shapeless chunk of
experience, the artist's load; bearing it home to his
ancient and comfortless shore; to work on it hard and
long, for God knew how long—it was the moment of
vision for which a lifetime is often too short. (pp.
163–64)

The grotesqueness of Los Angeles has provided this vision, and the California girl Aimée, who boasted of the way bodies were "transfigured" by embalming at Whispering Glades cemetery, has become his muse.

Homecoming and transcendence are also the obsessive goals in Joan Didion's *Play It as It lays,* sought by the tortured California girl who is its heroine, Maria Wyeth, on the "flawless burning concrete"[9] of the freeways and in the desert, the major symbols of the novel.

The language of Los Angeles, writes Reyner Banham, is movement. For Banham, who learned to drive in order to "read

Los Angeles in the original,"[10] the freeways are among the wonders of the world. Banham learned the exhilaration of the freeways, learned that "the extreme concentration required in Los Angeles seems to bring on a state of heightened awareness that some locals find mystical." Didion quotes this passage approvingly in her essay "Bureaucrats" and observes that to participate in (as opposed to merely driving on) the freeways "is the only secular communion in Los Angeles."[11]

Thus the thousands of miles Maria logs on the Corvette are her way of seeking this temporary transcendence:

> She drove it as a riverman runs a river, every day more attuned to its currents, its deceptions, and just as a riverman feels the pull of the rapids in the lull between sleeping and waking, so Maria lay at night in the still of Beverly Hills and saw the great signs soar overhead at seventy miles an hour. . . . Again and again she returned to an intricate stretch just south of the interchange where successful passage from the Hollywood onto the Harbor required a diagonal move across four lanes of traffic. On the afternoon she finally did it whithout once braking or once losing the beat on the radio she was exhilarated, and that night she slept dreamlessly. (pp. 15–16)

In a life where "nothing applies" (p. 4), the participation in the freeways is a way of creating order through the exercise of skills. It is an action recalling that of Hemingway's characters, and suggests, also, through the image of the raftsman, the competency of the pioneering ancestors whose self-reliance Maria (if no one else) believes she inherits. Above all, the communion of the freeway is a method for Maria to escape the house in which she imagines the embryo of her aborted second child choking the plumbing, a house that can never be home.

As she roams the freeways, Maria's itinerary becomes a projection of her inner drama. She drives everywhere, but most often she is drawn into the desert, that vast and troubling presence which most Angelenos would like to ignore. The paradox of Los Angeles, geographically, is that it is both a seacoast and a desert city. In spite of the ocean and apparently plentiful water for domestic use, Los Angeles is a fragile growth, like the imported vegetation of its urban landscape, that would wither without irrigaton. As Evelyn

Waugh noted, the ecology of the city is so fragile that it cannot hope to survive very long; at some point the aqueducts that are its arteries will fail (they could be snapped at any instant by a few terrorist bombs) and the city will disappear, leaving only scattered strange artifacts like the statues of Forest Lawn, over which the archaeologists of a future age will puzzle.[12] The desert, lurking in the east, is the city's doom. Out of the desert blow the Santa Ana winds, drying the hillsides and spreading the brush fires which smoulder in the background of the novel. "The city burning," Didion wrote elsewhere, "is Los Angeles's deepest image of itself."[13] Thus the echoes of Eliot's *The Waste Land* and Yeats's "The Second Coming"—the language of apocalypse—come naturally enough from the city's perilous setting.

For Maria this sterile land is many things, beginning with the childhood home she has lost. Silver Wells, Nevada—a gas station, a diner, and a railroad siding—must have been unbearably bleak to her, but even its name suggests the vaguely legendary aura of the mining days of the frontier, a spirit perpetuated by her father and his partner Benny Austin, men with great appetites, hopes, and willingness to gamble. When Maria flees Los Angeles on one occasion, driving a Ferrari she has taken from an actor who has brutalized her, she drives deep into the desert, confusedly seeking her father's grave. But in other moods Maria knows that the past— her own childhood, and the optimism of the old West—cannot be recovered. "There isn't any Silver Wells," Maria tells Benny Austin at their last meeting. The pathetic town has been replaced by a missile range. The only legacy of the frontier now appears in the prefabricated images of Hollywood westerns, such as the one her husband, Carter, is shooting in the desert.

Deserts always have been places of prophecy and truth-seeking, and the message of this desert, "the hard empty white core of the world," is annihilation, nothingness. There Maria hears the story of the man who walked into the desert seeking God and was killed by a rattlesnake. There she finally accepts the precept that "nothing applies." This is the lesson taught by BZ, the character who best expresses the meaning of the landscape. The conversations of BZ and Maria, on the location of Carter's western movie, beome increasingly cryptic, the exclusive code words of master and disciple moving into occult brotherhood:

"You're getting there," BZ said.
"Getting where."
"Where I am." (p. 192)

BZ's final lesson is his suicide, committed in Maria's presence because she alone understands its meaning, has been with him "out there where nothing is."

If Maria knows "what 'nothing' means," yet "keeps on playing," it is, as she tells us, for Kate, her daughter. Images of "the family they might have been" float through Maria's mind. Confined in an expensive sanitarium after BZ's death, she still has her "plans": "(1) get Kate, (2) live with Kate alone, (3) do some canning. Damson plums, apricot preserves. Sweet India relish and pickled peaches. Apple chutney. Summer squash succotash" (p. 210). This is courage in the face of nothingness, existential self-definition, yet infinitely sad and pathetic. It is only "on film they might have seemed a family." In the work of art she might have found transcendence and home. But Maria is only an actress, not a film maker, and the film will never be made.

II

Didion's picture of Los Angeles is perhaps the most compellingly bleak of any writer's. The key event of the book is Maria's abortion, and sterility is its dominant mood. Yet it is not just Los Angeles that is sterile: it is the whole modern world, the way we live now. Didion makes no smug contrasts between arid freeways and the humane sidewalks of New York. Maria's first breakdown, in fact, occurred in New York, and the pattern of her destructive relationship with men began there. The author's own account of her eight years of life in New York, though she loved the city, includes the very words eastern critics always apply to Los Angeles: "exotic," "mirage," "temporary," "hallucinatory." Didion describes how she came to understand that "it is distinctly possible to stay too long at the Fair,"[14] and returned home to the solid reality of California.

Yet "home" is an ambiguous term to Didion, as it is to most adult Americans, an ambiguity which she explores in her often-reprinted essay "On Going Home." The term means for her both the Sacramento home where she grew up, and Los Angeles, where she works and lives with her husband and daughter. Didion is both an outsider and an insider in the city, possessing a combination of knowledge and distance reflected in her savage, clinical, painful novel.

Marc Norman's *Bike Riding in Los Angeles,* like *Play It as It Lays,* is a brief novel with lots of blank white space, and most of the causal relationships left out. Yet the books are quite different. Didion's is a work of entropy, where things fall apart because "nothing applies." Norman, like other California writers of the fifties and sixties (especially Richard Brautigan, whose influence is perhaps too apparent here), works in the opposite way, making strange juxtapositions, forcing the reader to make new imaginative connections. Norman's hero, Bike Rider, pedals through the city in search of its past and its meaning, and his own.

Thus a key chapter of the book is "Old Neighborhood," Bike Rider's homecoming to the section of the city "between Pico and Venice, and Hauser and Fairfax." The streets are quiet and empty as he rides through them, and he remembers that it was always so: "There are no voices, no shouts from the kitchens, no whoops from the halls, no radios on, no kids out in front damming the gutters with Popsickle sticks" (p. 39). These are the silent streets that have struck Wilfrid Sheed and other eastern pundits as eery and sinister, proof of the alienation of the place, so devoid of the jostling life and casual curbside meetings of eastern cities; of everything, in fact, that traditionally defines "neighborhood." Understanding this, Bike Rider is disturbed:

> All this barrenness bothers him, bothers him a lot, both as a writer and as a child of the neighborhood.
>
> As a writer, selfishly he supposes, but then this is supposed to be his first-novel neighborhood. All the other writers he knows have one—some special corner in a mad city, some great soup from which they ladle all those wonderful laughing Italians and those charming drunk Irish and the candy-store ethics and the strong widows and all the lovers padding around in their socks with their shoes in their hands, all those rich chunks of things that give his friends' novels their tang and truth. (p. 40)

Not having this sort of neighborhood to remember, to come home to, Bike Rider feels cheated, and wonders, with a shock, if he has grown up "as bland and arid" as the street. This fear, which corresponds to frequent criticisms of Southern Californians, provokes as a response a quotation from Louis Adamic's 1932 novel, *Laughing in the Jungle*, which describes the creation of residential Los Angeles by Americans who came "with a conception of the good community, which was embodied in single-family houses, located on large lots, surrounded by landscaped lawns and isolated from business activities" (p. 41). Bike Rider is heir to these immigrants who came to California's shore fleeing those first novel neighborhoods, considering them "congested, impoverished, filthy, immoral, transient, uncertain"; and recognizing himself as created by their historic dream, Bike Rider can resolve to accept and "be kind to himself."

So Bike Rider's first novel, which we are reading, is not like those eastern first novels of his friends, with the laughing Italians and other fixtures that he gently parodies. It is, instead, a novel of alternatives, constructed out of fragments of his own California dreams and those of Angelenos who preceded him and left their traces on local history and on the Los Angeles cityscape. He explores "Los Angeles Dream Zones," recalling Abbott Kinney, the cigarette tycoon who developed the fantasy landscape of Venice, and remembers Edward Doheny, who "dreamt of oil," and whose derricks transformed the economy of Los Angeles and coincidentally ruined the "placid lagoons and glittering canals" of Venice. In a fantasy sequence he meets Andreas Pico and discusses with him the days of the old Californios, whose memory survives only faintly in Southern California place and street names like Pico Boulevard, Nieto Lane, Yorba Street, Verdugo Road, and Dominguez Hills.

In naming himself Bike Rider, and making the first event of the book the purchase of a bicycle, the hero-narrator commits himself to a Los Angeles novel in which freeways and cars are scarcely mentioned. The city, blurred by the automobile's speed, comes into sharper focus on a bike, allowing the narrator to discover, for example, an overlooked cornfield near Olympic Boulevard where he talks with an aging Japanese gardener, relic of an earlier era, and muses over the patterns of ethnic settlement. But

the bicycle has a still greater significance, based on its representing a symbolic alternative not only to the automobile but to the
whole contemporary matrix of destructive technology. This symbolism is dramatized by a movie which Bike Rider watches on
television. The film is an espionage melodrama (Norman's fabrication, of course) in which the Wright brothers, horrified by the
use of their invention in World War I, volunteer to penetrate the
German lines and destroy the warplanes of Von Richtofen's famous
squadron. The first airplanes, after all, were created with bicycle
technology. But if the bicycle's progeny have become corrupt machines which serve mankind's rapacity, the bicycle itself remains
incorruptible; it is the one completely benign machine, which (as
Norman imagines, at least) cannot be put to destructive use. In a
novel written in the sixties, with the Vietnam War shadowing its
margins, the celebration of the bicycle suggests a way to return,
culturally, to a point of missed opportunity and choose the road
not taken.

In his search for this new future, Bike Rider is tutored by
Phantom Bike Rider, a nude figure riding a gold and sugar bicycle.
Phantom Bike Rider is a distant relative of such fictional California gurus as Norris's Vanamee, Steinbeck's Doc, Kerouac's Japhy
Ryder, and perhaps even Didion's BZ, characters who combine
practical skill and a mystical harmony with the landscape. Thus
Phantom Bike Rider can announce to the narrator, as they sit in
Hussong's Cantina in Ensenada, that the moment has arrived when
they occupy "the center of the universe." By the end of the novel,
however, Norman implies that Phantom Bike Rider is renouncing
his role, and his symbolic title, in favor of his successful disciple.
He is last seen with a basket mounted on his legendary bicycle, do-
mestically carrying the picnic lunch packed by his new girlfriend,
Sunny. Before they leave, Sunny tells Bike Rider that "Charles"
speaks of him often: "He says you're not very holy, but you're
working on it" (p. 120). The novel ends at a moment of expected
transcendence for the narrator, and a hint of transcendence for society as well. The last chapter reports that Bike Rider's old ortho-
dontist, charged with treason for aiding draft resisters, has "packed
the Continental and fled the country" (p. 122). "Good News," he
titles his last chapter, and closes the book by again chortling,
"Good News" (p. 122)!

III

Bike Rider's gentle zaniness and his hope for renewal are certainly products of the 1960s, yet grounded (as were many extravagances of that era) in the history of California. At times Bike Rider's optimism seems naive, at least now, but it usually is redeemed by irony and a sense of play. Thus Bike Rider's account of being wakened by the "Great 1971 Earthquake" leads him to imagine that "a bicycle might have come in handy if things had been worse. He could have gotten his family out on a bike. While the freeways collapsed and the chasms gaped, he could have made it with them, twining among the jammed cars and portaging around the rubble" (p. 102). In evoking the image of the earthquake, Norman is sporting with the greatest of California nightmares, which, in Los Angeles literature, is often blended with the apocalyptic vision of the city burning.

The horror of earthquake seldom has been captured successfully in fiction. Perhaps this is because earthquakes are not only unpredictable (as yet), but lack anything like the ominous overture—the thickening skies, the swirling approaching clouds—that sometimes precedes tornadoes and hurricanes. Earthquakes are such abrupt, random events that they are difficult to weave into the order of a story. The obvious solution—to make the earthquake a correlative to the emotional climax of the characters—usually appears contrived and unsatisfying. Among the few works successful in portraying this fact of the Los Angeles landscape is Hisaye Yamamoto's gem-like story, "Yoneko's Earthquake."

Yamamoto recreates the rural surroundings of Los Angeles in the early 1930s, a time when the landscape was "one vast orange grove"[15] broken occasionally by a truck farm such as that operated by Yoneko's parents. It was a fading way of life, as the author knew, writing twenty years later. By the 1950s the towns near Los Angeles, with their feed and seed stores, their Sunkist and Pure Gold packing houses and P.E. lines, were fast losing their agricultural character and becoming indistinguishable suburbs. And, of course, the Japanese, who had played an important role in the development of California agriculture, had lost most of their lands. Yoneko Hosoume, born in 1923, would have spent most of her teens in a resettlement camp. All of this, known alike by reader and author, is unstated in Yamamoto's story. Instead, it is the Long Beach earthquake of 1933 that demonstrates the fragility of the dream of home nourished by Mr. and Mrs. Hosoume.

Yamamoto uses the narrative technique of James's *What Maisie Knew*, following the consciousness of the ten-year-old girl who understands only a part of the adult world around her. Yoneko plays with her little brother Seigo and watches the activities of the farm; she admires the young Filipino farm worker, Marpo, who explains the novel religion of Christianity to her; she loses her faith when her prayers fail to stop the aftershocks of the merciless earthquake; she grieves over the sudden departure of Marpo and the death (apparently from appendicitis) of her little brother. Other events, such as the secretive gift of a ring from her mother, and the trip to a Japanese hospital in Los Angeles, where the children had to wait outside in the car, are apparently without meaning to Yoneko.

The reader, however, sees behind these events to the tragedy of the Hosoumes' marriage. Yoneko does not understand that her mother, apparently much younger than Mr. Hosoume (a "half-opened rose," someone calls her), would be also attracted to the handsome Marpo. The earthquake causes a power line to fall across her husband's automobile, shattering his nerves and reducing him to partial invalidism, while Marpo and Mrs. Hosoume assume the responsibility for the farm. Surely the ring, which Mrs. Hosoume gives to Yoneko, telling her to say she found it, is a gift from Marpo, and indicates that they have become lovers. Though Mr. Hosoume joins his wife for a time in praising Marpo's indispensability, his suspicions and the tensions within the household rise. An argument between the Hosoumes about Yoneko's use of nail polish circles around the issues of American and traditional Japanese values, Mr. Hosoume's authority, and, distantly, the sexual implications of cosmetics:

> "That's quite enough of your insolence," he said. Since he was speaking in Japanese, his exact accusation was that she was *nama-iki*, which is a shade more revolting than being merely insolent.
> "*Nama-iki, nama-iki?*" said Mrs. Hosoume, "How dare you? I'll not have anyone calling me *nama-iki.*"
> At that, Mr. Hosoume went up to where his wife was

ironing and slapped her smartly on the face. It was the
first time he had ever laid hands on her. (p. 354)

At this point Marpo, "who happened to be in the room reading a
newspaper" intervenes, laying a hand on Mr. Hosoume's shoulder
and saying, "The children are here, the children."

Although Marpo is ordered to mind his own business, he
has voiced the tacit assumption in this drama: the children must
not understand. Naturally enough, the children are not told the
reason for the visit to the hospital, which occurs at the time of
Marpo's disappearance. The children are told only that Mrs. Hosoume had received "some necessary astringent treatment," and
are cautioned to tell no one of the trip to the city. The illegal abortion is the central event of the story (as Maria's abortion is the
central event of *Play It as It Lays*), and symbolically corresponds
to the earthquake that indirectly causes it. The Hosoume's idyllic
way of life is destroyed. After the death of Yoneko's brother, Seigo,
Mrs. Hosoume becomes emotionally unstable, a convert to Christianity (Marpo's religion), and believes that her son's death is punishment for her sins. "Never kill a person, Yoneko," Mrs. Hosoume
warns, "because if you do, God will take from you someone you
love." Yoneko does not pause to ponder the ambiguities of this
statement—was the person taken Seigo or Marpo?—but pours out,
"I don't believe in that, I don't believe in God" (p. 357). Her faith
and much of her home have been destroyed in the earthquake and
its complicated aftershocks; her parents' dreams no longer hold her.

The vulnerable child, however, has discovered a power that
she conceals from her parents. Throughout the story she has been
fascinated with songs, word games, and unexpected rhymes. Now,
"whenever the thought of Seigo crossed her mind, she instantly
began composing a new song, and this worked very well" (p. 375).
The theme of the story is the birth of Apollo: out of the Hosoumes'
suffering, the sterility and wreckage of Yoneko's earthquake, the
artist is created.

IV

Yamamoto's story reminds us that among the Americans
facing west from California's shores are many who see Asia as the
"land of maternity" in a more literal sense than as the shadowy

origin of European *völkerwanderung* imagined by Walt Whitman. A complete study of the ideas of home projected upon California would include those of its many ethnic groups, including the Chinese vision of Gold Mountain, the mythic Aztlán of the Chicano, and whatever shattered memories may remain among the California Indians to whom the place was home first. The paradoxes of California remain precisely as Whitman stated them; the "I" of the poem is far more complex, however, than he realized.

Bike Rider admits of Los Angeles that "nobody's ever explained why, with all those people, there's no sense of a city, no feeling for a shared geographical experience" (p. 67). The symbolic capital of the state—the capital of its symbols—Los Angeles expresses all of its historic contradictions. Alienation and disorder are of course the basic stuff of American literature; it is not surprising that this disturbing city has so often evoked what Waugh called that "zone of insecurity in the mind" which is the artist's frontier.

Notes

1. Like most Californians, I use the name Los Angeles for both the city proper, as defined by city limits, and for "greater Los Angeles," corresponding roughly to the Los Angeles basin.

2. Reyner Banham, *Los Angeles: The Architecture of Four Ecologies* (Harmondsworth, Middlesex, England: Penguin Books, 1971; Pelican ed., 1973; rpt. 1976), pp. 24–25.

3. Los Angeles novels, then, will not show the "geological determinism" defined by John R. Milton, *The Novel of the American West* (Lincoln: University of Nebraska Press, 1980). see esp. pp. 107–110. The best treatment of Southern California geography and cultural history remains Carey McWilliams, *Southern California: An Island on the Land* (New York: Duell, Sloan and Pearce, 1946).

4. Marc Norman, *Bike Riding in Los Angeles* (New York: Dell Publishing Co., Delta Books, 1973), p. 80. Further references to this work appear parenthetically in the text.

5. Wilfrid Sheed, "The Good Old Days in California: Memoir of a Campaign Drop-in," *Atlantic Monthly*, September 1968, p. 53. Sheed argues with great earnestness that Robert Kennedy was assassinated by an Arab because Californians do not speak with New York accents.

6. Evelyn Waugh, *The Loved One: An Anglo-American Tragedy* (Boston: Little, Brown and Co., 1950), pp. 87–88. Further references to this work appear parenthetically in the text.

7. Quoted by Malcolm Bradbury, "America and the Comic Vision," in *Evelyn Waugh and His World*, ed. David Price-Jones (Boston: Little, Brown and Co., 1973), p. 177.

8. My reading of the poem follows that of Daniel Hoffman. See *Poe Poe Poe Poe Poe Poe Poe* (Garden City, N. Y.: Doubleday & Co., 1972), pp. 60–63.

9. Joan Didion, *Play It as It Lays* (New York: Farrar, Straus & Giroux), p. 17. Further references to this work appear parenthetically in the text.

10. Banham, p. 23.

11. Didion, *The White Album* (New York: Simon and Schuster, 1979), p. 13. See Banham, pp. 214–15.

12. Waugh, "Death in Hollywood," *Life*, 29 September 1947, p. 73.

13. Didion, "Los Angeles Notebook," in *Slouching Towards Bethlehem* (New York: Dell, 1968), p. 220.

14. Didion, "Goodbye to All That," in *Slouching Towards Bethlehem*, p. 236.

15. Hisaye Yamamoto, "Yoneko's Earthquake," in *West Coast Fiction: Modern Writing from California, Oregon and Washington*, ed. James D. Houston (New York: Bantam Books, 1979), p. 346. The story was originally published in *Furioso* in 1952 and was included in Martha Foley's *The Best American Short Stories of 1952*. Further references to this work, from Houston's anthology, are indicated parenthetically in the text.

Bibliographic Note

My approach to this topic has been influenced by Kevin Starr's magisterial study, *Americans and the California Dream, 1850–1915* (New York: Oxford University Press, 1973), even though there is no overlap in authors or time periods discussed.

Other provocative general studies of the relationship of western landscape and western culture are William Everson's *Archetype West: The Pacific Coast as a Literary Region* (Berkeley, Calif.: Oyez, 1976), and John R. Milton's *The Novel of the American West* (Lincoln: University of Nebraska Press, 1980). Neither book, however, is concerned with Southern California. Most relevant and important—as other essays in this collection will attest also—are Reyner Banham's *Los Angeles: The Architecture of Four Ecologies* (Harmondsworth, Middlesex, England: Penguin Books, 1971) and Carey McWilliams's *Southern California: An Island on the Land* (New York: Duell, Sloan and Pearce, 1946). McWilliams' discussion of the geography of Southern California is excellent, as is his discussion of the history of ethnic minorities in the region, though the latter is dated. See also his *California: The Great Exception* (New York: Current Books, 1949). Both McWilliams books have been reissued by Peregrine Smith. A more recent study of California minorities is *The Other Californians* by Robert F. Heizer and Alan F. Almquist (Berkeley and Los Angeles: University of California Press, 1971).

The Case Against Los Angeles, as I call it, is too large and complicated an issue to document in a short article or bibliography. The literary tourist in California—that component for which I have made Wilfrid Sheed serve as representative and straw man—might be traced back to Henry James's comments in *The American Scene*. See Leon Edel's edition (Bloomington: Indiana University Press, 1968), esp. pp. 372, 411–12, 462. Another standard landmark along this tourist trail is Edmund Wilson's *The Boys in the Backroom: Notes on California Novelists* (San Francisco: Colt Press, 1941). The whole issue of Los Angeles as a symbol of chaos and collapse is admirably summarized by J. U. Peters in "The Los Angeles Anti-Myth," *Itinerary Seven: Essays on California Writers*, ed. Charles L. Crow (Bowling Green, Ohio: Bowling Green State University Press, 1978), pp. 21–34.

PART FOUR

Fiction as History

TEN

Los Angeles from the Barrio: Oscar Zeta Acosta's The Revolt of the Cockroach People

Raymund A. Paredes

In considering Los Angeles from a Mexican-American literary perspective, one begins with this fundamental fact: Los Angeles has been, since the mid-nineteenth century, a city uneasy about its Mexican-ness. The first several generations of Anglo settlers sought either to obliterate the prevailing Mexican character of the city or to make it over in their own preferred conceptualizations, both responses deriving from the widespread belief that actual Mexican culture was unworthy of recognition and preservation. By 1920, when the great surge in Los Angeles growth began, Mexican culture had been either effectively submerged or relegated to specified neighborhoods. For the new Anglo arrivals in the city, most of whom came from outside the southwestern United States and probably would have had difficulty distinguishing a Mexican from a Mongolian, the erosion of Mexican culture was not an issue of great importance. The inevitable consequence was best described by the Mexican poet Octavio Paz, who visited Los Angeles in the late 1940s. Noting that by then only a "vaguely Mexican atmosphere" lingered in the city, Paz wrote:

> This Mexicanism . . . floats in the air. I say "floats" because it never mixes or unites with the other world, the North American world based on precision and efficiency. It floats, without offering any opposition; it hovers, blown here and there by the wind, sometimes breaking up like a cloud, sometimes standing erect like a rising skyrocket. It creeps, it wrinkles, it expands and contracts; it sleeps or dreams; it is ragged but beautiful. It floats, never quite existing, never quite vanishing.[1]

Today, despite the fact that people of Mexican ancestry constitute a larger proportion of the city's population than at any other time in this century, Paz's observations remain apt. Anglo residents continue to acknowledge the presence of Mexican Americans grudgingly. Local newspapers and television newscasters rarely treat the Mexican-American community except to deplore the continuing influx of undocumented aliens and the persistence of gang violence. Producers of televison shows and films have demonstrated little inclination to feature Mexican-American characters and issues. As for fiction, few Anglo writers have seriously engaged Mexican-American aspects of Los Angeles life. One can recall a charming character, a charming story here and there—Ray Bradbury's "The Wonderful Ice Cream Suit" comes to mind—but very little of a sustained, thoughtful nature. In Anglo fiction of Los Angeles, Mexican-American characters appear primarily to lend stories or novels a touch of ethnic exoticism. When one thinks of literary Los Angeles, one thinks of values and life-styles associated with Hollywood, Beverly Hills, and the beach communities, but seldom with the sprawling barrio of East Los Angeles. As much as ever, Mexican-American culture seems curiously disconnected from general Anglo perceptions of the city, literary or otherwise.

Historically, Mexican-American literary activity in Los Angeles has not been sufficient to counterbalance Anglo indifference. Los Angeles Mexican-American writing dates from the 1850s, when *El Clamor Público* and other local Spanish-language newspapers began to publish poems and fictional sketches, some of which treated aspects of Los Angeles life.[2] But these works are of limited interest and the fact remains that extended fictional works about Los Angeles by Mexican-American authors did not appear until the 1970s. The reasons for this situation are not difficult to identify. Certainly, the relatively underdeveloped cultural environment of early Los Angeles was not conducive to the composition of novels, whether by Mexican Americans or Anglos. Furthermore, the record of literary activity among minority groups indicates that they generally express themselves in oral tradition and the briefer literary forms—poems, sketches, and stories—in most stages of disadvantage; the facts of bigotry and limited opportunity clearly stifle the production of extended fictional works. Hopeful Mexican-American novelists in early Los Angeles must certainly have been discouraged by the difficulties associated with publication. Their own community lacked the printing, distribution, and financial resources necessary to support their work; Anglo publishers in Los Angeles and other major American cities were generally antipathetic to Mexican-American writers, particularly the large majority that composed in Spanish. Only the publishing houses of Mexico City appeared potentially receptive but were so distant as to be virtually inaccessible. All Mexican-American authors in the Southwest who hoped to reach an audience beyond that for local Spanish-language newspapers encountered similar obstacles.

Not until the 1960s, as one of the consequences of the civil rights movement, did the prospects for aspiring Mexican-American writers improve. Young poets and novelists recognized the uses of literature as an instrument of social change and were encouraged by the appearance of several publishing houses founded specifically to issue their works. But even as Mexican-American writing has grown in volume, poems, stories, and novels with Los Angeles settings have remained relatively few in number. Over the past twenty years, Mexican-American authors have quite successfully depicted the circumstances of their people in the small towns of Texas and New Mexico, while in California a remarkable group of Chicano poets has emerged to portray vividly barrio life in cities such as San Jose and Fresno. But Los Angeles, despite its standing as the center of Mexican-American population and culture and despite its extraordinary recent contributions in painting, music, and film, has yet to produce a significant body of Mexican

ican writing. Undoubtedly, the sheer vastness of Mexican-American Los Angeles has proved daunting if not simply unmanageable. Richard Vasquez's highly publicized but unsatisfying novel *Chicano* (1970), with its randomness, its inability to locate the vital center of Mexican-American life in Los Angeles, and its ultimate collapse into banality, confirms the existence of this difficulty. Perhaps Octavio Paz's observation that Mexican Los Angeles "floats, never quite existing, never quite vanishing" best explains the problem confronting other Chicano writers. And it may be that the dearth of Mexican-American writing on Los Angeles is simply a momentary aberration which will have little importance over time. Nevertheless, the current scarcity is conspicuous. Among the available works, the one that portrays Los Angeles and its Chicanos most powerfully is Oscar Zeta Acosta's *The Revolt of the Cockroach People*.

By the time *Cockroach People* appeared in 1973, Acosta was already well established as a startlingly bizarre character and author in an era when eccentrics languished on park benches in every medium-sized American city. A friend of Hunter Thompson, Acosta had appeared in Thompson's *Fear and Loathing in Las Vegas* (1971) as the freaked-out Dr. Gonzo, a three-hundred-pound "Samoan" lawyer with a drug appetite to match his girth. Encouraged by Thompson, Acosta became an author himself and brought out his first book, *The Autobiography of a Brown Buffalo*, in 1972. As he tells it, Acosta's personal history is quite extraordinary. Raised in the racist rural community of Riverbank, California, Acosta picks peaches as a child and recalls the flour sacks his mother used to make dresses, shirts, and curtains. He begins to call himself Brown Buffalo for his complexion and obesity and because the buffalo is "the animal that everyone slaughtered."[3] After high school, Acosta launches himself out of Riverbank and into a remarkable series of careers: clarinetist in an air force band, Baptist missionary in Panama, copy editor for a San Francisco newspaper, and, finally, poverty lawyer in Oakland. In his last occupation, Acosta is miserable, frustrated by an endless procession of poor blacks and Chicanos who want divorces, restraining orders against brutal husbands, and relief from angry creditors. His personal life is equally wretched. Unable to sustain a romantic relationship and frequently impotent, Acosta indulges his secret wish for self-destruction: he drinks heavily, experiments with every variety of drug, and subsists on a diet of burnt hamburger for breakfast, tomato-beef chow mein with a quart of Pepsi for lunch, chili beans, apple pie, and beer for dinner. On top of his other difficulties, Acosta is a man very unsure of his identity. He remembers hardly any Spanish—although he spoke nothing else until he was seven— and knows few Mexican Americans intimately. In early 1968, Acosta begins to hear reports of Chicano activism in Los Angeles and so, anxious to find some worthy cause in his life and to reconnect himself to his Mexican-American origins, he embarks for "the home of the biggest herd of brown buffalos [sic] in the world."[4]

The Revolt of the Cockroach People treats Acosta's involvement in various Chicano political activities in Los Angeles from 1968 to 1971. The book is rendered in Acosta's version of Hunter Thompson's "Gonzo Journalism," a literary technique that requires the author's participation in the very events he is in the process of recording. Thompson also rejected the conventional journalist's practice of carefully revising his materials, maintaining that rewriting only destroyed the immediacy and passion of the reporter's initial observations. As Thompson described it, Gonzo Journalism resembles nothing so much as stream-of-consciousness fiction: rambling, highly personal if not idiosyncratic, sometimes overheated. Certainly, *The Revolt of the Cockroach People* seems more a novel than traditional reportage. To be sure, Acosta focuses on actual events—the assassination of Robert Kennedy in 1968 and the Los Angeles Chicano Moratorium of 1970 as two examples—but his presentation of these and other experiences is impressionistic without any significant concern for objectivity. Acosta exhibits the novelist's fondness for irony, figurative langauge, and characterization. He never hesitates to rearrange history for dramatic effect, and he employs hyperbole and outrageousness to push his readers toward his nihilistic and apocalyptic vision of contemporary life. His Los Angeles is, typically enough, chaotic, schizophrenic, and violent, qualities Acosta's Gonzo style—the literary equivalent of a Molotov cocktail—is admirably suited to convey.[5] Indeed, the affinity between Los Angeles and Acosta transcends style. As his own literary creation, Acosta embodies the very excesses and paradoxes that give Los Angeles its distinctiveness: quite simply, Los Angeles never drew the attention of a writer so much like itself.

Acosta arrives in Los Angeles with little money and consequently checks into a "sleazy downtown hotel." After resting a-while, he takes a walking tour of the surrounding neighborhood and is immediately repelled:

> . . . already my bones have told me that I have come to the most detestable city on earth. They have carried me through the filthy air of a broken city filled with battered losers. Winos in tennies, skinny fags in tight pants and whores in purple skirts all ignore the world beyond the local bar, care about nothing except where the booze comes cheapest or the latest score on the radio. Where I am, the buildings are crumbling to pieces. The paint is cracked and falling to the streets covered with green and brown phlegm, with eyeless souls who scuttle between tall buildings hoping to find a bed, a bottle, a joint, a broad or even a loaf of bread. Streets filled with dark people, hunchbacked hobos [sic], bums out of work, garbage of yesterday and tomorrow; with black men and women in bright garish clothes, brown men with mustaches to boost themselves up a notch, coffee-drinking people, wine-sipping sods who haven't had more than five bucks at a time since the last war.[6]

As Acosta moves about the city, he registers his predictable distaste for general features of Los Angeles: the smog, the seemingly endless freeway system, the pervasive drabness. But as a self-styled cultural outlaw and ally of the downtrodden, Acosta invariably focuses his attention on those areas and features of Los Angeles that represent a disturbing reality far removed from the affluence of Bel Air and Malibu. From the central city, Acosta ranges eastward to the barrios and quickly recognizes that Mexican-American Los Angeles is a city apart, not merely a collection of neighborhoods, but a distinctive, embattled community with its own language, culture, and long-standing resentments.

Physically, East Los Angeles resembles the central city, with its "streets of dogs and cats and trash, narrow jungle paths of garbage cans, beat-up jalopies, mudholes and dogshit" (p. 35). But whereas the central city is populated by "battered losers," the barrios bristle with energy and expectation. Acosta arrives in Los

Angeles just as the local Chicano movement is getting under way. East Los Angeles is in a state of imminent convulsion, brought to this point by a long history of injustices.

As Acosta begins to understand the circumstances of the Mexican Americans in Los Angeles, he discards his notion of them as "buffaloes" and comes to regard them instead as cockroaches, an image from a traditional Mexican song that captures the extent of their degradation. Cockroaches are those people who live in squalor and oppression and are reviled by others with higher economic and social status. Cockroach people, as the lowest of life forms, are exterminated even more casually than buffaloes. Acosta explains that cockroach people are found all over the world: in Vietnam, in South Africa, wherever violent oppression persists. The metaphor, however, fits the Mexican Americans of Los Angeles best, underscoring their remoteness from the hygienic glamor and easy living, superficial or otherwise, commonly associated with the city.

In Acosta's mind, the most notable variety of Mexican-American cockroach is the *vato loco* (literally, "crazy guy"), who is found in virtually all urban areas with a substantial Chicano population but who seems nowhere so much at home as in Los Angeles. The *vato loco* is the descendant of the pachuco, the zoot-suited rebel of the 1940s and 1950s. Fortified with "pills, dope and wine," he is the Mexican-American community's contribution to the bizarreness of Los Angeles and a symbol of destructiveness and moral anarchy. In the following passage, Acosta charts the stages of development in the *vato loco's* life:

> You learn about life from the toughest guy in the neighborhood. You smoke your first joint in an alley at the age of ten; you take your first hit of *carga* before you get laid; and you learn how to make your mark on the wall before you learn how to write. . . . And when you prove you can take it, that you don't cop to nothing even if it means getting your ass whipped by some other gang or the cops, then you are allowed to put your mark, your initial, your sign, your badge, your *placa* on your turf with the name or intitial of your gang: . . . Quatro Flats, Barrio Nuevo, The Jokers. . . . (p. 91)

Acosta admires the *vato loco's* disdain for conventional Anglo-

American values and his willingness to mount a guerrilla war against the dominant society, but the *vato loco* is ultimately a tragic and isolated figure, another victim of Los Angeles's particular pathology.

The anger and alienation of the Mexican Americans of Los Angeles, so well embodied in the *vato loco*, rises out of the realization that the city has become prosperous at their expense. Acosta insists vehemently that Los Angeles—as well as virtually the entire Southwest—was stolen from Mexicans in a brazen act of imperialism. To compound the outrage, Anglo Americans signed the Treaty of Guadalupe Hidalgo to end the Mexican War and then promptly violated all its key provisions: Spanish and Mexican land grants were voided, assurances regarding bilingual education were forgotten. In a deftly ironic scene, Acosta and other activists visit Olvera Street, the original center of Los Angeles and now little more than a tourist trap in a rundown neighborhood. Across from Olvera Street stands a monument of mounted soldiers "driving away *bandidos* and near-naked savages" placed to commemorate the decisive local battle in the Mexican War. Acosta and his friends resent that such a monument has been placed adjacent to one of the few areas in the city, meager though it is, that officially celebrates the Mexican past. The monument, to Acosta and his companions, symbolizes the Anglo sense of superiority and dominance. One of the activists shouts obscenities at the monument; Acosta and another activist spit on it.

Acosta's participation in the Chicano movement demonstrates to him that the traditional aversion of the Los Angeles Anglo community to Mexican Americans has not decreased. He discovers, for example, that Chicano political activities are generally relegated to the back pages of the local newspapers and then badly distorted. He learns that the Catholic hierarchy in the city is controlled by Irish priests insensitive to the needs of their Mexican-American parishioners. The most dramatic instance of the local establishment's hostility to Mexican Americans occurs when Acosta, by now working as a lawyer once again, asks the coroner's office to conduct an autopsy on the body of Robert Fernández, a teen-ager who had allegedly hanged himself while a prisoner in the county jail. The young man's family suspects that he had actually died of a beating by police. At first, the coroner refuses Acosta's request; he acquiesces only after Acosta holds a television news conference that attracts wide public attention. The coroner, however, attaches a stipulation to the proceeding: Acosta must attend the autopsy. Acosta reluctantly complies, watching in horror as a team of pathologists cut out chunks of the boy's face, neck, and chest in their search for indications of a beating. Quite literally, the doctors hack the body to pieces. Later, the coroner releases his report stating that the evidence for a fatal beating is inconclusive. The experience reminds Acosta, in the strongest possible terms, that in Los Angeles, Mexican Americans, dead or alive, count for nothing. Robert Fernández was simply another cockroach. Little wonder that Acosta, a cockroach himself, insists repeatedly that Los Angeles is "the most detestable city on earth."

To Acosta and his fellow activists, it becomes clear that the only way to improve the lives of Mexican Americans in Los Angeles is to challenge those institutions that are most oppressive. The task is staggering, for the very social and political structure of the city seems contrived to hold Mexican Americans in a perpetual state of peonage. Still, the activists push on, organizing boycotts of barrio high schools to protest their failure to provide courses in Mexican-American history and culture. Acosta and his comrades venture out to gleaming, prestigious Wilshire Boulevard to picket St. Basil's Catholic Church, "the richest temple in Los Angeles." A five-million-dollar "monstrosity" of white marble and black steel, the Church mocks the poverty and humble piety of Chicano Catholics. As Acosta watches, the Anglo parishioners arrive from their Beverly Hills mansions in pearls and diamonds. They mutter insults at the demonstrators as they enter St. Basil's to offer prayers to the "Christ Child of Golden Locks and Blue Eyes." A scuffle between the demonstrators and police erupts, a development that Acosta regards as momentous. Not since the Aztecs resisted the Spaniards at the temple of Huitzilopochtli had "Chicanos" fought for their rights in a place of worship. This outburst of "religious warfare" indicates to Acosta that Chicanos are now ready to destroy those institutions that will not allow for their needs and interests. As the anger of the cockroach people intensifies, Los Angeles finds itself closer to immolation.

The Chicano activists of Los Angeles encounter their most tenacious enemies in the courtrooms where, as Acosta tells it, the entire judicial system, from policeman to superior court judge, is arrayed against them. Forced to take up the practice of law once more, Acosta, cynical as he is, nevertheless is startled by the degree of corruption in the local halls of justice. As he defends a parade of Chicano activists against inflated, irresponsible charges, he faces witness after witness, prisoners and police officials alike, who lie under oath. An eminent judge openly flaunts his bigotry. Chicano jurists, in the employ of the government, exhibit uncommon hostility to the activists. Not surprisingly, Acosta's trials deteriorate into farce. As the prejudices of the judge, the prosecutors, and their witnesses become obvious, Chicano spectators and Acosta himself explode in frustration. Courtrooms are cleared and Acosta is cited for contempt time and again. For months, Acosta spends his weekends in jail. All of these experiences Acosta implicitly connects to the special character of Los Angeles. On several occasions, Acosta looks out the windows of the high-rise courtrooms to note the smoggy skies, the sheer feeling of dirtiness about Los Angeles. He sees the people moving about on the streets below, struck by how small they appear. Los Angeles is a gigantic city that reduces human beings to the size of insects: perhaps ants, perhaps cockroaches.

Anglo Los Angeles is simply incapable of providing Acosta any relief from his disillusionment. He raises money for his legal expenses in the westside liberal community but dislikes the experience, presumably because he considers the donors condescending. At UCLA to speak about Chicano activism, Acosta finds the affluent students lacking in true commitment to social justice. When local organizers for a presidential candidate donate $10,000 to the activists' defense fund in hopes of winning Mexican-American votes, their check bounces. In an extraordinarily bizarre incident, Acosta is invited to the mayor's office for a talk. The mayor has been embarrassed by various Chicano demonstrations and hopes to win Acosta's assistance in curtailing them. Acosta wants the district attorney's office to drop charges against his clients in exchange. But the mayor wants no part of a deal with Acosta and begins to shout: "I'm telling you that picketing is over. . . . the blacks picketed for years . . . but . . . they didn't get a thing until they had Watts. . . . And I'm telling you, until your people riot, they're probably not going to get a thing either" (p. 73). So it has come to this: the mayor of the "world's biggest armpit" daring Acosta and his friends to escalate their activities, to resort to violence.

The insanity of the mayor's challenge is symptomatic of the lunacy that Acosta finds rampant in Los Angeles. It's not enough to say that Los Angeles simply reflects the chaos and pathology of contemporary existence. For Acosta, the city is uniquely destructive, an urban horror that nurtures violence, injustice, and human folly to an extent unmatched in any other city Acosta knows. Los Angeles is the city that Charles Manson found congenial and in which he masterminded his campaign of murder. Acosta finds a terrible appropriateness in the fact that Robert Kennedy, a friend of cockroaches and of César Chávez, is assassinated in Mexican-hating Los Angeles. For his part, Acosta struggles mightily to preserve his fragile sanity every day he lives in the city. He suspects that his association with those quintessentially Los Angeles types, the *vatos locos*, is turning him *loco*. After an especially bad day in court, Acosta observes:

> We walk out of the courthouse into the dirt and slime. Even in spring, the smog sits on the city like moldy orange juice. I look back. For years I have been walking in and out of that building, into the icebox of justice and then out into the garbage. Nobody has to tell me I'm sick. Nobody has to say, [Acosta] you look like shit. I stand there, staring backward like an idiot. (p. 220)

The stress of Los Angeles living is so severe that Acosta occasionally runs away, the farther the better. At one point, Acosta and some friends travel to Lake Elsinore, about a two-hour drive from Los Angeles, to enjoy fresh air, swimming, and drugs. The trip turns out badly when the group wanders onto some private property and is run off by the owner with a shotgun. Apparently, Acosta has better luck in his old hometown of San Francisco, where the citizens, to his mind at least, seem more tolerant and less prone to violence. Acosta's best moments, however, are spent in Acapulco. Here, Acosta is able to relax completely. Acapulco is attractive to Acosta precisely because it is so unlike Los Angeles. He enjoys quiet walks, cool, clean breezes, spectacular views, and the proximity of unspoiled nature. In Acapulco, Acosta feels no sense of being a cockroach. His happiness is unbroken until the morning he reads a newspaper acount of a "Chicano riot" in East Los Angeles.

The report of the riot draws Acosta back to Los Angeles to defend his activist friends who have been arrested. He learns that the so-called riot had actually been intended as a peaceful demonstration against the war in Vietnam and the disproportionate number of Chicano soldiers dying there. Acosta watches a film of the Chicano Moratorium and concludes that the police, not the demonstrators, had triggered the bloodshed. In Acosta's view, the police, as agents of the local power structure, were intensifying their campaign of extermination, carrying it deeper into the barrios and destroying not only the cockroach people but their culture and neighborhoods as well. After the Moratorium disaster, East Los Angeles resembles a battlefield:

> Whittier Boulevard is burning. Tooner Flats is going up in flames. Smoke, huge columns of black smoke looming over the buildings. Telephone wires dangling loose from the poles. Everywhere the pavement is covered with broken bottles and window glass. Mannequins from Leed's Clothing lie about like war dead. Somehow a head from a wig shop is rolling eerily down the road. Here a police van overturned, its engine smoking. There a cop car, flames shooting out the windows. Cops marching forward with gas masks down the middle of the debris. An ordinary day in Saigon, Haiphong, Quang Tri and Tooner Flats. (p. 217)

Even as the images of devastation grow more vivid in Acosta's mind, he enters the despised courtrooms of Los Angeles one last time to fight for the activists' rights. Acosta performs spectacularly, clearing all seven of his defendants of felony charges. His victories, however, bring him little joy. He thinks of Roland Zanzibar, the foremost Chicano journalist in Los Angeles, who had been killed during the Chicano Moratorium while quietly sitting in an eastside bar. He thinks of the mutilated corpse of Robert Fernández. He recalls the cover-ups and lies and concludes that the power structure of Los Angeles had absorbed its minor defeats rather easily. Soon after his final trial, Acosta participates in the bombing of the

Los Angeles Hall of Justice. With this final display of contempt for Los Angeles, Acosta heads north for the more congenial surroundings of San Francisco.

Ultimately, Acosta's depiction of Los Angeles tracks a familiar course. His image of Los Angeles aflame recalls, obviously, the imagery of Nathanael West and, more recently, of Joan Didion. His view of Los Angeles as sprawling, ugly, dirty, impersonal, and schizophrenic is also conventional enough. Even his focus on one of the least glamorous areas of Los Angeles, although certainly not common, is not unique in the fictional record of the city.

What sets Acosta apart from other writers on Los Angeles is the linkage he establishes between the unsavoriness of the city and its long-standing abuse of its Mexican-American population. Somewhat like Faulkner's Yoknapatawpha County, Acosta's Los Angeles is a region cursed by its subjugation of a people and its willful destruction of a standing, vigorous culture. The schizophrenia of the city is rooted in its rejection of its very soul. Indeed, Hollywood's endless inventions and modifications of the city's image and identity are at least partially attributable to the vacuum caused by the obliteration of its Mexican past. Los Angeles is a "nowhere city" largely because its Anglo residents have traditionally refused to recognize its inescapable self. Not until Los Angeles confronts its Mexican-ness and begins to meet its obligations to its Mexican-American residents, argues Acosta, can it be at peace with itself.

The Revolt of the Cockroach People, not yet a decade past its original publication, is already badly dated. The book's shrillness has not worn well, and many of Acosta's proposals—notably that Mexican Americans strive to regain possession of the Southwest—seem hopelessly naive. Still, Acosta portrays the disappointments and resentments of the Los Angeles Mexican-American community in the heyday of the civil rights movement quite vividly. And it bears mention that many of the injustices suffered by Mexican Americans in Los Angeles cited in Acosta's work have yet to be adequately addressed.

One last note, slightly digressive. Not long after the publication of *The Revolt of the Cockroach People,* Acosta dropped from sight. He has not been heard from since and, as far as this writer knows, none of his friends or members of his family can say whether he is dead or alive.

Notes

1. Octavio Paz, *The Labyrinth of Solitude,* trans. Lysander Kamp (New York: Grove Press, 1961), p. 13.

2. This tradition continues to the present day. *La Opinión,* the largest Spanish-language newspaper in the city, regularly publishes literary items, mainly poetry.

3. Oscar Zeta Acosta, *The Autobiography of a Brown Buffalo* (New York: Popular Books, 1972), p. 253.

4. Ibid., pp. 254–55.

5. For a fuller treatment of this feature of Acosta's work, see Bruce-Novoa, "Fear and Loathing on the Buffalo Trail," *MELUS* 6 (1979):39–50.

6. Acosta, *The Revolt of the Cockroach People* (1973); rpt. New York: Bantam Books, 1974), p. 15. All subsequent quotations from this volume will be indicated with page numbers in parentheses.

Bibliographic Note

As indicated in the above essay, Mexican-American Los Angeles fiction is scarce. In addition to the Acosta work, Richard Vasquez's novel, *Chicano* (Garden City, N. Y.: Doubleday & Co., 1970) and J. L. Navarro's collection of stories, *Blue Day on Main Street* (Berkeley: Quinto Sol, 1973) have Los Angeles settings. See also *201: Homenaje a la Ciudad de Los Angeles/ Latino Experience in Literature and Art* (Los Angeles: Self Help Graphics, 1982) for a selection of fiction, poetry, and graphics on Los Angeles. A recent well-executed novel that treats Mexican-American life in Los Angeles is Danny Santiago's *Famous All Over Town* (New York: Simon and Schuster, 1983).

ELEVEN

History As Mystery, or Who Killed L.A.?

Paul Skenazy

People used to write detective stories for money, and read them to escape. Now readers and writers look for less secure retreats or measurable profits. Written with purpose and read as art, our newer, more self-conscious detective tales expand the traditional crime-and-punishment formula to include the mysteries of life on the one hand, and the corpses of political motive and historical event on the other.

John Gregory Dunne's *True Confessions* (1977) and Thomas Sanchez's *Zoot-Suit Murders* (1978) are two very different, but compelling and instructive, literary products of this conversion of the once low-brow genre to high purpose. We might call them novels of historical memory, or near history. Self-conscious attempts at historical reanalysis, both novels fictionalize unsolved Los Angeles police cases: the "Black Dahlia" murder of Elizabeth Short in June 1947, and the so-called Zoot Suit riots of June 1943 in the East Los Angeles barrio. These events, still vivid to the memory, allow

Dunne and Sanchez to speculate on the social implications of our concepts of culpability, and to challenge traditional legal forms of reasoning which assume individual culpability. Both novels serve as useful object lessons in the problems of writing about the Los Angeles past, the contradictions involved in historical revision, and the difficulties encountered in turning the melodrama of news headlines into the stuff of tragedy.

I

> It's not like real life,
> detective stories.
> *True Confessions*[1]

The complex moral and aesthetic issues in *True Confessions* frame, and develop from, a traditional investigative police yarn. A woman is found naked, her body cut in half, a candle in her vagina, a rose tattoo on her abdomen. Dubbed the "Virgin Tramp" by the newspapers, she is discovered to be Lois Fazenda, a sometime hooker and pornographic movie actress who has come to Los Angeles seeking fame and fortune. Tom Spellacy and Frank Crotty, ace homicide detectives, work from clue to clue, fending off cranks and reporters and ambitious superiors eager to build their careers on a rapid solution. They accumulate the details of Fazenda's life. They eliminate some suspects; they discover others. Except for the fact that Dunne streamlines his summaries of evidence more than most detecive writers, the story is a good mystery. A killer is eventually discovered, a motive named, an arrest made.

And like most tough-guy fiction since Hammett and Chandler, the story is encased in a climate of political and social corruption and greed. Fazenda's story is a classic Hollywood tale of failed dreams of stardom. Los Angeles is portrayed as a dense, layered structure of interrelationships among business, the church, government, and the police, in which public behavior is shaped by private needs and ambitions. The tone remains consistently smutty and hard-nosed. We are assaulted by a cruel, trashy, violent male language. Dunne seems anxious to violate us bodily with his vocabulary, leaving no illusions of failed innocence:

> Hustling and the payoff were the perimeters of their knowledge of each other. She knew everything there was

> to know about coming, and as a matter of course she told
> him about the number of free fucks it took to buy a
> grand-jury transcript and the cost of a deputy chief. . . . It
> was a slum of a relationship surrounded by acres of
> indifference. (p. 227)

Everything from human relationships to the Catholic church is soiled, grimy. The landscape is a string of run-down amusement parks, restaurants smelly and snobby, abandoned buildings housing voyeuristic citizens. Businessmen are on the make in schools and cathedrals, on golf courses and at home; priests muse on finances while dispensing the Host. The city is a garbage dump of civilization, full of rot and decay, breeding disease.

But the solution to Lois Fazenda's killing, and even the detailing of social corruption and moral decay, are more Dunne's excuse than his objective. While *True Confessions* is a conventional tough-guy novel about the connections between person and institution, crime and government, the little guy and those in power, Dunne also departs from the aesthetic and moral conventions of the genre through his story of Tommy and Desmond (Des) Spellacy. The two are Irish Catholic brothers, one a homicide detective without prospects of advancement, the other an ambitious, highranking priest and potential successor to the Archbishop of Los Angeles. Their intimate personal and professional brotherhood represents the relationship of crime to sin—the alliance, and the incompatibility, of state and church. The men and the institutions they serve are diametrical opposites and mirror images: the clerical and legal, the otherworldly and just plain worldly.

Both men work to maintain order and the illusion of sanity in a world of chaos and derangement. Both live in a world of "games" in which "those that want something [play] with those that have something." The two men reciprocate favors. Tom quietly removes the dead body of a priest from a whorehouse to prevent scandal; his job is spared during an investigation of police payoffs because of Desmond's usefulness to a politically powerful man.

Each brother, then, sees himself as a servant of order and decency in an imperfect world of compromises. Each is at the edge of, and seeks, perfection and purity: Tommy through his pursuit of solutions to crimes, Desmond in his eager hope to feel a calling in the church. Yet each accepts the notion that everyone makes deals to get through, so morality must remain a relative rather than absolute condition. Both are resigned to life in a limited world of partial certainties.

The two men are linked to the Virgin Tramp case through the figure of Jack Amsterdam, a prominent citizen famous for his philanthropic civic and church work. A building contractor, Amsterdam is also a gangster involved in whorehouses, pornographic films, the running of illegal aliens from Mexico, the numbers rackets, and dope distribution. Knowing he is soon to die, Amsterdam tries to buy his way into heaven through church donations while continuing to profit from building contracts acquired through Desmond. Lois Fazenda was once his mistress, then a whore he loaned to prominent political friends; he introduced her to her eventual killer.

Despite some obvious evidence, however, Tommy knows that Amsterdam did not kill Lois Fazenda: "killing the girl was stupid and Jack had never drawn a stupid breath in his life. Nor had he ever confused a fuck with grand passion" (p. 316). And Tommy also knows how Amsterdam can implicate him and Desmond if threatened with arrest. But the actual killer turns out to be one of the least culpable of the woman's acquaintances. So Tommy arrests Amsterdam for the crime in a self-destructive act of revenge that ends both his and Desmond's careers. The exposure of Amsterdam is self-exposure, his arrest a form of public penance Tommy makes for his own role in the death of Brenda, a whore, and as a form of revenge against his brother. Amsterdam "confesses" to his associations with Fazenda, his earlier police payoffs, his church arrangements with Desmond, and a chance meeting between the girl and the priest one night; then he conveniently dies while in prison awaiting trial. Everyone is implicated in, and implicated through, the woman's life and death. Justice is neither served nor even acknowledged.

But Dunne wants more than a political and psychological understanding of institutions, or individuals. His church is not only a diocese, and hence a bureaucratic structure; it also signifies the incomprehensibility of contemporary life. His tale of detection is similarly an effort to make the mysterious comprehensible, and undercut those assurances of clarity that have become so much a part of the detective genre. The novel challenges not only our faith in social structures, but in ontological systems.

Religious and artistic systems of meaning-making are satirized throughout the novel. There is a deliberate play with and against history, with and against the detective form, and with and against all other institutional forms. At several points, for example, Dunne introduces parodies of mystery stories: three of the great detective writers of the 1940s try to discover the Virgin Tramp's killer for the newspapers; Tom Spellacy and the Cardinal exchange comments on Father Brown (pp. 225, 267–68).

The solution to the murder, when it finally occurs, comes as much through accident as work, and reflects a macabre, comic illogic which Dunne sees ruling human experience. Attempting to make sense of the accumulating evidence, Tommy realizes that the

> whole business was too neat, too much like a story on the radio, and it had been from the start. There were no loose ends, everything seemed to be connected, and that was what bothered him. . . . No, that wasn't how things worked. (pp. 316–17)

After he sees that Jack Amsterdam did not do the killing, Tommy reverses himself: "On this one, nothing crossed. All that work and nothing crossed, that was the biggest joke of all" (p. 330).

Finally, Tommy must accept the fact that the "biggest joke" is that both visions are true: from one angle there is only disconnection; from another, only intersection. But what crossings there are come through a skewed, jumpy, and finally insane logic made up of fragments of greed, ambition, lust, chance, and hate. Tommy discovers "the definite pattern" while reviewing files at his office because he won't go home to bed with his wife, just returned from the mental institution. And he recognizes the pattern only because of his years trying to make sense of his wife's demented comments and wandering associations: "Linear thinking was irrelevant when you tried to follow Mary Margaret. You followed the bouncing ball." "The years spent tracking . . . monologues" bounce him from the Virgin Tramp to the victim of a car accident later the same night: "Nothing crossed. And everything did" (pp. 334, 346).

The solution to the crime is without meaning. Tommy's

final realization reveals very little; rather, it confirms the power of "chance. That great fucker-up of lives." The real killer is not he who killed, but those who have participated in and endorsed the tangle of lives and the idealized, prosperous structure of church and state with its inhuman foundation in whores and drugs and pornography. Tommy's and Des's brotherhood is the symbolic underpinning of Dunne's fictional world of mirrors, where the religious and secular reflect each other in their pragmatism, their corruption, their hierarchical power structure, and their financial dependence on the rich and unscrupulous.

A retrospective frame encloses the story of the Virgin Tramp. The "now" of 1974 introduces us to the "then" of 1947; at the end of the novel, we are thrown back into the present once again. Part of Dunne's subject is the absurd joke time makes of human effort. The book begins:

> None of the merry-go-rounds seem to work anymore.
> There is a Holiday Inn across from the coroner's office.
> And Lorenzo Jones is our mayor.

When we return to the 1970s at the end of the novel, Tommy summarizes the consequences of the Tramp investigation in a series of macabre paragraphs that read like a parody of those reassurances about the future one finds in the last pages of an Austen, Dickens, or Eliot novel. Jack Amsterdam died three weeks after his arrest. The police officer credited with the solution to the murder choked on a steak during speeches at the dinner celebrating his promotion. Corinne remarried and developed cataracts. Frank Crotty collapsed of a heart attack on a golf course in Palm Springs right after shaking hands with Bob Hope and Arnold Palmer. Desmond dies and is buried in the desert, and Tommy survives to tell the story, "in the pink" at 72.

Dunne plays with hopes both private and public, idealistic and selfish, and then chides the vanity of all such dreams. Aging, time, and fatalities horrible and comic throw people together and split them apart. Knowledge and self-discovery only provide amusement in a world of absurd accidents and chance encounters. History, as an ordered sequence of events linked through cause and consequence, gives way to a wry, caustic vision of life as an uncharitable joke—cosmic, or perhaps only sophomoric. The importance of a day, a moment, an event, a life, even a city's destiny is mocked by the strange links among disparate elements of experience. The process of converting incident into narrative is subverted.

Dunne's cynical view of the reality of those narratives we inherit as history is apparent even before the story begins, in the seemingly innocuous disclaimer that precedes the plot:

> THIS IS A WORK OF FICTION. THE AUTHOR IS AWARE OF THE
> ANACHRONISMS AND AMBIGUITIES IN THE SOCIAL AND
> CULTURAL PUNCTUATION OF THIS BOOK, AS HE IS AWARE OF
> DISTORTIONS OF TIME AND GEOGRAPHY.

It is easy to interpret this as simply a warning that Dunne makes no claim to historical accuracy. In the context of the book, however, it also suggests that Dunne resists and even disparages inherited versions of these events as he depends on them as his starting point. He wants his words, and his narrative, to echo off these recorded circumstances in the reader's memory, but he refuses to accept responsibility to preserve events as time has accepted them. The statement seems almost a brag of inaccuracy, as if fiction could correct and improve upon the material provided by history. Or perhaps we are only meant to see fiction as another, equally valid, plot structure, no more (if no less) significant or truthful than the historical record.

Either way, the disclaimer is a philosophical claim as well as an artistic aside. Our reformation of the past in narrative is linked to present circumstances, needs, and assumptions. The past serves as Dunne's register of change, an ironic re-creation of a different time meant to emphasize the continuing, similar patterns of violence and corruption that link it with our own. The anachronism, ambiguities, and distortions of the novel and of life itself merge in the erratic misalignments and plotless occurrences that join and disjoint our days.

If there is a significance to be found in Dunne's world, it comes in the various, ironic meanings of the title. The story of the past is cast as an act of confession, unfolding from Desmond's statement to Tommy that he is dying, concluding in Tom's apology for causing Des's fall from grace, and in Desmond's response:

"You were my salvation, Tommy. . . . out here in this
Godforsaken place, I am useful. . . . There's a kind of
peace in that, Tommy. I can't help it if you don't believe
it, but it's true." (p. 370)

The novel is a series of partial, or cautious, confessions both true
and false, which turn into feeble efforts at communion: lover to
lover, criminal to police, cop and gangster to priest, novelist to
reader. The two brothers' lives are bound by the confessional—
most concretely, perhaps, when Corinne acts as their conduit to
the private places of each others' souls. When she confesses her
adultery with Tommy (and pregnancy by him) to Desmond, she
forces the brothers to share responsibility for her life as they have
refused to do for each others' destinies. Desmond slyly offers the
possibility of a morality founded in one's peculiar personal view
of the world when, instead of the church's ritual absolution, he
offers her only freedom of choice:

"Goddamn you, you talk less about sin than any priest
I've ever met."
"I'm here to let you consider the possibilities."
"And that's all. . . . My penance?"
Without hesitation, Desmond Spellacy said, "Do the
right thing."
"If that's your idea of an easy penance, I'd rather have a
rosary."
"I never give them." (pp. 215–16)

But it is hard for a reader to believe even such meager forms
of faith in human capacity. Dunne's cynicism is so multiedged that
it undercuts itself. He defies the reader's expectations. Writers like
Hammett, Chandler, and Macdonald undermined the cozy affir-
mations provided by the resolutions of crime in a traditional mystery novel, but they maintained the comfort provided when the
detective was able to resolve—and realign—circumstances through
his investigation and his dual commitment to truth and client.
Such closure confirmed the power of the individual to understand
and find order in the seemingly chaotic, to rearrange the haphazard events and clues into the meaning provided by narrative, and
to alter the lives of others through his contol of the crime's solution. The detective's life was built on the assumption that inexplicable acts were causally linked, that there was a logic embedded

even in violence and self-destruction. Chandler's Marlowe played chess each night; while he knew that no case would ever resolve itself into the pure exact beauty of the game, his habits at the board carried over into his view of people and their circumstances.

Dunne manages to mock such presumptions. His evil is closer to Iago's "motiveless malignancy"—an incomprehensible passion for disorder and corruption which tests even the most self-protective and calculating survival arrangements individuals design. Finally, in fact, Dunne seems to want to challenge the possibility of design itself. Seeking to move beyond a simple revision of historical events, Dunne designs a hall of mirrors in which actions and reactions are denied consequence. The uncontrollable powers of chance and madness and the leveling powers of time give a final, ghoulish twist to the extreme circumstances of the Virgin Tramp—and Black Dahlia, and Los Angeles—stories.

Even Tommy's survival seems an ironic joke of circumstance by the end of the novel. What more sense is there in writing about such madness than in living within it, in reading about it than in trying to resist or accept it? All stances—social, political, artistic, metaphysical—are mocked by the misaligned happenstance of existence, and we are condemned to remain passive spectators of our times. The lesson of history seems to be that it is irrelevant; there is no lesson to learn, nothing worth knowing in or of the past. But neither, of course, is there much satisfaction in the not knowing.

II

> The man spoke quickly in a small
> voice, determined that his history
> of the past could help Younger
> reach his destination more easily.
> *Zoot-Suit Murders*[2]

Zoot-Suit Murders uses a quite traditional detective framework to tell the story of the Mexican-American barrio, a "deadend trap for the thousands who came across the border to find an honest day's work." Attempting to revive a lost heritage, Sanchez has written a revisionist history. The novel is meant to be fiction from the bottom up, affirming an early moment of Chicano rebellion too often neglected in Anglo texts. The portrayal of the Los Angeles ghetto and the greedy and fanatical groups that prey upon it brings to mind the depictions of Harlem one finds in black writers like Ellison, Baldwin, Claude Brown, Malcolm X, and Chester Himes. The fights between the zoot-suiters, or pachucos, and the military that occurred in Los Angeles in May and June 1943 highlighted the impossible working and living conditions of the Mexican-American community at the time.[3] The pachucos expressed their frustration and rage in their extravagant costumes, which were a parody of Anglo business suits and a declaration of the Mexican American's distinction from the surrounding white world. As Octavio Paz noted, "The *pachuco* [had] lost his whole inheritance: language, religion, customs, beliefs." To Paz, the zoot suit provided common identity and protection for the pachuco while differentiating and isolating him. It was a suicidal gesture of defiant malehood within the Anglo culture.[4]

The rhetoric of racism in the 1940s was exacerbated by suspicions that the barrio citizens were either un-American or vulnerable to the fifth column strategies of Fascists. Fascist-led Sinarguista groups from Mexico had supposedly infiltrated the barrio, urging Mexican Americans to sabotage needed war work. There were also suspicions that Communists were gaining recruits among the discontented, jobless, and underpaid workers. And, at the outskirts of this supposed conspiratorial activity, there were powerful cults like the I-Ams and Mankind, Incorporated. Each of these religious factions and save-the-world campaigns made a pitch for the Mexican American's loyalties; each was suspected of being a Communist or Fascist front organization; each presented an explanation of and solution to the war, and to the poverty.

It is this political climate of competing international forces, public suspicions, and inhumane social conditions that Sanchez chooses as his entrance into the barrio world, "a concentration camp [with] a quarter of a million people living in terror." His central character, Nathan Younger, is a home-front white "soldier" sent to live among the Mexican Americans and investigate subversive political activity—specifically, Mankind, Incorporated, led by the mysterious Kathleen LaRue. Plainclothes F.B.I. agents are killed during a riot, supposedly by some pachucos. While tensions within the barrio and between the pachucos and the military build in intensity, Younger tries to understand the sources of this incident. The solution to the crime coincides with the most violent of the zoot-suit riots, in early June 1943.

The novel effectively anchors events within the historical circumstances of Los Angeles. Headlines and letters from the front highlight the war; clandestine meetings at a local ball park register the color line in sports; travel to the Navy docks and the Hollywood hills take us through streets dotted with Schwab's Drugstore, Graumann's Chinese Theater, and Aimee Semple McPherson's Angelus Temple. Best are the descriptions of conditions in the barrio itself; the feel of fighting; the street environment; comments on the Mexican Americans' fears and the racial hatred they experienced; the life of the pachucos, with their defiant slang and extravagant suits:

> *"Ese, que pasa!"* . . .
> "You ask me what's happening! . . . Look at yourself!
> Wearing a *tando,* and a *pachuco* hat, *tramados,* pants
> with reet-pleats, dago chains hanging all over, a real
> Zootie! A *bato loco,* a crazy street-cruisin' dude!" (p. 61)

Sanchez also captures the feel of the city in two brilliant scenes set against the twelve-foot-high letters that spell HOLLYWOOD just below the RKO radio tower atop Mount Lee. "All that's left standing of an expensive dream," the letters are an eerie symbolic architecture of crumbling hopes and eternal promise, a ruined dream evoking the past within the beautiful California landscape. The juxtapositions of the natural and artificial, gilt-edged and wild, suggest a world at the edge of dissolution. It is here that Younger waits for a clandestine contact to appear, terrified of a night filled with unknown enemies:

> He would wait for the light of morning, wait until the
> letters were exposed. . . . Even in his dreams, after he
> went to sleep at the foot of the giant sign and the coyote
> had long since ceased its solemn lament, and the rising
> sun stunned the vastness of the distant Pacific Ocean
> holding back the sprawl of highways clawing concretely
> out from the heart of Los Angeles, even then he did not
> know what he expected to find up there. (p. 179)

But despite the power of individual scenes like these, the book as a whole is disappointing as a reevaluation of *pachuismo,* as a record of barrio life, and as a detective tale. The problems begin with the attempt at historical recreation. While it is clear that Sanchez has done his homework, much of the period material seems forcibly inserted. More problematic is the investment of viewpoint in Younger. As his name implies, Younger is meant to be comparatively too innocent, a "good American" who believes in and works for "the American way." His fierce emotional loyalty to the Mexican-American community wars with his naive faith in his country.

Sanchez is ironic about Younger's idealism, but even this tone cannot sustain the long series of Younger's shocked reactions to racism which we are expected to take as significant and searching comments. While one can nod approvingly at Younger's political sentiments, one also nods off reading them; they seem too set, too much like soapbox orations:

> "Most [barrio residents] are good Americans, not what the newspapers make them out to be. Most of those people are fighting this war every bit as much as you are. . . . Everybody's been using them—the Fascists, the Communists, even us. It's got to stop, because when this war ends those people in the Barrio are going to go on hating us, never understanding the truth. Those people have rights just like every other American, and if we destroy those rights what the hell is the whole goddamn war for anyway." (pp. 243–44)

This is the voice of disillusionment, the culmination of Younger's "growth" from Andy Hardy to social dropout. But the knowledge hardly seems to represent a valuable accumulated profit from the harsh events he has witnessed; it comes across as both trite and obvious, a plea for kindness rather than an understanding of social reality.

The most glaring problem, however, comes in the simplification of politics. *Zoot-Suit Murders* attacks the way groups like Mankind, Incorporated play on fear, and the paranoid suspicions that dominate governmental decision making, but the novel falls prey to its own form of scapegoating. The story is formed on a paranoid model of the detective plot. Evil is personified. Younger's— and Sanchez's—mind is dominated by a "bad-guy" approach to problems, a search for "this man," a single source of tension in the barrio.

The end of the novel is a political and aesthetic muddle in which the plot is resolved at the expense of the content. Conspiracy becomes the watchword as the actuality of barrio life disappears in the rhetoric of accusation. The complicated texture of racism is reduced to the political maneuvers of Communists, Fascists and the American government, as means are equated with ends. No distinctions are made among these groups according to their ideas or stances on issues; instead, they are all made to exemplify the manipulative, inhuman program of politics itself.

This is most apparent, and appalling, in the climactic confrontation. Younger learns that Kathleen is a Communist agent who has killed the FBI men, that his brother has died in the war, and that a friend was murdered by the Communists. Betrayed by country and woman, he rushes to Kathleen's apartment to confront her. He finds her with the man who is the Voice of Mankind, Incorporated and who, on Younger's entrance, commands her as a "comrade" to kill him.

The revelation that Kathleen is a Communist is meant to explode backward across her passionate affair with Younger, establishing the irreconcilability of political and personal alliances. But their relationship has been too vapid, and her character too eccentric, for the conflict of person and party to seem significant. So Younger's final appeal for an end to politics is laughable rather than convincing: "I'm sick of the ideologies. What good are they if they destroy people? Both sides have made us killers. . . . We can't let them kill us, Kathleen" (p. 252).

Mexican-American life and historical revision disappear into this Anglo love story. Two men struggle for control of Kathleen, reducing the political conflict to a contest between the Party and the heart, Communism and personal relations, Russia and America. The only humane choice, of course, is the personal option. Yet it is ideology, of a more sophisticated sort than Younger can understand, that has denied the pachuco a viewpoint and existence. In his pursuit of closure, Sanchez seems to have ignored, or forgotten, the ideological traps built into the cult of free choice and personality.

To break down existing categories of interpretation of the past is to open new freedom in interpreting the present. It is Sanchez's failure to appreciate, or utilize, this fact that makes the ending of his novel so disappointing. By way of contrast, in Luis Valdez's play *Zoot Suit* (1981), we get a more ritualistic version of pachuco life. Based on the so-called Sleepy Lagoon murder of 1942 and the subsequent trial of 22 pachucos for the crime, the drama avoids suggesting a solution to the killing. The dead man is beaten not by a realistic character, but by the figure of El Pachuco, an ominous and lovable tyrant who serves as the Mexican-American gang's adviser, alter ego, better self, and macho devil. This mythic cultural version of malehood acts as a counterforce to the pachuco's struggles with Anglo racism and oppression.

By courting that fine line between legend and everyday circumstances, Valdez keeps issues of ideology before his audience. The personal actions and destinies of his characters are engulfed in the racial hatreds and terror of the times so that issues of "who done it" become political questions about the whole city's moral responsibilities. And the mythic figure of El Pachuco also provides a perfect bridge across time, lending a contemporary quality to Valdez's analysis of the past. While particular conditions may have changed, he suggests, the forces of distrust between Anglo and Chicano, and the avenues of validation and self-affirmation open to the poor, remain much the same.

The play ends by exploding outward, emphasizing the representative quality of the experiences and characters. A newspaper reporter gives us a "factual" account of a doomed pachuco leader's future—more time in prison, another killing, hard drugs, an early death "of the trials of his life." But *El Pachuco* rejects this Anglo stereotype of victimization and suggests "other ways to end the story": a Congressional Medal of Honor; a marriage and five kids, "three of whom are now attending universities, speaking pachuco slang and calling themselves Chicanos." The ambiguity serves as both challenge and possibility, allowing Valdez to avoid stereotypes without succumbing to sentimental optimism.

III

The detective story proper could
not [flourish] until public sympathy
had veered round to the side of
law and order.
Dorothy Sayers, *The Omnibus of Crime*

The reclaiming of the past is a form of Affirmative Action in which voices of economic protest demand historical parity. History is a kind of coded empowerment, reflecting our contemporary dilemmas and providing shadows against which to measure our lives. Women, blacks, Chicanos, Asians, and Native Americans reminded us in the 1970s how much the past verifies our right to exist as individuals and cultures.

Through the efforts of these groups, we have gained access to new stories. The question has switched from *what* happened in the past to *why* what happened to *whom.* Part of the reevaluation involved a challenge to the methodological assumptions of history. We began to accept the notion that history is plural, that it varies with the viewpoint, needs, and times of the historian, that narrative is by nature interpretation, and that the stories we had been told, and had come to believe, represented an ideology; they confirmed the nature of reality as those in power would have it.

Narrative retelling became a way of conferring significance. We found our ancestors in that forgotten world. We developed new heroes and heroines and new culpabilities. Our history books admitted shame, and started retelling the story of the American migration in terms of Native American as well as white populations; of the South from the black as well as the white perspective; of California as it looked to an Okie, or an interred Japanese civilian, or a Chinese railroad worker, or a Chicano farmhand, or barrio resident.

Implicit in every retelling of the recent Los Angeles past is a compelling set of questions: How had this city happened? What has made it what it is? Why has it developed its peculiar legends? Its reputation? Its status? The film *Chinatown* was the first of many recent historical investigations into such questions to use the detective genre, a form in many ways ideally suited to an examination of this city's past.

From Chandler to Macdonald, the greatest achievements of the tough-guy tale have been rooted in Southern California. The detective tale established an intimate connection between the popular, antiestablishment, sentiment-edged cynicism of the period and the myths and history of the region. These hard-boiled fictions developed in the 1920s and 1930s as part of an interest of the time in the styles of life and language of a newly emergent migratory urban class. And its success in representing that class and its world of violence and unrest is confirmed by our continued association of the form with the times; Chandler's image of Los Angeles maintains a hold on the imagination that defies the most accurate of historical correctives. The tough-guy tradition has tended to sympathize with the dispossessed and relate stories of the underdog and the down-and-out. It has developed a stylized, colloquial language of the streets, preferring four-letter words of protest to the four-syllable pieties of politics.

Tough tales are also traditionally investigative. There is an assumption within the genre that the most important parts of institutional life are hidden, but subject to discovery. Detection challenges accepted understandings; it endorses one's right to know one's own world, and one's ability to "save" that world by solving it. Detective stories claim that one can clarify what happens by asking why, by assuming cause and effect relationships among events. Seeking facts that might reveal these relationships, the detective connects events across time.

There is an implicit faith in the genre that knowledge can subvert the status quo, then return the world to a more stable, because more fully comprehended and comprehensible, balance. The detective functions as the designing narrator, borrowing the skills of both the novelist and revisionist historian. It is only a small step from the kinds of reconstruction of past events in a character's life that are part of the resolution of a mystery to the recreation of an earlier period in a city's history, linking social events to private circumstances by giving a period the significance of "clues" waiting for discovery. Our century has provided enough actual stories of public corruption and betrayal of social trust for personal gain to make integrations of political collusion and private morality believable.

But there are also some structural limits to the detective story as a vehicle for profound social or political analysis. By tradition, the genre is heroic, which is to say romantic and individualistic. Someone—the criminal—acts, and someone else—the detective—reacts, to find him or her out. Personal culpability of this sort, however, belittles political and class influences. The tough-guy tradition develops social causality of a sort through its massive accumulations of background detail, embedding crime in the circumstances of environment. But too often this cultural evidence becomes the mitigating rather than responsible factor in the action. In a recent, supposedly overt political film like Brian de Palma's *Blowout*, for example, the explanation of political criminality as psychological derangement deflects the evil from the realm of politics into the personal sphere. The explanation through madness evades the representative quality of crime, focusing instead on the case history of the aberrant. Even the more socially sophisticated conclusion of *Chinatown*, with its equation of political hubris, racial and class privilege, and egomania with incest, suffers from this problematic contradiction between private motive and public meaning.

Finally, the detective story establishes some very firm expectations in both reader and writer. One must, for example, confront the problem of closure, which is a narrative confirmation of the reign of law. Solutions don't come easy in the world of politics, and historical clarity is not a wholesale commodity. The accusation of blame, on the other hand, is a form of mastery, an act of dissociation of narrator from doer, accuser from accused. The many contemporary masterpieces that have borrowed strategies from the detective form—Faulkner's *Absalom, Absalom!*, all of Thomas Pynchon's novels, Doctorow's *The Book of Daniel*, Robbe-Grillet's *Le Voyeur*—scrupulously avoid, and go on to challenge, solution. Dunne provides and mocks his revelation; Sanchez is undone by his.

Thomas Pynchon's *The Crying of Lot 49* (1966) suggests one way the artist might use investigative procedures to reinterpret the past while maintaining historical pluralism. Pynchon creates his own history—or parody of history—by mixing the actual and imaginary until fact and fancy merge, making us reevaluate the acts of perception and belief. He satirizes the paranoid pattern of causality in so many mystery stories while developing a paranoid mystery of his own: whether significance is embedded in the Southern California landscape, and whether that vision, if discovered, works for or against life.

The plot immerses us in an atmosphere between private madness and public pattern. Seeming clues are available everywhere, from garbage cans to Jacobean plays, Porky Pig cartoons to

deaf-mute conventions and housing projects. The central character moves from revelation to revelation, less and less sure that she
is discovering rather than creating her associations, so inextricably linked are they to her desperation.

But however narcissistic, the *search* for significance offers
the only possible alternative to the entropic, uncommunicative
system of civilization which Pynchon details. Meaning, such as
it is, comes in the quest for it, and the conviction that it does,
indeed, exist; or at least the hope that it might.

Such open-endedness is a stance of cultural suspicion: it pre-
cludes pat answers while avoiding cynicism, demanding collusion
and complicity from the reader. It assumes the power of cultural
scripting over our existences, but also challenges these preesta-
blished texts. It asks us to consider authority in the form of an
aesthetic question: Who will be responsible for plotting, and nar-
rating, our lives? In this way, it provides a motive for the recreation of history. The exclusion of finality from works like Pynchon's
suggests the power that vision and revision have to shape existence; significance, along with culpability, are still at issue. The
possibility remains that knowing more about the past might ena-
ble us to know more about our assigned roles, the alternative cultural dramas available, and the voices our times provide for telling
tales out of school.

Notes

1.   John Gregory Dunne, *True Confessions* (1977; New York:
Pocket Books, 1978), p. 268. Further references to this work are indicated
parenthetically in the text.

2.   Thomas Sanchez, *Zoot-Suit Murders* (1978; New York: Pocket
Books, 1980), p. 173. Further references to this work are indicated parenthetically in the text.

3.   A vivid description of both the events and the climate of feeling in Los Angeles can be found in Carey McWilliams, *North From Mexico:
The Spanish-Speaking People of the United States* (Philadelphia: J. B. Lippincott, 1949; reprinted New York: Greenwood Press, 1968), pp. 227–58.

4.   Octavio Paz, *The Labyrinth of Solitude*, translated by Lysander
Kemp (New York: Grove Press, 1961), pp. 13–17.

Bibliographic Note

On the experiences of Mexican Americans and other minorities, see Carey McWilliams, *North From Mexico: The Spanish-Speaking People of the United States* (Philadelphia: J. B. Lippincott, 1949; reprint New York: Greenwood Press, 1968); Roger Daniels and Spencer C. Olin, Jr., *Racism in California* (New York: Macmillan Co., 1972); Matt S. Meier and Feliciano Rivera, *The Chicanos: A History of Mexican Americans* (New York: Hill and Wang, 1972); and the first chapter of Octavio Paz's *The Labyrinth of Solitude: Life and Thought in Mexico,* translated by Lysander Kemp (New York: Grove Press, 1961; first published in 1950).

No one has yet undertaken the kind of thorough social and political analysis of Los Angeles through the detective or police procedural genres that one finds in Maj Sjöwall's and Per Wahlöö's extraordinary ten-volume Martin Beck series on life in Sweden. But recent detective novels have incorporated new groups of citizens as subjects (Joseph Hansen's Dave Brandstetter series on the gay population, for example), and have become more overt in their political and social interests (Roger Simon's *The Big Fix* remains one kind of model; Jospeh Wambaugh offers another in his police works). Many writers have turned to the past for both plot and atmosphere, though most of their fictions waver uncertainly between nostalgia and populism: Stuart Kaminsky's playful Hollywood stories, Gordon DeMarco's recent *The Canvas Prison* (on Frances Farmer), Andrew Bergman's *Hollywood and Levine* (on blacklisting). David Geherin's *Sons of Sam Spade: The Private Eye Novel in the 1970s* (New York: Frederick Ungar, Publishing Co., 1980) offers a thoughtful, if overly appreciative, reading of Simon and Bergman (along with Robert B. Parker, author of the Boston-based Spenser series).

Critical works on Thomas Pynchon continue to appear with alarming frequency; the interested reader might begin with Joseph Slade, *Thomas Pynchon* (New York: Warner Books, 1971) and George Levine and David Leverenz, eds., *Mindful Pleasures: Essays on Thomas Pynchon* (Boston: Little, Brown and Co., 1976). Pynchon's moving article on Los Angeles inner city life, "A Journey Into the Mind of Watts," *New York Times Magazine,* 12 June 1966, pp. 34–35, 78, 80–82, 84, appeared the same year as *The Crying of Lot 49.*

TWELVE

Chinatown,
City of Blight

Liahna K. Babener

Almost from the beginning, imaginative portraits of Southern California have searched out the region's darker side. A whole dystopian literature has emerged which makes Los Angeles a definitive emblem of false promise and venality. The paradoxes of the city's history underscore its ironic plight as Fallen Garden. Once Los Angeles was viewed as Canaan rising anew from the wasted desert (John Gregory Dunne has noted that the climate of Los Angeles exactly duplicates that of Bethlehem),[1] the land of celestial sunshine, curative oranges, and fast fortune. The legend inevitably collapsed under the weight of its overblown promise. Among writers who survey the ruins, a counterfable has evolved to challenge and vitiate the Edenic image: sunshine mutates into what Edmund Wilson has called "the golden air of death"[2] oranges putrefy in the fetid air; easy money gives rise to easy virtue. A survey of the titles of twentieth-century writings about Los Angeles confirms this notion of a world gone wrong: *The Devil to Pay, The Day of the Locust, The Nowhere City, The Slide Area, The Celluloid Asylum, Queer People, Naked in Babylon, Souls for Sale, Die on Easy Street, The Dangerous Edge, Love Among the Cannibals, I Should Have Stayed Home.* Where it once epitomized the collective hopes of a people, the city has come to typify a charnel house for dreams.

Set in the langorous, sun-washed Los Angeles of the 1930s, the film *Chinatown* is an allegorical retelling of the Fall of Paradise, drawing on scandals from the region's history and the tainted private lives of its patriarchs to expose the foundations of greed and thievery upon which the metropolis was built. *Chinatown*, released in 1974, is the quintessential Los Angeles film. It was written by Robert Towne, a self-consicous disciple of such Southern California countermythmakers as Nathanael West, Raymond Chandler, and Ross Macdonald, and directed by Roman Polanski, whose funereal vision of the city no doubt draws impulse from the atrocities visited upon him there by Charles Manson and his homicidal band of California cultists.

The amber tones of the film capture and crystallize a vision of Los Angeles in the moment of transition from lotus land to wasteland. Penetrating through the shimmering subtropical light to the contaminated underside of the city, *Chinatown* offers up a cinematic version of the Fall of the New World Garden. As Kevin Starr has written: "Something happened in Southern California during the 1930's. Some new vision of evil rushed in upon the American consciousness. Roman Polanski has of late caught that '30s feeling of moral depravity and impending doom in the film *Chinatown:* a sense of brooding evil abiding just beneath the movietone surface of Southern California life."[3] The 1930s were a time of radical change in the American sensibility owing to the convergence of a number of economic and historical factors. The pall of the depression hung over the nation, mocking its rags to riches mythology. The dark memory of World War I and the rise of militarism and fascism in Europe undercut optimism about world peace. Widespread crime and growing poverty put the lie to sentimental cant about "a better tomorrow for everyone." Los Angeles, traditionally perceived as a city of refuge, washed in the mist of a cleansing ocean to the west, might seem to have escaped the menacing trends elsewhere, but as Polanski makes clear, the surface glow veils a foundation of deceit and wickedness which emerges in all its odium during the course of the film.

Polanski's moral parable, fittingly described by many of its reviewers as "serpentine" or "Byzantine,"[4] is constructed upon a plot that deftly intertwines public scandal and private perversion to suggest the scope and depth of the iniquity which has permeated the city. Jake Gittes, a private detective in the tradition of Philip Marlowe and Sam Spade, jaded on the outside but unsullied at heart, sets about to unravel the two puzzles, which gradually prove to mirror and ultimately merge with each other.

The first centers on the intricate scheme of Noah Cross, a rapacious city father and water magnate, to manipulate the Los Angeles water supply in order to create an artificial drought. Cross hopes thereby to win voters' support for a bond issue financing a costly dam that will irrigate the surrounding countryside and, not incidentally, augment the value of agricultural acreage to the north, which he has been buying surreptitiously. The inspiration for this tale is the city's own history, rife with instances of water rights usurped from neighboring regions, fraudulence in municipal government, profiteering in real estate, and ill-advised dam building resulting in catastrophe. The old riparian rights controversies are alluded to in the film when Hollis Mulwray is introduced. Mulwray is the chief engineer of the Los Angeles Water Commission, whose opposition to the raising of the dam for safety reasons leads to his murder. "Hollis Mulwray" is an anagram of Mulholland, the name of the turn-of-the-century master builder who designed and erected the Los Angeles aqueduct system and who also engineered the ill-fated St. Francis dam. Entrepreneur and money-man Noah Cross is himself a composite portrait of several greedy moguls and selfish visionaries. When Jake Gittes finally exposes Cross's avaricious scheme, he asks the old man what he intends to purchase with the spoils of his theft. Cross's response suggests how his greed masquerades as philanthropy: "Why, the future, Mr. Gits [*sic*], the future." It remains for Jake to expose the horror behind that twisted idea.

This tangled tale of land swindling and civic double-dealing, traced back to the omnivorous Noah Cross, is paired with a second and equally labyrinthine plot line. Gittes must unriddle the marital mystery revolving around Evelyn Cross Mulwray, troubled daughter of Noah Cross and wife of the apparently adulterous Hollis Mulwray. By the time he disentangles the convoluted network of treachery and deception and uncovers the sordid truth, Gittes is a changed man.

At the film's opening, Jake is not much better than a high-class voyeur reporting assorted indiscretions and fornications for a fee. "Matrimonial work is my metier" he tells us flippantly, crudely pronouncing the word "meaty air."[5] But the Jake Gittes who finally comprehends the sexual crime at the center of the maze—the incest between Noah Cross and daughter Evelyn—is transformed by his entry into the world of sin and sorrow. As Gerald Forshey has observed, the moment of revelation in which Jake finally extricates the truth from Evelyn—that Catherine is both her sister and her daughter—"approaches the moral and dramatic power of Oedipus' recognition scene."[6] Noah Cross has defiled his child as he has defiled the virgin land of Southern California. Robert Towne himself calls attention to the parallel between civic and sexual culpability: "The great crimes in California have been committed against the land—and against the people who own it and future generations. It was only natural that the script should evolve into the story of a man who raped the land and his own daughter."[7]

But Cross's incursion against his daughter is ultimately even more injurious. When Gittes confronts Evelyn with the incest, she denies that she was raped. Cross's true sin was to inveigle his daughter cynically into his own depraved world, to make her an accomplice in her own perversion. She has been made to view herself as a seductress rather than a victim. It is guilty self-knowledge rather than mere shame or fear that has shattered the woman. No wonder she stutters noticeably whenever her father's name is mentioned. Evelyn Mulwray is thus both daughter and "wife" to Noah Cross, roles which have become grotesquely fused in her mind. Her name is a variant of Eve, whom God first punished for her trespass in the Garden of Eden with the words: "And I will greatly multiply thy sorrow and thy conception; in sorrow shalt thou bring forth children. And thy desire shall be to thy husband and he shall rule over thee." Evelyn does conceive and bear her child in sorrow. As film critic Garrett Stewart has suggested, Noah Cross is in this sense Evelyn's true husband: "Mrs. Mulwray's personal stationery, as Gittes notes with strange interest, bears the letterhead E.C.M., and this middle initial stands for no mere maiden name: in effect, her father has been her first husband and has given her his name" through incest.[8]

The original transgression against his first daughter is amplified by the potential transgression against his granddaughter, or second daughter, Catherine, whom Evelyn has managed to secrete from him. Near the end of the film, after Evelyn's grisly death in a futile attempt to escape her father's tyranny, Catherine is led from the scene in the obscenely protective arms of Noah Cross, and we shudder to anticipate the re-initiation of the entire unspeakable cycle.

The two thematic strains of *Chinatown*—the double violation of property and of progeny—are adroitly woven into the fabric of the film as a whole, reinforcing and reflecting each other through a complex series of pairing. Gittes's quest to uncover the sexual secret that blights the marriage of Evelyn Mulwray is soon interlocked with his mission to expose the water fraud. Hollis Mulwray is murdered because he is the obstacle to the fulfillment of both criminal designs: he has refused both to build the proposed dam and to divulge the hiding place of his wife's daughter, sensing a larger peril in both instances. The two intrigues have *crossed* in the demented mind of the old progenitor, who equates the making of a city with the birthing of offspring, a pathological fusion of capitalism and lust.

Verbal doublings and analogies between characters also reinforce the correspondences between the two themes. For example, early in the story Gittes's nose is sadistically cut by a pugnacious, baby-faced gangster in Noah Cross's employ (played by Roman Polanski). He issues a warning to Jake about the fate awaiting "nosy" detectives. The image of Jake's maimed nose is reiterated later in a scene of hostile banter with a sneering cop who taunts Jake about his lashed face while they inspect the corpse of a murder victim. Jakes turns the joke against his detractor: "Your wife got excited and crossed her legs a little too quick." Thus Jake's wounded nose is associated with both political and sexual intrigue. Note too the additional pun on Noah Cross, whose sexual villainy lurks behind virtually every reference to copulation in the film.

The pattern of disfigurement is repeated in the case of Evelyn Mulwray, whose erotic allure for Gittes stems in part from a color defect in her left eye which she tellingly labels "a birthmark." As she stands over Gittes, disinfecting his lacerated nose, he stares up at her flawed iris and the first true emotional communion between them has begun. The defective eye, of course, marks Evelyn's doom. In the final catastrophe, played out on the streets of Chinatown, she is shot through the back of the head by a bullet that emerges dead center through it. Ironically, her assassin is the very policeman who had mocked Gittes about his gashed nose.

The motif of the impaired eye also underlines the theme of illusion central to the film. At the close of the same scene, Noah Cross leads Catherine from the killing ground, his hand shielding her eyes from the carnage, and from the truth behind it that might have saved her. In an earlier scene where Jake and Evelyn first kiss, the moment is triggered by Evelyn's remark, "You have something in your eye." His vision is indeed obstructed, not only by the duplicity of the world, but also by his own moral innocence, which prevents him from grasping the full horror of the truth he uncovers. Like Oedipus, slow to appreciate the enormity of his discovery, Jake cannot fathom the magnitude of Cross's evil or the pervasiveness of is power.

The convergence of public intrigue and private taint is conveyed by means of a rich and evocative symbolism. Water imagery forms the most insistent design in the film, prompting many reviewers to notice implicit references to the Watergate scandal, at its height in 1973 when the film was in production. Indeed, Cross's plot to manipulate the city's reservoirs by drawing off water illicitly through sluice gates invites such correspondences. But the imagery is much more suggestive: the siphoned water becomes an emblem of the twisted libido of Noah Cross. As Mike Wilmington has argued, Cross's "crooked entrepreneuring and his sexual perversion are identical; the symbolic and concrete levels of action become one. The reservoir's water, dammed up during the day and then shooting forth in clandestine bursts at nighttime, recalls Noah's secret lusts. . . . Water, like Cross' sexual appetites, can represent creation or destruction, a drive toward life or death."[9]

Indeed it can. Water is frequently used as the instrument or harbinger of death in the film. Two characters are drowned, one a hapless drunk who has passed out in the arid channel of the Los

Angeles River and is submerged in the raging currents when the sluice gates are opened. Gittes himself is almost overpowered by the sudden torrents which gush through a trough he has been using as a vantage point for his sleuthing. The methodical dripping of a faucet ticks off the suspenseful seconds as Gittes moves slowly toward the discovery of a woman's corpse. The backyard lily pond at the Mulwray house serves both as the drowning pool of Hollis Mulwray (murdered by Cross), and as the inspiration for one of the old man's deranged monologues on procreation. He tells Jake the story of his self-decreed role as sire of Los Angeles, when he had brought life-giving fluid to the parched land, "letting the water percolate down to the bedrock," and thus begat the infant city. Cross's pretentious portrait of himself as father-creator recalls the old adage about Southern California: "What's the recipe for instant Eden? Add water and stir." But Cross's Eden is a despoiled one from the start. The lily pond is the resting place for a corpse. "That's where life begins, Mr. Gittes," Cross proclaims ironically, "in sloughs and tidepools." The remark is unwittingly incisive, for Cross's corrupt world is indeed a slough, a place of moral contagion and rot. Not surprisingly, even the vegetation of this adulterated Eden reflects the pervasive decay. In one vivid scene, the camera lingers on the squalor of a spread of rotting groceries, strewn across the floor where they guide the viewer's eye inexorably toward another of Noah Cross's murder victims.

As the unscrupulous manipulator of the city's water supply, Noah Cross lives up to the implications of his Old Testament name.[10] His bibical forebear was charged with the responsibility of saving the creatures of the earth from the Deluge, an instruction which the latter day Noah has inverted for his own dishonest ends. Cross has inflicted upon the residents of Los Angeles a life-threatening drought by which he means to enrich himself and then win recognition as a public benefactor by building the dam as a reprieve. Ironic recollections of the first Noah's directing the animals aboard the Ark are evident in one scene when a group of local farmers supporting the construction of Cross's dam interrupts a meeting of the Los Angeles Water Commission by driving a flock of noisy sheep down the center of the meeting hall. Moreover, Cross himself calls attention to his role as father of the waters when he quips abut his scheme for inducing the city to annex the

Valley farmland he has been acquiring at paltry prices: "If the water won't come to Los Angeles," he says in a burlesque version of the old parable about Mohammed, "then Los Angeles must go to the water."

Allusions to the scriptural Flood are of course appropriate for a city besieged by the fluctuating calamities of drought and deluge. From the beginning, water has been of obsessive interest to Southern Californians. Mythology and geology combine to emphasize the importance of water to those who are ever conscious of its scarcity or overabundance. Joan Didion meditates in *The White Album* on the meaning of water to a civilization hovering at the edge of a desert: "Some of us who live in arid parts of the world think about water with a reverence which others might find excessive."[11] When Noah Cross violates the trust placed in him as steward of the city's water supply, his treachery is tantamount to sacrilege.

In the Old Testament, God commands Noah to oversee the regeneration of the world's population following the ravages of the Flood, another responsibility that his movie namesake has warped to fit his own depraved impulses. *Chinatown's* pervasive water imagery and the ironic parallel with the first Noah thus assist in the merger of the themes of political and familial guilt. Noah Cross desecrates his paternity just as he desecrates his assigned role as protector of the city.

The perversity of Cross's mission is magnified by contrast to the genuine beneficence of Hollis Mulwray. In keeping with the ethic of sham and duplicity which permeates the city, Mulwray is made to appear the guilty one: he seems to be an adulterer and a perfidious politician. But, in fact, it is he who saved Evelyn and sheltered her daughter Catherine from Cross's voracity, and it is he who is trying to rescue Los Angeles from the profiteer's greed. Mulwray is the rightful steward, but his integrity in a sullied world only ensures his destruction.

Perhaps the most compelling symbolism of the film, which also serves to unite the themes of social and personal taint, is the abundant pattern of Oriental imagery carried by the title. Chinatown is much more than the Chinese neighborhood of Los Angeles, though it is that too. Polanski's Chinatown is the unknowable and unfathomable city within a city, the ultimate metaphor for enigma, corruption, and doom—and thus the fitting scene for a modern reenactment of the Fall. Drawing upon conventional images of the mysterious East,[12] the film exploits the connection between the professional puzzlement of the detective, lured into an increasingly baffling mystery, and the cryptic world of Chinese culture, suggested to the viewer by a profusion of Oriental icons and visual details. In Chinatown, things are not what they seem, and this is the first lesson of the story. The film opens with a series of still photographs depicting copulation, flashed in succession across the screen, and counterpointed on the sound track by a series of groans. Though we expect the lascivious pantings of a voyeur, we get the embarrassed cries of a hoodwinked husband scrutinizing the evidence of his wife's infidelity. This teasing paradigm of deceit and violated expectation is central to the story proper, where illusions repeatedly masquerade as truths, and truths are dismissed as hallucinations.

When the Oriental gardener at the Mulwray estate laments that the salt water of the garden pool is "bad for glass," he seems to mean "grass." But Gittes tosses the unintentionally suggestive phrase about in his brain for the duration of the film before he sees its ulterior significance, then dispels the riddle when he dredges out of the pond a pair of broken glasses (another allusion to impaired vision) that ironically lead him to the solution of Hollis Mulwray's murder. Even these are not what they appear. Gittes's assumption that the spectacles belong to Mulwray correctly marks the backyard pool as the site of the man's murder. But in fact they belong to Noah Cross, as we discover later, and it is this revelation which identifies Cross as Mulwray's killer.

Chinatown is a place of mystery, but also a place of corruption, and the film is fraught with references to the insidious pollution there. Ever since the days of opium dens and decadent Oriental pleasure palaces, Chinatown has served the Western imagination as what one critic has called "the country of guilty legend."[13] Of course, it is not chiefly the Chinese who have denigrated their own house; much that is sinister in Chinatown is a result of the venal institutions and ethics of white culture, fed by centuries of Sinophobia. In the Chinese ghettos of California hundreds of thousands of dispossessed immigrants to the "land of the Golden Mountain" watched their dreams die in the face of poverty, abuse, and cultural exile. In the film, the profligacy of the white world is epitomized by the racism of the Los Angeles police force and the exploitative policies of a city government run by robber barons like Noah Cross whose villainy and greed have debauched Chinatown. For Jake Gittes, once a cop on the beat in the Chinese quarter, Chinatown was where the policeman's code was "do as little as possible" and "look the other way." At a more basic level, the corruption is sexual. Jake hears and retells a lewd joke about a Chinaman, which leads back to deception and sexual taint.

But the film's Chinese references go even beyond this symbolic function. Ultimately, Chinatown becomes the territory of doom, to which all roads—and clues—inevitably lead, for, as one writer argues, "the specter of Chinatown is vigorously signalled as the plot's inexorable destination. . . . The way out is the way back in."[14] In this sense, the figurative link between the film and the Fall is most truly understood. The murky memory of Gittes's former assignment in Chinatown is rehearsed a number of times, but in one particularly revealing scene, Jake, who has just made love to Evelyn Mulwray (looking her most exotic or "Chinese" as some reviewers put it), reminisces about the nightmarish experience he'd had there: "I tried to keep the girl from getting hurt," he says. "But I ended up making sure she *was* hurt." The horror of the memory is that the well-meaning but naive guardian ended up in effect leading the lamb to slaughter.

But Jake's nightmare is destined to be replayed once more. He concocts an elaborate plan of escape for Evelyn and her daughter, but his fatal mistake is to trust his old partner on the Chinatown beat, Lieutenant Escobar, who has risen in the police ranks because he has never deviated from the unofficial decree to "do as little as possible." In the climactic scene, Gittes reenacts his past error by luring Evelyn and Catherine unwittingly right to the center of the police dragnet on the streets of Chinatown. In a gruesomely ironic sequence, Gittes attempts to divert Escobar's shooting hand, aimed at the Mulwray getaway car, but he only succeeds in positioning the second cop (his snide adversary on the matter of the nose) for the kill. So his role as inadvertent bringer of catastrophe is recapitulated. True to form, Escobar advises him to "Forget it, Jake. It's only Chinatown." The film ends as Jake, disabused of his romantic illusions, wanders inward to the inscrutable core of Chinatown. Here, in the heart of darkness, the themes of personal and political corruption merge in a vision of irremedial determinism just as they did in the first Garden of Eden.

Notes

1. John Gregory Dunne, "Eureka! A Celebration of California," *New West*, 1 January 1979, p. 31.

2. Quoted in Alan Cheuse, "Edmund Wilson's Critical Eye on California Novelists," *Los Angeles Times Book Review*, 6 July 1980, p. 3.

3. Kevin Starr, "It's Chinatown: James M. Cain," *The New Republic*, 26 July 1975, p. 31.

4. "Serpentine" is a reminder of the Garden of Eden. "Byzantine" evokes the East, as does Chinatown and all the Oriental imagery in the film.

5. I am grateful to David Elliott for this punning phonetic spelling which he includes in a review of *Chinatown* in *Film Heritage* 10 (Fall 1974):44.

6. Gerald Forshey, "Exploring the Uncharted Depths of Depravity," *The Christian Century*, 18 September 1974, p. 860.

7. From an interview, "*Chinatown*'s Robert Towne," by Peter Rainer, in *Mademoiselle*, November 1974, p. 235.

8. Garrett Stewart, " 'The Long Goodbye' from 'Chinatown,' " *Film Quarterly* 28 (Winter 1974-75):31.

9. Mike Wilmington, "Roman Polanski's 'Chinatown,' " *Velvet Light Trap*, no. 13 (Fall 1974):15.

10. The casting of John Huston in the Noah Cross role was a kind of cinematic *double entendre*, since Huston had portrayed a benign Noah in his own earlier film *The Bible*.

11. Joan Didion, "Holy Water," in *The White Album* (New York: Simon and Schuster, 1979), p. 59.

12. Mark Royden Winchell has suggested to me that the Oriental milieu of the film may serve as a reminder of the Fall in another sense. If Los Angeles is a western Eden, then the film's imaginative movement to the eastern ambience of Chinatown may be a reenactment of Adam and Eve's expulsion from paradise to the east of Eden.

Certainly, Los Angeles, the city at land's end, has been viewed as the terminus of one frontier (the American West) and the gateway to another (the Pacific and the Orient). Many accounts of the region celebrate the siren lure of the exotic east felt on the Southern California coastland. When detractors condemned Los Angeles for its aura of unreality, natives could always point to the greater mysteries of Cathay beyond.

13. Richard T. Jameson, "Son of Noir," *Film Comment* (November 1974):33.

14. Stewart, p. 28.

Bibliographic Note

Although many consider Polanski's *Chinatown* to be one of the finest American movies ever made (an opinion I share), there is relatively little critical analysis of the film. *Chinatown* was amply reviewed when it was released in 1974 and most of the film's critical consideration is to be found in the original reviews. Two incisive essays are mandatory for any serious student of *Chinatown*. These include Mike Wilmington, "Roman Polanski's 'Chinatown,' " *Velvet Light Trap*, no. 13 (Fall 1974):13–16; and Garrett Stewart, " 'The Long Goodbye' from 'Chinatown,' " *Film Quarterly* 28 (Winter 1974–75):25–32. Both essays trace image patterns and explore moral themes in the film, and both are indispensable. A third critical study is Richard Jameson's "Forget it Jake, It's Chinatown," *Movietone News*, no. 33 (July 1974). However, though listed in bibliographies, this article is virtually unavailable. I could not locate a single academic library that carries the relevant issue of *Movietone News*, and letters and phone calls to the Seattle Film Society which published the journal went unanswered. An instructive note by William D. Bottiggi, "The Importance of 'C——ing' in Earnest: A Comparison of *The Maltese Falcon* and *Chinatown*," *The Armchair Detective* 14 (Winter 1981):86–87, discusses the problem of failed vision in the film through sustained puns on the verb "to see."

Among the reviews of *Chinatown* which I find thoughtful and substantive are Gerald Forshey, "Exploring Uncharted Depths of Depravity," *The Christian Century*, 18 September 1974, pp. 860–61; William Pechter, "Everyman in *Chinatown*," *Commentary*, September 1974, pp. 71–74; and reviews by Stanley Kauffmann in *The New Republic*, 20 July 1974, pp. 6 ff; William Walling in *Transaction Society* 12 (November 1974): 73–77; Robert Hatch in *The Nation*, 6 July 1974, pp. 29–30; John Simon in *Esquire*, October 1974, pp. 14 ff.; David Elliott in *Film Heritage* 10 (Fall 1974):44–45; Tom Milne in *Sight and Sound* 43 (Autumn 1974):243; Colin Westerbeck, Jr., in *Commonweal*, 26 July 1974, p. 405; Hollis Alpert, "Jack, the Private Eye," *Saturday Review/World*, 27 July 1974, p. 46; Kenneth Turan, "In Chandler Country," *The Progessive*, September 1974, pp. 53–54; Jay Cocks in *Time*, 1 July 1974, p. 42; and Paul Zimmerman in

Newsweek, 1 July 1974, p. 74. Kevin Starr's brief piece on James M. Cain, "It's Chinatown," *The New Republic,* 26 July 1975, pp. 31–32, contains piquant description of the Los Angeles ambience in the film.

A new book on the life and career of Roman Polanski, *Polanski* by Barbara Leaming (New York: Simon and Schuster, 1982), discusses *Chinatown* only marginally.

Several articles on Robert Towne, who won an Academy Award for his *Chinatown* original screenplay, have appeared. Three that touch on this film are Peter Rainer, "Chinatown's Robert Towne," *Mademoiselle,* November 1974,pp. 166 ff.; Martin Kasindorf, "Hot Writer," *Newsweek,* 14 October 1974; and "Doctor Towne," in *California Magazine,* May 1982, pp. 90 ff.

Contributors

David Fine teaches English and American Studies at California State University, Long Beach. His publications include a book, *The City, the Immigrant, and American Fiction, 1880–1920* and articles on urban immigrant literature and on the Los Angeles fiction of Nathanael West and James M. Cain.

Richard Lehan has published books on Theodore Dreiser and F. Scott Fitzgerald and articles on a variety of topics and authors. Currently he is at work on a book on the city in literature. He teaches at UCLA.

Gerald Locklin is a poet, short story writer, and critic. He has published articles on Fitzgerald and West. Locklin teaches at California State University, Long Beach.

Paul Skenazy teaches American literature and American Studies at the University of California, Santa Cruz. He is the author of *The New Wild West: The Urban Mysteries of Dashiell Hammett and Raymond Chandler* and of various articles on detective fiction. His reviews of contemporary culture appear regularly in *In These Times*, the *San Francisco Chronicle Review* and *The Threepenny Review*. He is writing a critical study of James M. Cain.

Liahna K. Babener teaches English and American Studies at Grinnell College and is vice-president of the Popular Culture Association and chair of its American literature section. She has published articles on the California detective novel and other topics. For this collection she served as assistant editor.

Jerry Speir has published books on Ross Macdonald and Raymond Chandler and is presently writing a police novel set in New Orleans. He lives in Oxford, Mississippi.

Mark Royden Winchell teaches at the University of Southern Mississippi. He has published books on Joan Didion and the novels of William Buckley, a monograph on Horace McCoy, and critical essays and reviews on, among others, Robert Penn Warren, Norman Mailer, Joan Didion, and James Dickey.

Walter Wells is the author of *Tycoons and Locusts: A Regional Look at Hollywood Fiction of the 1930s*, a book cited repeatedly as a source in the notes and bibliographies accompanying the essays in this collection. He is also the author of *Mark Twain's Guide to Backgrounds in American Literature* and has most recently collaborated with Alain Robbe-Grillet on a novel/textbook called *Djin, or the Evanescent English Teacher*. He teaches at California State University, Dominguez Hills.

Charles L. Crow is director of graduate studies at Bowling Green State University, in Ohio, where he has developed a course on California writers. He has published articles in *Western American Literature* and *American Quarterly* and is coeditor (with Howard Kerr) of a collection of essays entitled *The Occult in America* and coeditor (with Howard Kerr and John W. Crowley) of a collection of essays entitled *The Haunted Dusk: American Supernatural Fiction.*

Raymund A. Paredes teaches at UCLA and has published widely on Mexican-American literature and American views of Mexico in such journals as *MELUS* and the *New Mexico Historical Review.*

Index of Authors and Titles

261